HAIL CALEDONIA

THE LURE OF THE HIGHLANDS AND ISLANDS

ERIC SIMPSON

AMBERLEY

The author and
his son Fraser on
Derry Cairngorm,
August 1991.

This book is dedicated to the memory of my beloved son and friend, Fraser,
who was my companion on many hill-walking trips in the Highlands and
who gave invaluable assistance in the preparation of this book.

Fraser Ewan Simpson (1964–2017)

First published 2017

Amberley Publishing
The Hill, Stroud
Gloucestershire, GL5 4EP

www.amberley-books.com

British Library Cataloguing in Publication Data.
A catalogue record for this book is available from the British Library.

ISBN 978-1-4456-4004-4 (hardback)
ISBN 978-1-4456-4014-3 (ebook)

Map and table design by Thomas Bohm, User design.
Typesetting and Origination by Amberley Publishing.
Printed in the UK.

Contents

About the Author

Eric Simpson is a native of Buckie, Banffshire, but now stays in Dalgety Bay in Fife. After teaching in schools from Orkney to the Borders, he was a tutor in teacher education in Edinburgh and also lectured in History for the B.Ed. of Edinburgh University. In addition, he was a part-time adult education tutor for Edinburgh and St Andrews Universities, and still is for the WEA. His books include *Going on Holiday, Discovering Moray, Banff, and Nairn, The Auld Grey Toun: Dunfermline in the Time of Andrew Carnegie 1835–1919*, and *Dalgety Bay: Heritage and Hidden History*. He also has four titles with Amberley Publishing, the most recent being *Wish You Were Still Here: The Scottish Seaside Holiday*. He was historical adviser for the BBC television series *Grand Tours of Scotland* for four series. His hobbies include cycling and hill walking; the latter included climbing all 282 Munros (Scottish 3,000 ft-plus mountains).

Reviews for *Wish You Were Still Here: The Scottish Seaside Holiday*:

'This book is a pleasure and an education' (*Review of Scottish Culture*)
'A thoroughly enjoyable read' (*History Scotland*)
'This book is a superb read. It reeks of wet sand, ozone and damp swimming costumes' (*Scottish Local History*)

COOK'S TOURS IN SCOTLAND

Introduction

In the summer of 1745 a French ship dropped anchor in Loch nan Uamh on the west coast of Scotland. A small party of men were rowed ashore, but this was no tourist outing. The leader was Prince Charles Edward Stewart, known to history as Bonnie Prince Charlie. He had returned to Scotland to claim the throne of Britain for his father, a throne which he and his followers believed had been unjustly lost when his grandfather, James VII and II, had been ousted in the revolution of 1688–89. He had come to Scotland, to the Highlands in particular, because he believed that it was the place where he had the best chance of securing a sizeable support. It was the very distinctive nature of Highland society that enabled Charles Edward Stewart – or rather the clan chieftains who backed him – to raise a formidable fighting force in an incredibly short time. Ironically, it was the nature of that very different society that deterred outsiders from visiting the Highlands at that time and for long after.

The Highlands and Islands were seen as remote, mountainous and difficult of access. Even worse, not only did the Celtic Highlanders of the Scottish mainland and western isles speak an incomprehensible language, but they were seen as primitive, warlike and barbarous, though it was far from being the complete picture – that was the perception not just of Sassenachs from south of the border but also of a large proportion of Lowland Scots. These views were reinforced by the threat of the largely Highland Jacobite army, which in 1745 had marched as far south as Derby and had caused panic in London. In the second half of the eighteenth century, perceptions began to change with the long-term result that in the Highlands and Islands today, tourism is a major industry. How and why and with what consequences these changes occurred is the subject of this book.

Consequently, more and more southern travellers began to explore the landscape and culture of what not so many years earlier was regarded as bandit country. James Macpherson from Kingussie set the literary world in ferment with his translations from alleged ancient Gaelic epics. Other cultural change, namely new notions about how to appreciate what many had once seen as a horrid and fearful landscape, brought increasing numbers of tourists. For the Victorians, Scotland had become fashionable, thanks in no small part to the writings of Sir Walter Scott. Scotland and the Highlands in particular thus came to be recognised as a place of picturesque beauty and romance and, after Queen Victoria bought a holiday home on Deeside, it was one that had gained royal approval. It was not just the Gaelic-speaking area that was affected. Some tourists went even further north to Orkney and Shetland. There too visitors could see a society that was also distinctive, but because of influences that were Scandinavian rather than Celtic. In the nineteenth century improvements in transport by land and sea meant that a trickle of tourists became a flood and this continued into the following century. Indeed, without these improvements there would have been no tourist flood. It may fairly be said that men like road and canal builder Thomas Telford and steamboat pioneer Henry Bell have as much claim as anyone to be the progenitors of Scotland's tourist revolution.

There were a variety of reasons why so many tourists ventured north. Some were sportsmen with rod and gun; some headed to the mountains; some took to the sea; and others sought health resorts. It is the purpose of this book to show, with text and illustration, why and how this tourist influx came about and how it impacted on the people of the Highlands for good and for ill. It was for ill, many would argue, that glen after glen was cleared of their people to make way, first for sheep and then for deer forests. In Victorian times, tourists came from the moneyed classes. The twentieth century brought new kinds of tourists and coach tour parties brought welcome relief for hard-pressed hoteliers. Young folk, students and factory workers tramped the hills and cycled the byways, finding cheap accommodation in the new youth hostels. Working men like the young Tom Weir tackled difficult routes on cliffs and snow-packed gullies. The Highlands, once a playground confined to the well-to-do, was now open to all classes.

Nowadays, with the Highlands as a playground for all, a wide variety of sports and pastimes are on offer. There is skiing, ice wall climbing, mountain biking, caving, canoeing, sailing, bird watching, wildlife tours and many more. Many, though, just want to appreciate the scenery. For them the Highlands and Islands retain their appeal as an area of singular charm and beauty.

Chapter One

Caledonia, Stern and Wild

It was a bleak and cold day on Drumossie Muir, near Inverness. A ferocious battle was underway. The troops of one side, Highlanders for the most part, were in flight. Their commander, in tears and hardly comprehending the scale of defeat, was led off a battlefield that was strewn with kilt-clad corpses. The date was 16 April 1746 and the defeated general was Charles Edward Stewart, known to history as Bonnie Prince Charlie. This battle, named by the victors after the nearby Culloden House, was the last throw in a dynastic conflict that had lasted nearly sixty years. The myth that the Stewarts from James VI and I onward had a divine right to rule was shattered on the bloody field of Drumossie Muir. It ended the hopes of the Stewarts to regain the throne that James VII and II had lost in the Revolutions of 1688–89. The victory over the Jacobites at Culloden meant that King George II was safe on the throne. His younger son, William Duke of Cumberland who led the government army to success, was feted; on the battlefield he was Billy to his huzzaing troops. In London an old tune that had only recently gained new words achieved unprecedented popularity – the opening words being 'God Save the King'. Handel wrote 'See the Conquering Hero Come' to greet Cumberland on his return to London. Later a flower, Sweet William, was named after him. As for his opponent, Prince Charles Edward Stewart, he was on the run – a hunted man with a huge price on his head, but in an odd sort of way the vanquished prince in the long run was the victor. It is the image of Bonnie Prince Charlie that adorns the lid of the proverbial shortbread tin, not that of 'Butcher' Cumberland.

Battles and wars lead to all sorts of unintended consequences. The defeat of the Jacobite clans in the long term made the Highlands safer for travellers. The pacification of the Highlands, brutal though it was, meant security for travellers and ease of passage through territory previously thought hostile. The Highlands and Islands before the Battle of Culloden had been a region like no other – indeed, they were a world apart, and quite distinct even from Lowland Scotland. As Edward Burt, a knowledgeable Englishman, remarked in about 1725, 'The Highlands are but little known even to the inhabitants of the low country of Scotland, for they have ever dreaded the difficulties and dangers of travelling among the mountains...' To Burt the Highlands were unappealing, and indeed repellent. Their 'stupendous bulk, frightful irregularity, and horrid gloom' rendered them hideous. Pleasure-seeking visitors were seldom seen. For outsiders it was definitely a path less travelled. Burt was an employee of the British Government and was writing just ten years after the defeat of an earlier Jacobite rebellion. This was the 1715 Rising, when the Earl of Mar led a Highland army almost to the gates of Stirling in an attempt to regain the throne of Britain for the exiled Stewarts. While this rebellion, the '15 as it was later termed, failed, the Jacobite threat to the new Hanoverian regime had been real enough. If it had succeeded, James Francis Stewart, the son of the former James II, would have been crowned as James III (the term Jacobite was derived from the Latin word for James). The fact that Mar had been able to raise a formidable force of fighting men was indicative of the very different nature of Highland society compared not just to the rest of Britain but also to the rest of Scotland as well.

After 1715, government troops were stationed in the Highlands to maintain law and order. Forts were built or strengthened and attempts were made to disarm the clans, although not very successfully as later events showed. As one of the measures to bring order to the Highlands, General Wade, Commander-in-Chief in Scotland between 1724 and 1740, and his successors set about improving roads and communications. Built for military use, these roads and bridges also benefited civilian travellers. Ironically, however, in the short term the new roads were used most effectively when the Jacobite army led by Prince Charles Edward Stewart evaded the government forces to march south and take a virtually unguarded Edinburgh. Although this largely Highland army won the initial battles, it was, as we have seen, crushed at Culloden, which was the last major battle fought on British soil. When Prince Charles was on the run, 'skulking' in the contemporary parlance, a price was put on his head followed by a major manhunt. Warships patrolled the coastal waters and redcoat soldiers combed the hills and glens. With some rebels also still on the loose and there always being the potential for French invasion, good maps, it soon became obvious, were essential. There was already one map of the new military roads, Rutherford's, published, ironically, in 1745. More systematic and more detailed mapping of the Highlands was essential and this was commenced in 1747 under the direction of the army's Board of Ordnance.

It was not just the English who had opposed Prince Charles' Highland army. The people of the Lowlands were mostly hostile. At the Battle of Culloden there were regular Scottish regiments on the government side, as well as a detachment of Highlanders – Campbell militia from Argyll. Within Scotland, the '45 was truly a civil war. After Culloden, the government in London was determined to cow the Highlanders into submission by measures that included removing the semi-feudal military power of the Highland Chiefs. This involved the disarming of the clans and the smashing of the military power of the clan chieftains. The kilt and the tartan were banned as emblems of a martial society, with even bagpipes were classified as weapons of war. The only exceptions were for military units under government control – the forerunners of the Black Watch. After the '45, Highlanders in general were regarded as disloyal savages. It was some time before tourists in any number dared to visit what was for Southerners still virtually unknown and uncharted terrain. The dangers, real or imaginary, of Highland travel meant that few Lowland Scots had direct experience of the Highland way of life. So unsafe did they consider it to be that some visitors made their wills before leaving the Lowlands. For travellers, particularly from England, to venture north, one essential requisite was the need to change attitudes and to counter anti-Highland prejudice – the kind demonstrated by a young officer serving in the army of occupation. This officer, a Lieutenant Wolfe, wanted to use Highland troops to combat King George's enemies in the American colonies. Highlanders were, he admitted, 'hardy, intrepid, accustomed to a rough country and no great mischief if they fall. How better can you employ a secret enemy than by making his end conducive to the common good?' In other words, Highland troops were expendable. Their loss meant fewer potential Highland rebels. Yet it was public appreciation of the contribution eventually made by Highland regiments in Britain's colonial wars that helped to bring about a diminution of the old prejudice against Scots in general and the rebellion-tainted people of the North in particular. Highland soldiers fought under the now General Wolfe in 1759 when Quebec was captured, thus opening the way to the conquest of Canada. The role of Highland troops in that battle and other victories of the Seven Years War (1756–63) earned the praise of William Pitt (the Elder), the man who had led the country to victory. The military successes of the Scottish regiments, the odd mutiny notwithstanding, helped as a counter-balance to the jingoistic nationalism, racism, and malignant Scottophobia of that time. In the 1750s and '60s there was a great deal of anti-Scottish racism in London, largely due to the number of Scots in high governmental positions. Even Dr Samuel Johnson, possibly best known nowadays for his book *A Journey to the Western Islands of Scotland*, had more than a tincture of anti-Scottish prejudice.

Lowland Scots too had to be won over. When the Revd Alexander Carlyle from Inveresk, near Edinburgh, toured Culloden battlefield in 1765, he went there not as a romantically inclined Bonnie Prince Charlie sympathiser but as one who had been a volunteer in the anti-Jacobite Edinburgh militia. He had been present, though not a combatant, at the Battle of Prestonpans when the Highlanders had swept all before them. In describing the dispositions of Cumberland's army, he referred to them as 'our troops'. But the fact that he did make a tour to the north, albeit only as far as Inverness, was a pointer to the kind of change that was underway. A few years earlier, in 1759, Lord Breadalbane noted that, 'It had been the fashion this year to travel into the Highlands.' However, unless they kept a journal like Sir William Burrell (1758), Bishop Pococke (1760), Bishop Forbes (1762) and Alexander Carlyle (1765), or entered the written record in one way or another, we have no way of knowing just how many tourists there were at that time. The likelihood is that there were very few. It should be noted that, although the term 'making a tour' was already in circulation, the word 'tourist' itself did not enter general use until about 1800, but it is too useful a word not to use it to describe travellers like the Revd Alexander Carlyle or Richard Pococke, an Englishman who held an Irish see. It is safe to say that Bishop Richard Pococke, an inveterate traveller, was a tourist. His interest in antiquities and acquiring souvenirs would indicate that he was a tourist in the modern mould. This indefatigable Bishop made his way north as far as Caithness and Sutherland, even crossing to Orkney. Even someone like the Scottish Episcopalian Bishop William Forbes, who travelled from Leith in 1762 to visit his remote Caithness flock, was tourist enough to be seduced into going off route to visit 'sights' like the hermitage at Dunkeld and the Falls of Foyers near Fort Augustus.

Not surprisingly, the various fortifications erected before and after the '45 drew most travellers' attention, particularly Fort George. English gentlemen travellers making a northern tour might at the very least expect to be given a guided tour of it. That was the case with Sir William Burrell, landowner, advocate and later a Member of Parliament, who toured England and Scotland in 1758. Burrell, an acute observer with wide interests, was not impressed by Fort William where 'the only thing to be seen is the fortification, strong neither by situation or art'. Fort Augustus he considered to be more of a barracks than a fortification. Fort George, on the other hand, merited a detailed description, with Sir William reckoning that this fort, when completed, would be the strongest in Britain. Unpublished in his own day, Burrell's journal, like most diaries and tour accounts, was written probably for his friends and families to read and for Burrell himself as a memento of his travels. Nowadays our travel *aide-mémoires* are recorded by camera and mobile phone. Oddly enough, that strangely matched couple – Dr Samuel Johnson and James Boswell – on their copiously documented tour of the Highlands in 1773 bypassed Culloden. Though they visited Fort George and dined with the officers, they made no reference in their tour accounts to the battle at all. Perhaps for both of them it was too hot a potato, as at various times both men had expressed Jacobite sympathies.

As time passed, however, fear and suspicion began to diminish. Governments needing to make financial cuts reduced expenditure on the northern garrisons. Observant travellers noted how things had changed. Thomas Pennant on his first tour in 1769 admired Fort George but observed that 'by reason of the happy change of the times, it seemed almost deserted'. Similarly, when making his way through Deeside, a hotbed of revolt in 1715, he visited Braemar Castle, which was still garrisoned but unnecessarily so, he thought. As we have seen before, Johnson and Boswell, touring in 1773, received hospitality from the officers at Fort George and Fort Augustus but made no comment on the size of the garrisons. On the other hand, the specially built barracks at Glenelg, according to Boswell in 1773, had a nominal garrison, just a sergeant and a few men. Another of the new post-1715 forts was located at Inversnaid by Loch Lomond, in the heartland of the unruly MacGregor clan. By the time, that Sir Walter Scott visited this fort in 1792, the 'Garrison', as it was called, was empty, with the key left under the door. When the poet Robert Southey visited Fort Augustus in 1819 he noted that, though a large sum of money had but lately been spent on repairs, the cannons had also been removed around the same time. The War Department, not for the last time, had wasted public money.

As the Highlander ceased to be regarded as an enemy, the Acts of Parliament that had led to the kilt and the tartan being banned were rescinded. The Highlander was no longer a savage in primitive dress but a North Briton in picturesque garb. Highland dress, banned after Culloden, came back into fashion, but mainly just with the upper-class. The Highland garb had become a tourist attraction, although visitors were often disappointed to find few adults wearing the kilt. Significantly too, the man who had led a Highland army that came close to rocking the foundations of the Hanoverian regime was also rehabilitated, metaphorically at least. Though in his later years a sad figure, the young Prince Charles of the '45 was increasingly seen as a figure of romance. Storytellers and songsters now celebrated the handsome prince who had charmed the ladies of Edinburgh during the brief Jacobite occupation of that city. Now no longer posing a threat to the established order, he could be seen as a storybook hero, featuring in bestselling histories and romances. He was the Young Pretender, a mere claimant to the throne but no more. In the popular imagination he was now the gallant and dashing Young Chevalier. As Bonnie Prince Charlie he had been transformed into a cult figure celebrated in sentimental story and nostalgic song. Robert Burns, who in 1787 toured the Highlands, composed songs that fitted the mood of the times, including 'It Was A' For Our Rightfu' King' and 'The White Cockade'. The latter was the Jacobite emblem. The songs of Lady Nairne (1766–1845) gave added impetus to this process of glorification. Songs like 'Will Ye No Come Back Again', 'A Hundred Pipers' and 'Charlie Is My Darling' showed where her sympathies lay. Even Queen Victoria professed an admiration for the man who had tried to depose her Hanoverian ancestor.

Bonnie Prince Charlie's hardships and adventures, as the 'Prince in the Heather' on the run for five months in the Highlands, added to his lustre. He was the archetype of the 'fugitive on the run' kind of story and film. The loyalty shown by many ordinary Highlanders and the help they gave at considerable risk to themselves and their families excited no less admiration. This too was a tale with feminine interest. Enter the modest heroine Flora MacDonald, whose deeds in aiding the Prince to escape gained the admiration of friend and foe alike. Nonetheless, she was arrested and imprisoned for some time in the Tower of London. Places associated with Flora MacDonald, such as her former homes, became stopping points on the Victorian tourist trail. The slab of marble that covered her grave in Kilmuir Kirkyard in Skye did not last long, with souvenir hunters destroying it piece by piece. Flora's memorials have not had the best of luck, as the next one, a huge Celtic cross, had to be propped up after being blown down in a gale. In Skye, Victorian tourists were also directed to Prince Charlie's caves and other hideouts. Even springs where he supposedly drank became tourist landmarks. In 1765, when Alexander Carlyle went to Culloden, there were no memorials to the fallen. Many graves, however, were discernible by their verdure. He was also able to trace the outline of the long trenches 'where the kill'd were buried by Twenties'. Commemorations to the slain at Culloden came rather late in the day. It was not until 1881 that the present large memorial, complete with patriotic inscription, was erected at the instigation of neighbouring laird Duncan Forbes of Culloden. At the same time, headstones were installed marking the supposed burial places of the slain from the different clans.

As Bonnie Prince Charlie was celebrated in song and story, the reputation of the victor suffered in retrospect. For Welshman Thomas Pennant, the victory was beneficial for Scotland. Culloden Moor was 'the place that North Britain owes its present prosperity to by the victory of April 16, 1746'. The Duke of Cumberland, according to Pennant, gained immortal laurels by this triumph. The atrocities carried out by troops under his command, many of them Lowland Scots, meant that Cumberland gained no posthumous praise in the Highlands, where he was vilified as 'Butcher' Cumberland. Yet most Lowlanders had celebrated his victory and Glasgow University awarded him an honorary doctorate. On the other hand, some years later when Alexander Carlyle visited Culloden, he was anxious to inquire into the atrocities alleged to have been committed. After being told of wounded Highlanders being shot, he concluded, 'It is certain that the Duke's name is abhor'd which never happens to a merciful Conqueror.' Cumberland may have been Sweet William in England, but in the Highlands his commemoration came with the name given to the weed common ragwort – Stinking Billy.

Highland clansmen on the march, as imagined by a Victorian artist.

Braemar Castle.

After the 1745 Rising, Braemar Castle, a traditional tower house, was fortified with additional outer defensive walls and was garrisoned until 1831. Today it is privately owned but is open to the public.

By 1815 it was possible to erect a monument at Glenfinnan as a tribute to the clansmen who lost their lives during the 1745 Rising. This is where Bonnie Prince Charlie's standard was raised. The kilted Highlander on the top of the monument is not, as is sometimes supposed, a sculpture of the Prince, but depicts a typical Highland warrior of the eighteenth century.

In 1896 a statue of Flora MacDonald was erected on the Castle Esplanade in Inverness. Note the symbolism of the faithful hound.

The Clan Fraser memorial stone at Culloden. The Fraser clansmen were in the Jacobite centre and with the men of Atholl and other clans broke through the government front line, but were slaughtered by the second line of defence. Their chief, Simon Fraser of Lovat, who was not present at the battle, was captured afterwards and executed at Tower Hill in London – the last man to be publicly beheaded in Britain.

Chapter Two

The Beginnings of Change – New Roads and New Ideas

'If you had seen these roads before they were made, you'd have lifted up your hands and blessed General Wade.'

Whereas the Duke of Cumberland's name was soon blackened, in Scotland at least, another Hanoverian commander, General Wade, earned posthumous praise, even though it is in a rhyme of dubious origin and one also that is often applied to roads for which he had no responsibility. As outlined earlier, the government in London built forts at strategic points to keep rebellious Highlanders under control. It was the intention also that these forts and barracks were to be linked by new military roads. We thus see the beginnings of major improvements in transport in the Highlands. Systematic road construction in the Highlands only started after General Wade had been appointed Commander-in-Chief for North Britain in 1724. In this capacity he was responsible for the construction of about 250 miles of roads, with the most important being the 'Great Highland Road' from Perth to Inverness. The most difficult to construct was the 28-mile-long crossroad from Dalwhinnie to Fort Augustus, which was completed in 1731. Going via the Corrieyairack Pass this road went as high as 2,500 feet, and with its eighteen hairpin bends the Corrieyairack soon gained a reputation as a difficult and dangerous route – so much so that some tourists preferred to take the long way round by Inverness. This fine feat of engineering aside, Wade built forty important bridges, which included crossing major rivers like the Upper Spey with Garva Bridge and the Tay at Aberfeldy. The Aberfeldy Bridge was an important link on the road that connected Crieff on the fringe of the Highlands to Wade's Great Highland Road and thence to Inverness. The extension southward from Crieff to the important fortress town of Stirling was, however, the work of Wade's successor Major Caulfeild.

The early tourists found their passage eased by the military roads and inns, but they also benefited from having maps of at least parts of Scotland available for their use. The Jacobite threat meant that to ensure military control of the Highlands, more up-to-date and accurate maps were required. Mapping of the Highlands was commenced in 1747 under the direction of the army's Board of Ordnance with a Scotsman, William Roy, in charge. As the state kept the completed map locked away, it was of little use to contemporary travellers. Most existing maps were based on the depiction of Scotland in Blaeu's Atlas, published in the Netherlands as far back as 1654. And that, in its turn, was based largely on the surveys carried out by Timothy Pont around 1600, with corrections and additions being made by Robert Gordon of Straloch and his son James. By the mid-eighteenth century, however, maps that were being produced for civilian use did at least show Wade's military roads, or 'His Majesty's roads'. Not that these commercial maps were very accurate, especially and not surprisingly in depicting the north-west Highlands. Travellers going up the east coast were better served. James Dorret's 'accurate' map of Scotland of 1761 showed a road up the east coast as far as John o'Groats and then a continuation westward, but only as far as Durness. Later travellers, as we shall see, were better served.

Of course, the people of the Highlands and Islands had managed to travel around the country without roads and maps. Specialist herdsmen drove large numbers of cattle and sheep to southern markets, like the major trysts at Crieff and Falkirk. These drovers followed ancient trails or drove roads, which, over the course of many, many years, became well-trodden. Going from the Western Highlands to the south and east, drovers and other travellers had a choice of routes – some later transformed into modern highways and others now featuring as popular trails for walkers and climbers. There were well-established drove roads through the Cairngorms by the Lairig Ghru and Glen Feshie passes, and the Grampians too were penetrated by a number of hill passes. Welsh traveller Thomas Pennant used one when he rode from Blair Atholl to Braemar in 1769 going by Glen Tilt – 'The most dangerous and most horrible [road] I ever travelled.' Travellers and cattle droves often intermixed. In late August 1762 Bishop Robert Forbes was travelling south in a chaise on Wade's Great Road. Near Dalwhinnie he counted eight droves of black cattle, totalling around 1,200, heading to the Crieff Tryst. At least one batch, the Bishop ascertained, had come all the way from Skye. That would have involved the cattle swimming across the dangerous strait at Kylerea. In more lawless times, when cattle theft was part of the Highland way of life, some trails were known as thieves' roads, and even with military occupation cattle reiving continued for many years.

Major William Caulfeild, who had the responsibility for military roads in Scotland from 1740 to 1767, like Wade before him, often followed the line of traditional drovers' routes. The major actually built many more roads and bridges than General Wade ever did. While Wade's and Caulfeild's roads did ease the way for tourists, not all of the military roads proved suitable for civilian use, with the gradients being just too steep. The 'Devil's Staircase' section of the Stirling to Fort William road was one such, with Thomas Pennant considering it 'very injudiciously planned'. Although Pennant considered the military roads in general to be excellent, this was a road that was often 'scarce surmountable'. It would have been better, he thought, if the road engineer had followed the track used by the local people. Like the Corrieyairack Pass route, the Devil's Staircase was eventually abandoned and replaced by a road that went via Glencoe and Ballachulish Ferry. It may have been abandoned as a highway, but the Devil's Staircase is now one of the more challenging parts of the West Highland Way – a popular long-distance hiking path.

The construction of the new Wade military roads had been accompanied by the building of a number of new inns, often erected on the sites of soldiers' work camps. These inns, accordingly, were called King's houses. The King's House on Rannoch Muir was the best known and was often portrayed in disparaging terms. Pennant mildly described the inn of his day as 'in a manner unfurnished'. Robert Southey and Thomas Telford, staying at the King's House in 1819, fared better than some other travellers, being served 'turkey as well as hen's eggs, a shoulder of lamb, and cream for the tea'. Dorothy Wordsworth, however, sixteen years earlier, had never seen 'such a wretched, miserable place'. Some of the innkeepers there, Robert Southey tells us, ran a sideline in salt smuggling, a commodity which at that time was very heavily taxed. The present-day hotel on this site, which retains the original name, is popular with travellers and climbers.

Until the early nineteenth century, although their strategic function had long gone, the military roads were maintained by army personnel. In 1788 English visitor Elizabeth Diggle, touring the Highlands in a chaise, saw soldiers at work in Glen Croe in Argyll: 'Soldiers' tents here and there enlivened the scene. The men are employed to mend the roads which were originally made, and are still kept in repair by the military.' These road improvements and the new sense of security following the disarmament of the Highland clans saw increasing numbers of visitors crossing the Border, with some proceeding even further north into the Highlands and Islands. An earlier visitor, Sir William Burrell, touring in 1758, was certainly appreciative of the difficulties the military must have had when road building in 'savage and barbarous' Glen Croe. So thankful were the troops of the 93rd Regiment on reaching the summit of this section that they erected a stone with the inscription 'Rest and Be Thankful'. To this day this route still goes by the name of the Rest and Be Thankful Road. Today that stretch in Glen Croe, completed in 1748, is brought back into use when the main highway is blocked by landslip. Burrell, en route between Inverary and Tyndrum, noted the contrast between the new and the old:

> The instant we left the new road we found ourselves in the most horrid paths that can be conceived, up and down steep hills, through bogs in some places, in others filled with large loose stones where our horses had no firm footing or, what was worse, now and then staircases of solid, craggy rock.

Two years after Burrell went that way another visitor, Bishop Richard Pococke (1704–1765), found few signs of improvement. Like Burrell, Pococke found the road to Loch Awe very bad in places, but the Bishop was not someone to be deterred by poor roads. He was an unusually experienced traveller, having already spent three years travelling on the Continent and another five in the Middle East, including Egypt, Palestine, Syria and Cyprus. While he had also made two previous short excursions into Scotland, this tour of 1760 was much more extensive, taking him well beyond the range of the military roads – even as far as Orkney.

As with many other travellers, Pococke's account is derived from letters sent to family members. These were later amplified, corrected and copied into manuscript volumes, which eventually ended up in the British Library. It is evident from the text of the letters that the good Bishop had done his homework by reading most of the available histories of Scotland and other books. These works were of their time, of course, with the authors accepting stories and legends that are now discredited. Standing stone circles and other prehistoric structures in Britain and Ireland for instance were erroneously attributed to the druids, which was a misapprehension that long persisted. As with many scholars of the time, the Bishop had an obsession with the druids. Eighteenth-century travellers knew their Classics and the stories related by Julius Caesar and other Roman writers about this high-ranking priestly sect. Without any real justification, they tended to assume that standing stones and other prehistoric structures were druid temples – built for sacrificial ceremonies. With regard to defensive earthworks, the standard explanation of the day was that they were the work of the Danes or Romans. Pococke, an assiduous antiquarian, was on the lookout for such works. The search for supposed Roman forts gave him at least one fruitless side-tracking journey.

Iona was, of course, an obvious target for a bishop. Crossing to Mull, he set out for Iona using local ponies, his own horses having been sent overland to Fort William. Though unshod, the Mull ponies he declared to be very hardy and sure-footed in rough ground. Iona naturally merited a full account of the history of the island and its abbey, and likewise a detailed description of the ruins and monuments. Pococke's account of the ruins is valuable as he wrote about features that no longer exist. The Bishop had a keen interest too in finding out about the ways of life and beliefs of the people he met. On Iona, he noted that the islanders, as was their custom apparently with all strangers, ceased their work and followed him all round the island. He passed on the information, too, that, as he had been told, the islanders had a talent for poetry 'chiefly of the lyric kind', in which they were only exceeded by those of Skye. The islanders' funeral practices also fascinated him, commonly spending three days at it. Evidently a social occasion, they spent their time eating and drinking 'very plentifully'.

On his return from Iona he sailed to Lismore, which was of interest to him as it had once been the seat of the Bishop of Argyll. He noted the fertility of the island, with the soil bearing excellent barley and oats. Pococke was seemingly unaware that the name Lismore can be translated as *Big Garden*. Of the medieval cathedral, nothing remained but the choir, the doors and the seats for the officiating priests. The medieval features that he saw had been incorporated into parts of the new parish kirk. While still on the mainland, the Bishop had acquired some souvenirs – the bones of an auroch that had been found in a Lismore bog. This was just the kind of trophy that the Bishop prized, as aurochs were the long-extinct large, wild cattle that were the ancestors of today's domestic breeds.

Back on the mainland he rode north on horses, presumably borrowed or hired, via Appin to Fort William and then via the military road to Inverness – 'a very pretty town'. As a loyal subject of the King, the Bishop was shown over Fort George and the battlefield of Culloden. Pococke provided a fairly detailed account of the battle, including a diagrammatic sketch of the formations on both sides. The Bishop concluded by writing: 'Thus ended this day of such consequence to the British Dominions, and Crowned the Duke [Cumberland] with immortal Lawrels.' The indefatigable Bishop made his way north even as far as Caithness and Sutherland. He thoroughly explored these northern counties, retracing his steps on many occasions. He even got to Cape Wrath, being first ferried across the Kyle of Durness. Like many later visitors, Pococke was taken to see the 'very beautiful' Smoo Cave, where a small underground lake is to be seen. A journey to see the broch Dun Dornaigil was, of course, a must. This 'round castle', as Pococke described it, was duly sketched, providing, with his exterior and interior views, the earliest depictions of this notable broch.

The Bishop later crossed to the Orkney Isles, landing in Hoy. It is evident that his main interest in Hoy was to see 'that famous stone commonly called the Dwarfie Stone … into which a room is cut'. This 'room', he wrongly concluded, was without doubt the habitation of a hermit. Known locally as the Dwarfie Stone, this large free-standing rock had long aroused curiosity as to its origins and purposes. A gap had been cut in the rock, giving access to an inner chamber with smaller cells on either side. Long before the Bishop arrived, the large stone sealing the entrance had been removed and the contents of what had been a prehistoric family or tribal burial place had been removed. A later antiquary, Sir Walter Scott, was so fascinated with the Dwarfie Stone that he brought it into his novel, *The Pirate*. Scott used its name to make it the home of a dwarf Trolld – a name already familiar from the Norse sagas.

From Hoy the Bishop's party sailed to Stromness on the Orkney mainland – a town described by him as very irregularly built and full of publicans and shopkeepers. These latter served ships seeking shelter from storms and also provisioned with stores vessels bound for Hudson's Bay. Orkneymen who were used to boats and hardship were in demand to serve in the lonely trading posts of the Hudson's Bay Company. In Stromness, Pococke, always on the lookout for information about strange people, wrote down accounts he was given describing the way of life of the Indians and the 'Askeomies' (the Inuit people). Procuring a horse in Stromness, the Bishop set out to tour the sights on the west side of the Orkney mainland. This trip shows the breadth of his interests. He visited the spectacular sea cliffs at Yesnaby, where his interest was mainly scientific. The Standing Stones and other ancient monuments at the Loch of Stenness were grist to the mill of an antiquarian. These he described and sketched and, of course, attributed to the druids. Before departing from

Orkney he visited Kirkwall, the principal town of the archipelago. As with Stromness, Kirkwall's irregularity did not meet with his approval. Ill-built was his assessment. On the other hand, the town's Norse-built cathedral and the ruins of two palaces he found to be full of interest. Kirkwall Town Council decided to present the Bishop with the freedom of the town, but he couldn't delay his departure for a personal investiture. It is interesting to note that Bishop Pococke was granted the freedom of no fewer than nine Scottish burghs. Important visitors were evidently rather rare at that time. His return to Caithness took him past the ruins of 'Johnny Grott's House' (John o'Groats). He returned south down the east coast where there were plenty of ruined castles, 'Picts houses', and other so-called druidical remains to keep him happy, and many of which he sketched, albeit somewhat crudely.

Important personages like bishops did not travel unaccompanied. Usually with travellers' accounts their servants are voiceless and seldom even get a mention. Bishop Pococke, we know from another source, was accompanied by four servants including a valet and a groom. We have, however, an eyewitness account of Bishop Pococke on the road in Cornwall. 'I saw … a cavalcade of horsemen approaching on a gentle trot, headed by an elderly chief in clerical attire, who was followed by five servants, at distances geometrically measured, and most precisely maintained'. Pococke finished the Scottish part of his tour on 27 September at Coldingham, having commenced at Portpatrick on 30 April. In that time he covered 2,496 miles. If we include the Irish and English parts of his journey, it is estimated that he had travelled 3,391 miles – a remarkable achievement for a man of fifty-six. The good bishop's travel diaries were not published until the nineteenth century, but Thomas Pennant had probably seen these diaries and was perhaps influenced by them when he decided to tour the Highlands. Pennant referred to one of the Ballachulish area hills as one that 'my old friend, the late worthy Bishop Pococke compared … to Mount Tabor'. The Bishop, it may be said, was very fond of making biblical comparisons, even comparing the situation of Dingwall to Jerusalem.

Another of the early post-Culloden travellers for whom we have some records was another bishop. This was Robert Forbes, a bishop in the Scottish Episcopalian Church, who travelled widely in the Highlands in 1762 and again in 1770. As the newly consecrated Bishop of Ross and Caithness, the Right Revd Robert Forbes (1708–1775) was actually doing his job when in 1762 he headed north from his base in Leith. Formally it was a 'visitation' or inspection visit to his clergy, but the details as recorded in his journal make it clear that at times he behaved like a tourist. He took time to see the same kind of wonders and curiosities as any other tourist would. On his way north, Bishop Forbes halted for breakfast at the ferry inn at Dunkeld. After breakfast, 'the landlord, Johnson, told us of a curious summer-house built on the bank of the River Braan … and kindly offered to conduct us to it'. This was the now well-known tourist hotspot that we call the Hermitage. Bishop Forbes gave a full description of it and also gave an account of how it came to be built. It was built by a nephew of the Duke of Atholl, the proprietor of the land, to surprise his uncle. Bishop Forbes mentioned in his journal that his fellow bishop had been there before him. The innkeeper informed him 'that the Bishop of Ossory spent several hours in this delightful Hermitage, and wrote a good deal in it'. That was Bishop Richard Pococke's title, he being a Bishop of the Church of Ireland, which was also an Episcopalian denomination.

In addition to those few travellers that we know about, there must have been others who passed through the Highlands without leaving any record. In 1759 the Earl of Breadalbane wrote from Taymouth in Perthshire to his daughter: 'It has been the fashion this year to travel into the Highlands, many have been here this summer from England, I suppose because they can't go abroad.' This would have been because Britain and France had been at war for the previous three years and it is very likely that that war (the Seven Years' War of 1756–63), as with the later French Revolutionary and Napoleonic Wars, did bring some tourists into Scotland, who might otherwise have embarked on a continental tour. This handful of pioneering tourists might not have been aware of it but they had arrived in the Highlands on the cusp of a new era, when there was an awakening of interest in the Highlanders and the land they inhabited. More and better roads and bridges helped to increase the number of visitors to the Highlands and Islands but there were other factors at play. Views on landscape were beginning to change. Like other travellers, Sir William Burrell found Glen Croe to be savage and barbarous and Glen Kinglas 'equally horrible, barbarous and disagreeable'. On the other hand, when he visited the already famous Falls of Foyers he considered its gorge to be 'extremely romantic, covered with shrubs from top to bottom.' Burrell's view that the Foyers gorge was 'romantic' is an indication of how elite attitudes to wild and lonely places were beginning to change.

Strangely enough, it was some literary forgeries that did most at that time to increase interest in what to most southerners was still a strange and distant land. These forgeries were the product of the imagination of a young Highlander, James Macpherson. It was in 1760, the same year Bishop Pococke made his tour, that James Macpherson from Kingussie burst on the literary scene with a work entitled *Fragments of Ancient Poetry Collected in the Highlands of Scotland and Translated from the Galic or Erse Language*. These, he claimed, were translations of traditional Gaelic verses passed on through oral tradition. He followed this up with *Fingal, an Ancient Epic Poem, in Six Books*, which, like the *Fragments*, was supposedly the work of Ossian, an ancient Gaelic bard and, like Homer, blind. Ossian, according to Macpherson, was Fingal's son – Fingal being an ancient Celtic hero who was King of Morven in the West Highlands. Tales and legends about Celtic heroes had long been current in both Highland Scotland and Ireland, and indeed their Celtic-world legends were intertwined. The name of the warrior Fingal appears in the mythology of both countries. While in the Highlands he was generally known as Fingal, in Ireland he was Fionn MacCumaill (anglicised as Finn MacCool), and both titles frequently crop up in place names. Although the legends were known, they were passed on through oral transmission. Macpherson's achievement was to produce what he claimed to be a written epic.

The publication of *Fingal* in 1761 caused a sensation in the literary world, both at home and abroad. While *Fingal*'s authenticity was challenged, this work and successor epics generated a lot of interest in the Highlands and in ancient Celtic culture. With the burgeoning interest in romantic literature and art, Macpherson's poems, written in what we would now regard as high-flown language, made an enormous impact. *Fingal* was lauded by continental literary giants like Goethe, Chateaubriand and Mme de Stael. For French poet Lamartine – 'The Harp of Morven is the emblem of my soul.' Napoleon too was an enthusiast, taking a copy of *Fingal* on his campaigns.

We see the effect of this in tourists' diaries and memoirs. Witness how the poet Thomas Gray, making a short Highland tour in 1765, was overwhelmed by the sublime nature of the natural landscape. The grotesquely shaped rocks at the Pass of Killiecrankie rose 'like the sullen countenances of Fingal and all his family frowning on the little mortals of modern days.' For French romanticist Charles Nodier, visiting in 1821, even the very mists and clouds could be construed as Ossianic. At Loch Lomond he was enchanted by 'the accidents of light and shade in the circuits of these profound glens … the whimsical appearance of vapours which hang on the summits of mountains, which has consecrated, if I may say so, the mythology of the clouds.'

Not every tourist was convinced by Macpherson's claims. The always outspoken Dr Samuel Johnson was not fooled by 'as gross an imposition as ever the world was troubled with'. While on his Scottish tour in 1773, Johnson continued to question the authenticity of Macpherson's work, continually baiting his defenders. Modern opinion would agree with Johnson that Macpherson's so-called translations were almost entirely his own work. *Fingal*, however, continued to sell well and it was widely translated. Forged the poems may have been, but many Scots of that time convinced themselves that Macpherson's epics must have been based on people who had lived at some remote period of time.

The prime example of Ossianic mania is to be found at the hermitage in the Duke of Atholl's Dunkeld estate, although, in its first form, its construction may have predated the Ossianic cult. As is clear from Bishop Forbes' account of his visit there in 1762, the hermitage was a cross between a folly and a viewing chamber. In this it was fairly typical of the ornamental follies erected by Georgian landowners to embellish their estates. In England and Wales, no less than in Scotland, landowners were inventing traditions to add interest and spectacle to the improvements they were then bringing to their estates.

Today the Dunkeld hermitage is still a tourist attraction, albeit of a more low-key nature. It is a convenient halting place for travellers on the A9 road to Inverness. Even if Macpherson's supposed translations were in doubt, the Fingalian legends were an intrinsic part of the Highlander's culture. Tales of the deeds of the Ossianic heroes – the Fiann or Fianna, Fingal's warrior band – were passed down through the centuries. In consequence their names were written into the landscape and these names, many of which might have been forgotten, entered the tourist guidebooks and other literature. All over the Highlands there are rocks, pillars, standing stones, cairns and other monuments with Gaelic names associated with Ossian, Fingal, and other figures of the mythological past. A stone in the Sma' Glen, the Clach Ossian, was supposed to be the burial place of the legendary poet. As it is located by the Wade road joining Stirling to Inverness, it was a feature pointed out to travellers. William Wordsworth went this way through the glen, passing by this 'still place where remote from men, sleeps Ossian in the narrow glen'. A nondescript standing stone in the village of Killin is, according to local tradition, the burial place of Fingal. The Fianna or Fiann are also commemorated. These warriors, the legends say, roamed widely over the hills and glens on hunting expeditions, tethering their hounds to stout stone pillars. The ancient sea stack, known as the Dog Stone (Clach a'Choin), which is close to Oban, is one such pillar. Its proximity to Oban ensured that this lump of rock featured in all the tourist literature.

Above: In this section of the Lairig Ghru the line of the old drove road can be traced alongside the River Dee. The author was on his way up the Devil's Point, a mountain which in the original Gaelic was named the Devil's Penis.

Left: In this SYHA image a rain-coated hiker surveys the Devil's Staircase section of the old military road, which was one of Major Caulfeild's roads. It is now part of the West Highland Way, a popular hikers' trail.

Right: After leaving
Lismore Bishop
Richard Pococke
sketched Castle
Stalker while en route
to Fort William in his
1760 tour.

Below: We see
continuity of military
use in this image.
The Devil's Elbow
was a notoriously
difficult corner on the
1750s-built Caulfeild
military road from
Blairgowrie to
Braemar.

Castle of Tene Stalcar.

A DANGEROUS TURN- THE DEVILS ELBOW, ABOVE BRAEMAR

Where there are no bridges, fast-flowing burns like this one in Glen Affric can be hazardous to cross when in spate.

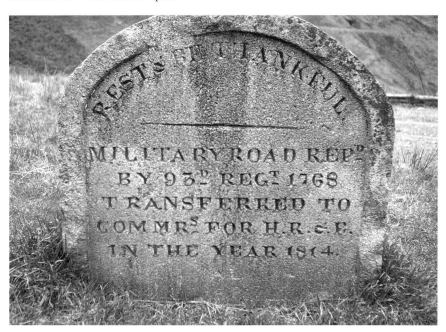

The present 'Rest and Be Thankful' stone at the head of Glen Croe is a replacement for the original, which was erected by redcoat soldiers in 1748. They were marking the completion of this section of the military road from Dumbarton to Inverary.

Chapter Three

A Fashion for Travel

'Away let us fly to the renowned cities of Asia! My soul flutters in anticipation, and my eager feet rejoice.' (Catullus, *c.* 84–54 BC)

As the above quotation from the Roman poet Catullus indicates, the idea of travel for curiosity and pleasure goes back a long way. Catullus expresses the sense of excitement that travel evokes. Among the British social and political elite too, foreign travel as part of one's education had become fashionable from the seventeenth century onward. Francis Bacon (1561–1626) had recognised its value when he wrote, 'Travel, in the younger sort, is a part of education.' Touring for pleasure became more common in the eighteenth century, as means of transport and communications improved and as political conditions became more stable. It then became established practice for wealthy young men to extend their education and experience of life by going on a tour. The most extensive type of tour was the so-called Grand Tour involving young men of rank rounding off their education by visiting places of cultural and historic interest in Western Europe. Italy, with its art treasures and antiquities, was the prime destination, especially since knowledge of the classical languages was a key component in the education of these fortunate young men. Long before he embarked on his Highland tour with Dr Johnson, the young James Boswell had done the Grand Tour, visiting Holland, Germany, Switzerland, Italy, Corsica and France. Travelling for the purpose of widening one's horizons was by no means confined to the Continent. While the aristocratic rich still favoured the Continent, others, mainly men but some women too of the gentry class, took off for the wider reaches of their own country. In England the Derbyshire peaks and the Wye Valley had their devotees. At the same time, the number making a tour in Scotland was on the increase, though initially that did not necessarily incorporate much or any of the Highlands. As for the Hebrides, it was a rare and unusual traveller who ventured that far. Boswell himself, when visiting France, told Voltaire, the great French thinker and philosopher, of the ambition of Dr Samuel Johnson and himself to visit the Hebrides. 'He looked at me,' Boswell recorded, 'as if I had talked of going to the North Pole.' 'You do not insist on my accompanying you?' Voltaire asked in mock concern.

Voltaire certainly didn't come to Scotland, but others, as we have already seen, did and some wrote about their travels in journals and diaries. These as with later tour accounts can, if used with care, help towards our understanding of life in the Highlands and Islands at the time of their visit. How much outsiders really understood the society of the North and West is quite another matter for, excepting the Northern Isles of Orkney and Shetland and a large part of Caithness, the language of the people was Gaelic. It is trite to say that much can be lost in translation and that, with many tourists, was obviously the case, but the scope for misunderstanding is so much the worse when no competent translator is available.

If there is one traveller who did try to analyse, and report on, this very distinctive society, it was Welshman Thomas Pennant. Pennant, in the course of two separate tours, travelled to the more remote parts of the Western and Northern Highlands and thus blazed a trail for others to follow. This Welsh gentleman had wide interests, including the study of antiquities and natural history. In the latter sphere, his three-volume work on *British Zoology* had been instrumental in his election to a Fellowship of the prestigious Royal Society. Of more importance perhaps was the fact that he was an experienced traveller and an adventurous one at that. To Dr Johnson he was 'a sad dog', but that was because Pennant was a political moderate compared to the High Tory Johnson. As a travel writer, though, Johnson conceded that Pennant was the best he had ever read: 'He observes more things than anyone else.' An obituarist wrote on his death in 1782 that his book on his first tour in 1769 opened up Scotland, 'a country at that time as little known to its southern brethren as Kamtschatka [a peninsula in the far east of Russia]'.

On his first visit in 1769 Pennant covered an extensive area of Scotland, reaching as far north as Caithness, travelling on horseback. Two years later he published an account of his journey, *A Tour of Scotland*, which indicated to southerners that the northern parts of Great Britain might now be visited with safety. This book was well received and seemed to have influenced Dr Johnson when he decided to proceed with his own tour in 1773. Although he had gone as far north as Caithness by the fairly well-established east coast route, Pennant realised, however, that his knowledge of the country was incomplete without seeing the Hebrides. Accordingly, he returned in 1772 and spent more time on this occasion on the west of the country, including some of the islands. Prior to his second tour, he had placed a notice in *The Scots Magazine* seeking useful information about the places he hoped to visit. Explaining his reasons, he wrote:

It is now becoming fashionable among the English to make a tour into Scotland for some few weeks or months; and there is a moral certainty of this fashion increasing, as the foolish prejudices against the country and its inhabitants daily decrease.

It was a pity, Pennant went on to say, that 'an intelligent curious traveller from England has no proper helps to assist him'. By 'helps' he clearly meant guidebooks, so he asked 'Gentlemen in the several parts of Great Britain' to assist by giving him useful information about their localities. His long list of suggested topics came to no less than ninety-seven, even including a query about the price of rabbits. It was Pennant's stated intention to publish the fruits of his investigations and this was duly achieved when his second book, *A Tour in Scotland and Voyage to the Hebrides*, was issued in 1776.

On his 1769 tour Pennant entered the Highlands at one of the traditional gateways, the Pass of Birnam, which he described, in picturesque phraseology, as 'awefully magnificent'. On this tour – which Pennant made on horseback – he was able to make good use of the military roads. On his second journey in 1772, however, he was venturing well beyond the safety blanket provided by the Hanoverian garrisons and military road system. On the other hand, Pennant had the company of a sizeable back-up team. He was accompanied much of the way by two clergymen – one an expert naturalist and the other knowledgeable in Gaelic. There were three servants too, with one Moses Griffith being a competent artist who provided illustrations for the travel book on Scotland he was to write. Pennant's high-level contacts secured too the use of a 90-ton cutter, *The Lady Frederic Campbell*. This vessel provided Pennant with a hop-on hop-off facility. Starting from Ardincaple, the present-day Helensburgh, skipper Archibald Thompson took the cutter to Bute and then Arran, allowing Pennant five days to explore the latter island. These Clyde islands, he reported, were Gaelic speaking, but this was before they became popular tourist destinations. Then, while the cutter sailed round the difficult waters off the Mull of Kintyre, Pennant went ashore to have a look round Campbeltown, where he was made a freeman of the town. This was quite common practice in those days, with town councillors considering it an honour to have distinguished guests in their midst no matter how short their visit. Bishop Pococke, as we have seen, collected nine 'freedoms' on his tour. In Kintyre, Pennant noted that a great deal of bere (a kind of barley) was grown. Unfortunately, although food was often scarce, the inhabitants were 'mad enough to convert their bread into poison' – whisky, in other words. The principal landowner, the Duke of Argyll, tried to discourage this business, but the trade was so profitable that 'many persist in it, to the great neglect of manufactures'. Whisky distilling continued to be profitable, it may be said, long after Pennant's day. In Victorian times there were twenty-eight distilleries in Campbeltown. Today there are three.

After crossing Kintyre on horseback, Pennant was ferried to the Isle of Gigha, where the cutter was awaiting his arrival, and this on-off process was repeated several times on the journey north. Everywhere he landed, Pennant was welcomed and entertained by the local gentry and clergymen. On Jura, for instance, the leading proprietor sent horses for the use of his party. Pennant, nevertheless, was certainly an able pedestrian. While on Jura he climbed Beinn an Oir, which at 2,578 feet is the highest of the Paps of Jura – 'a task of much labour and difficulty.' Judging by the number of manmade cairns around the summit, he was by no means the first to climb this hill. The stupendous view from the summit, however, made the effort worthwhile. Looking down on the two lower Paps, they were, Pennant considered, well named, all of them being 'perfectly mammillary'. Pennant was evidently a keen climber as later in Skye he ascended Beinn na Caillich, which, he noted, was also topped by a cairn – an enormous one that was supposedly the burial place of a Fingalian giantess. The Jura peak is a target for today's hill walkers who are ticking off Corbetts, a category of Scottish hill between 2,500 and 3,000 feet. Hills over 3,000 feet are Munros.

Pennant's journal, which was the basis of his later book, is full of scientific details about the geology and the fauna and flora of the places he visited. The fishing industry was one aspect that Pennant took a particular interest in, with the migration of herring being one of the subjects he dealt with in his book on *British Zoology*. At Campbeltown he had seen a flourishing industry, with 800 sailors being employed in the herring fishery using drift nets. This town, he wrote, was created by this fishery. Herring caught in Loch Fyne and elsewhere in the Firth of Clyde found a ready and large market in Glasgow. Further north in the Highlands the industry was seasonal but with vast shoals of herring being harvested in Loch Broom, Loch Hourn and other sea-lochs. The people of the West Highlands certainly played their part in harvesting these riches. At Loch Hourn Pennant saw over a hundred boats rowing towards the inner loch to lay their nets. Unfortunately, as Pennant recognised, they lacked the capital to be able to fully exploit the rich bounty of the western seas. Many of the Highlanders who lived along the coast combined inshore fishing with farming, and fishing was very much an ancillary activity. The boats Pennant saw in Loch Hourn in 1772 were small and carried few nets. Another traveller around the same time observed that, though there were fertile fishing grounds round Mull, there was, on that island, 'not a net or long line in all the island'. The people of Mull did catch fish, but it was with a rod from the shore.

The real profits from fishing came from curing and retailing the herring and this was in the hands of businessmen from the Clyde ports. In inner Loch Hourn Pennant saw 'a great fleet of busses [small two-masted sloops] and all the busy apparatus of the herring fishery'. The owners of the vessels that carried away the cured herring were Lowlanders from the Clyde ports. However, not all was sweetness and light between the locals and the interlopers. Visiting Loch Hourn fourteen years later, John Knox was told of trouble between 'the buss-men' and the native Highlanders, with the locals sabotaging the Lowlanders' nets and gear.

Time and again, however, Pennant was dismayed by the poverty of the people of the West Highlands. Canna, on first sight, with hundreds of cattle grazing, looked as if it should be prosperous. Pennant was soon disabused as the people were in much want, many having 'no bread or meal for their poor babes'. To compound their problems, their supply of fish hooks was almost exhausted. Pennant lamented that all he had brought as potential gifts were ribbons and other trifles, and that it would have been an insult to offer these to people in such a degree of misery. On Rum, while he did think that the people looked well and strong, he did add that in many years there had been no grain to harvest. On Islay, too, he had found a people 'worn down with poverty, their homes scenes of misery, and their food that which may rather be called a permission to exist rather than a support of vigorous life'. In the 'torn and convulsed' district of Assynt, the people, he considered, could have done more to help themselves. Nevertheless, at the same time Pennant witnessed crowds 'dispirited and driven to despair by bad management' heading for the east coast, where rumour had it that a vessel laden with meal had arrived.

Admittedly, the year before he arrived had been a particularly bad one in the Highlands. During the 'Black Spring' of 1772 an unending frost had meant that the ground was covered with snow for eight weeks. Even in better years, however, the ordinary people lived a little above subsistence level. Poor though they were, the people of Assynt were still hospitable: 'Kindness and hospitality possess the people of these parts. We scarce passed a farm but the good woman, long before our approach, sallied out and stood at the roadside, holding out to us a bowl of milk or whey.' As many other tourists testified, even the very poorest maintained the old tradition of hospitality to travellers. At the same time, Pennant was disgusted with the dereliction of the chieftains, who had been transformed into rapacious landlords. The manifold problems of the Highlands, Pennant argued, could be solved if the chieftains, instead of seeking the fleshpots of the south, were to return to their native heath. They needed to teach their people arts and skills and provide instructors and materials for manufactures. Unfortunately, few chiefs had the means or inclination to implement Pennant's proposals. At any rate many chiefs sold their estates and the new sporting landowners had other interests.

Shortly after Pennant returned, the two most celebrated tourists of this pioneering time of Highland tourism combined for a tour of Scotland, namely Dr Samuel Johnson (1709–1784) and James Boswell (1740–1795), who toured the Highlands and Islands in 1773. On the surface this was an ill-matched couple. They had different backgrounds and a disparity of age. Dr Johnson was nearing sixty-four and Boswell was thirty years younger. Johnson was an odd-looking figure – large and corpulent and walking with some difficulty. His head and sometimes his whole body shook with convulsive twitches. His face was marked with the scars of scrofula – the King's Evil as it was then called. Blind in one eye, Johnson was also somewhat hard of hearing. Nevertheless, he was active and hardy enough to undertake an arduous and strenuous tour, which took him and his friend Boswell well off the beaten track. When Dr Johnson embarked on this tour he was undoubtedly the outstanding literary figure of his time, his greatest achievement being the compilation of the first English dictionary, which was completed in 1755. Robust in his physique, he was also extremely robust in expressing his opinions. Johnson could be overbearing and irascible and it took a brave man to contradict 'the Great Bear' of literary London.

Johnson's companion, James Boswell of Auchinleck in Ayrshire, was another complex figure. Trained as a lawyer, he escaped a Calvinistic home background to seek out the fleshpots of London. In this he proved remarkably successful and, as his own astonishingly frank private diaries show, not just during his initial sojourn in London but at many times during his later life. Recurrent bouts of venereal disease were the unfortunate outcome. An attention seeker, he sought the company of the celebrities of the day and that, of course, included Dr Johnson. Their first meeting in 1763 did not go too well. Boswell, introduced to the great man as a young Scotsman lately come to London, said, 'Indeed sir I come from Scotland, but I cannot help it.' Johnson's reply was typical of the man: 'That I find is what a very great many of your countrymen cannot help.' Nevertheless, once they became better acquainted they became good friends and travelling companions, the best in the world according to Johnson. Boswell was naturally boyish and good-humoured, although occasionally suffered from depression. As his account of the 1773 tour shows, Boswell could draw people out and thus, as Johnson acknowledged, assisted him in his pursuit of information about the modes and customs of the Highlanders: 'Mr Boswell's frankness and gaiety made everybody communicative.' Boswell, too, had enjoyed literary success. As mentioned already, while on his European Grand Tours he had gone to Corsica, where he met and befriended Pasquale Paoli, the leader of the Corsican independence struggle against the Genoese Republic. The book he wrote on that subject was well received and gained him the nickname of 'Corsica Boswell'. While in Skye, Boswell was not just seeking information for the book he was to write on their tour, but he was also carefully noting his companion's every word for the biography he was eventually to write. His account of the life of Dr Johnson (which was published in 1791) enjoyed great critical acclaim and has been judged the greatest biography in the English language. Long after his death, he was to gain further posthumous fame when, in the course of the twentieth century, his other private journals came to light. These extremely self-revealing journals have been published in several volumes and consolidated his reputation as a very talented chronicler and diarist.

Johnson had long expressed a wish to visit the Highlands with Boswell. As a youngster Johnson had read and had been much pleased with Martin Martin's book on the Western Isles, which had been published way back in 1703. He had a copy with him on his journey and it was his hope to meet with a way of life that, as described by Martin, was unique in Britain. In the Hebrides they thought, as Boswell put it, that 'we might there contemplate a system of life almost totally different from what we have been accustomed to see'. It was their hope 'to find simplicity and wildness, and all the circumstances of remote time or place'. Their reasons for taking this journey reflect something of the contemporary preoccupation with primitive people and forms of society.

In preparing for the journey to the Hebrides, Johnson had provided himself with a pair of pistols. Boswell persuaded him that his fears of encountering robbers were groundless though and that he should leave his weapons behind. For literary men, more useful than pistols were their journals in which they set down their impressions of the people and places they encountered and were the basis for the travel books each was to write. Leaving Edinburgh on 18 August 1773, the two men began a lengthy tour of Scotland, which lasted until 22 November. They crossed the Firth of Forth to Kinghorn in Fife, where they boarded the vehicle that was to carry them on the first overland part of their journey. This was a post-chaise, a mode of travel only available to the wealthy. Since Boswell's servant, Joseph Ritter, accompanied them, they probably hired a four-wheeled vehicle. There would have been periodic change of horses at change-inns. The driver would likely have ridden, postilion-style, on the leading horse and once dismissed would have taken the chaise back to its starting place. The chaises themselves would have been changed less frequently. Boswell, who is more informative than Johnson on the mechanics of travel, mentions several places where they had a fresh chaise. The chaise they got at Banff he describes as very good and it was the same with the horses. Whereas their driver from Aberdeen to Banff had been rather slow, their Banff driver, the innkeeper himself, drove briskly. By eighteenth-century standards this was first-class travel. Johnson and Boswell arrived at Inverness on 28 August, ten days after leaving Edinburgh.

When they reached Nairn, en route to Inverness, Johnson noted that they were now on the verge of the Highlands, it being the first time he saw a peat fire and, more significantly, heard the Erse language (Gaelic). It was Boswell, though, who tells us about their forward planning for the visit to the actual Hebrides: 'Mr Macaulay (a local clergyman) and I laid a map of Scotland before us, and he mentioned a route from Inverness to Fort Augustus to Glenelg, Skye, Icolmkill (Iona), Lorne, Inverary, which I wrote down.' Along with the addition of the isles of Coll, Ulva and Inchkenneth, that was basically the route they followed. Since Macaulay had been to St Kilda, the most remote of all the Hebridean islands, his advice would have been valuable. Once the tourists left Inverness and the well-established east coast route to the north, they needed people with local knowledge to help them.

For their departure from Inverness on 20 September, the two travellers hired four horses – two for their own use, one for Joseph Ritter and another for their luggage. They also employed two Highlanders to serve as guides. Their route took them by Loch Ness 'as remote and agreeably wild as could be desired' to Fort Augustus, thence to Fort William and then over the Mam Ratagan Pass to Glenelg on the Sound of Sleat. The Mam Ratagan route was certainly a challenge for Dr Johnson. The very steep descent of 'Ratiken' greatly alarmed him and then the inn at Glenelg left him disgusted with both the food and the accommodation. Still, the next day his long-felt ambition was on the point of being realised: they were about to be rowed to Skye. First, having no further need for their guides, they paid them off. Their guides, of course, had to take their horses back to Inverness. Johnson commended them for their helpfulness and civility, adding, 'Civility seems to be part of the national character of the Highlanders.'

Their visit to Skye was undoubtedly one of the highlights of their Highland tour. It was but a half-hearted reception they received, however, from their first host on the island, Sir Alexander Macdonald. He did not conduct himself, they thought, in a way that befitted his position as Chief of the Macdonalds of Skye. Though his wife was a relative of his, Boswell loathed this self-important chieftain for his parsimony and the way he treated his tenants. Elsewhere, whether in a tenant-farmer's dwelling in Sleat or in the grand Dunvegan Castle, they were very well received. In Skye, as elsewhere in Scotland, their way was eased by Boswell's connections, his father Lord Auchinleck being a notable figure in the Scottish legal system. Johnson, the great arbiter of English letters, enjoyed celebrity status and was greeted accordingly.

When they moved on to the Isle of Raasay, their welcome and entertainment at Raasay House was the opposite of that at Armadale. While the Eton-educated Sir Alexander Macdonald had been stiff and formal, their Raasay hosts were friendly and open. Boswell tells us about this visit in some detail, including what the meals were like. On their first morning, he lets us know that he had goat's whey brought to his bedside. Once dressed, he enjoyed an excellent breakfast, including 'as good chocolate as ever I tasted, tea, bread and butter, marmalade and jelly.' Like most travellers whether in private homes or inns, Boswell remarked on the absence of 'loaf-bread'. There were, though, barley-bannocks and scones. The scones he did greatly enjoy, having at the same time to explain to southern readers that these were cakes of flour baked with butter. There was also cheese for breakfast, which, Boswell states, was the custom all over the Highlands, but not one to either man's taste. That aside, breakfast was a meal in which 'the Scots, whether of the lowlands or mountains, must be confessed to excel us'. The humble folk of Skye would have had few, if any, of these luxuries set out on the breakfast tables at Raasay House. Johnson and Boswell were not the last tourists to comment on the poverty and limited diet of the ordinary folk.

While on Raasay, Boswell took the opportunity with some other house guests to explore the island, including climbing Dun Caan, which was at 1,456 feet or 448 metres the highest point. At the summit he, together with Malcolm MacLeod, danced a reel. Macleod, in his dress and bearing, was in Boswell's view the epitome of the traditional Highland gentleman. Although MacLeod had been arrested and taken to London for aiding Prince Charles' escape, he avoided execution, with the evidence not being strong enough. Now, in defiance of the law, he insisted on wearing the full Highland costume. Johnson stayed back from this expedition. What he did enjoy was the entertainment at Raasay House. With lots of young people present there was a lot of dancing and singing: 'After supper the ladies sung Erse songs to which I listened as an English audience to an Italian opera, delighted with the sound of words which I did not understand.' One was a love song and another a farewell composed by an islander who was going, as Johnson put it, 'In this epidemical fury of emigration to seek his fortune in America.' Back on the Skye mainland Boswell joined in a dance they called 'America' – another instance of the way this 'epidemical fury' had impacted on Highland society. At this time large numbers of Highlanders were leaving for what, in 1773, were still the American colonies – for what they hoped would be a better life. This was voluntary migration, and not the forced clearances of the following century. On one occasion Boswell was an eyewitness: 'In the morning I walked out, and saw a ship, the *Margaret* of Clyde, pass by with a number of emigrants on board. It was a melancholy sight.' They chanced to see another emigrant ship in Portree harbour. Boswell, but not Johnson, went on board this 'very pretty vessel'. Boswell considered the accommodation for the emigrants to be very good. It was like a long ward with a row of similarly sized beds on each side, each bed being suitable for four people.

Dr Johnson, a typical rationalist of the Georgian Age, probed and asked questions about the whys and wherefores of emigration, taking no statement on trust. He then gave his reflections on the causes and possible consequences of emigration, concluding that the landowners were largely to blame. Some lairds, he stated. 'Of more prudence and less rapacity have kept their vassals undiminished.' From Raasay, he observed, only one man had been 'seduced' and on the Isle of Coll no one desired to go away. On other occasions on their Highland tour, the question of emigration came up. Earlier on their journey the landlord of the inn at Glenmoriston, Lachlan MacQueen – 'a sensible man' – informed them that seventy men had already left the glen for America and that he himself, since his farm rental had been raised to an unreasonable level, intended to go in the following year.

Back on the main island after leaving Raasay, Johnson and Boswell called at Kingsburgh House, which was at that time the home of Flora MacDonald. Flora had married her cousin Allan MacDonald, whose father had sheltered the Prince at Kingsburgh when he was on the run in 1746. Dr Johnson described her as 'A woman of middle stature, soft features, gentle manners, and elegant presence.' His praise for her courage was lavish: 'Flora MacDonald, a name that will be mentioned in history, and if courage and fidelity be virtues, mentioned with honour.' Boswell was amused to find that Dr Johnson was to sleep in the same bed that Prince Charles had used, as had Pennant before him. The MacDonalds, however, had financial problems, so in the following year, 1774, they too emigrated, arriving in America just in time for the outbreak of the American War of Independence. Like many other recent Highland emigrants to the colonies, they had the singular capacity for choosing the wrong side. In the fighting, Flora's husband Allan was captured. In due course they were able to return to Scotland, eventually returning to Kingsburgh.

Leaving Kingsburgh, Johnson and Boswell headed for Dunvegan Castle, the seat of the MacLeod chiefs. The chief was Eton-educated and, following a sojourn in England, Lady MacLeod had cultivated English manners. This ensured that Johnson was in his element, with everything quite 'civilised'.

From Skye, the travellers had intended to go to Mull, cross this large island and then head for Iona, visiting Inchkenneth, another small island, on the way. Bad weather, however, drove them off course. Seasick and in

Boswell's case terrified, they were glad to find a landing and shelter on Coll. Unlike Iona, Coll in the eighteenth century did not attract many visitors, since, as Dr Johnson observed, 'there is not much to amuse curiosity or to attract avarice'. They remained stormbound on Coll for ten days, which, although irksome for them, gave them time to explore the island and to quiz the islanders about Hebridean ways and customs. Many of Johnson's generalisations on Highland life and society were based on what he had seen and heard while on Coll. It was on Coll that Johnson saw 'more of the ancient life of a Highlander than I had yet found'. He met a farmer's wife, Mrs Macsweyn, who spoke no English and taught him Gaelic songs. Here was a glimpse of the 'primitive' life that Martin Martin had described and what he had travelled to see. This for him was what a tour was all about. Johnson had nothing but contempt for travellers who rushed through a tour, knowing only what they could see from the coach and heard about in the inns.

On 14 October they were on their way to Tobermory on Mull. Johnson was anxious to press on to Iona so they made their way across Mull, Johnson riding on a pony that was too small for him. Neither the pony nor the scenery was to his taste – 'The most gloomy and desolate that I had ever beheld.' From Mull they went first to the islands of Ulva and Inchkenneth and then from there to Iona, or Icolmkill, which was the name then in use. (Icolmkill is interpreted as the Isle of Columba's monastery.) The Isle of Staffa they just saw in passing, as the waves were too high to permit landing. In Iona they had to rough it, sleeping in a barn and using hay for bedding. What disappointed them, however, was finding the ruins badly neglected. The floor of the abbey church was full of mud and rubbish and the nunnery chapel had been used as a cow-house. In the previous year Pennant had paid some of the locals to remove a great quantity of the dung that covered the floor, so bringing into the light of day the tomb of the last prioress. As for Iona being the burial place of Scottish kings, Johnson, once again the rational man seeking 'attestation', is sceptical. He does, however, concede that, 'The Chieftains of the Isles and perhaps some of the Norwegian or Irish princes might well have been taken to this holy place for burial.' For Johnson, Iona, one of the cradles of British Christianity, was an island to be revered. It was an illustrious place 'whence savage clans and roving barbarians derived the benefits of knowledge, and the blessings of religion'. There is no doubt that Johnson was greatly moved to be on the island of St Columba: 'The man is little to be envied, whose patriotism would not gain force on the plain of Marathon, or whose piety would not grow warmer among the ruins of Iona.' Boswell, for his part, hoped that his own piety would grow warmer after being in this holy place. Unfortunately, his hopes of maintaining 'an exemplary conduct' were not to be realised.

Returning to Mull once again, the travellers moved quickly across the island in order to return to the mainland. 'We were now to leave the Hebrides,' Johnson reflected, 'where we had spent some weeks in sufficient amusement, and where we had amplified our thoughts with new scenes of nature, and new modes of life.' These 'scenes of nature' were clearly not to his liking, however. Johnson, as one accustomed to 'flowery pastures and waving harvests', was repelled by the sterility of the landscape – 'a naked desert'. What he did like were the Highland people of all classes who had entertained this clumsy, uncouth foreigner with unpretentious hospitality and kindness. As Johnson admitted, they had been treated like princes. Other travellers readily remarked on the hospitality offered, even by those who had very little. Tourists of those days, however, seemed to be oblivious to the disturbance caused when unexpected, and usually uninvited, visitors appeared. One Highlander complained that parties of tourists, flourishing letters of introduction, would turn up without warning, often at inconvenient hours and quite heedless of the trouble they inflicted on their hosts. The hosts, of course, would surrender their best rooms and beds while they and their families made do with very inferior accommodation.

On 22 October 1773, Johnson and Boswell finally departed from the western islands of Scotland. From Grasspoint on the east side of Mull they embarked on a ferry boat, the bottom of which was strewn with tree branches, and on these they sat. Sailing to the tiny port-settlement of Oban, they glimpsed the old castle of Duart in the distance, then in ruins but now restored. At Oban they stayed in what Dr Johnson described as 'a tolerable inn' and the next day they were on their way south.

Circumscribed as he was by lack of knowledge of Gaelic, Johnson, the complete outsider, nevertheless showed great insight into the nature of Highland society and the way the economy worked. The clans had been tamed and now, Johnson could see, they retained little of their original warlike character. The bonds between clansmen and chieftain had been broken by the post-Culloden pacification measures. All they had left was their poverty and their language and the latter he saw as being attacked on every side. Their poverty and the lairds' rapacity meant that their only recourse was to emigrate. It was not just the poor who left; many of the middle order of clan society also emigrated. These were the tacksmen – gentry who held land from the chief and sublet in turn to the humble folk, which made them the middlemen of the agricultural economy. The tacksmen had also served as the subordinate officers in the chain of the clan military command structure. With (post-Culloden) this function gone, the tacksmens' social status was diminished and, likewise, with the clan chiefs increasing their rents, their revenue too was curtailed.

Two years after the tour, Johnson published his account of their journey – *A Journey to the Western Islands of Scotland*. Boswell waited until 1785 to publish his book – *Journal of a Tour to the Hebrides*. Johnson had died in the previous year. Many of Johnson's judgements on some aspects of Highland society may have been acute, but they penetrated too far for some of his Scottish readers. Much of what he wrote did not go down well in the Highlands, and understandably some Highlanders were offended by what they saw as condescension and unjustified criticism of their way of life and culture. Many of his observations, whether openly stated or just implied, grated. Even in the course of the tour he offended their landlord at the Glenmoriston Inn when he expressed his surprise at the number of books he possessed. Not surprisingly, there were rejoinders to both books, some of which were vehement.

Later visitors, nevertheless, used Johnson and Boswell's books as guides. An English lady, a Miss Diggle, wrote to a friend relating how in the course of her 1788 tour she had sent for Boswell's book to see whether she was following in Dr Johnson's steps. Reading it, she ruefully had to admit 'that for exactness and prolixity, I am not at all comparable to Mr B.' While some travellers followed Pennant and Johnson by going to the more distant places, most, after seeing Edinburgh, confined themselves to the more accessible parts of the Highlands. For them what John Knox, writing in 1787, described as the 'the Short Tour of Scotland' sufficed. 'Strangers,' wrote Knox, 'who come to this place from motives of health or amusement, generally visit Glasgow, Loch Lomond and Inverary on the west; or Perth, Dunkeld, Blair and Taymouth on the north.' Short tour or extended expedition, north or west, the tourists still came and this continued into the following century and beyond. Many, while not following Johnson's book as an exact guide, have still referred to it and in some cases constantly. One notable outdoor man, Ben Humble, writing in the 1930s, asserted that all trampers (walkers) should know Johnson's book. After all these years Samuel Johnson's account of his travels in the Western Isles is still worth reading.

Loch Hourn from Ladhar Bheinn. Thomas Pennant, who described the loch and surrounding scenery as having an Alpine wildness and magnificence, was told that the name meant the Loch of Hell. The herring fishery, which he witnessed there, has long gone.

Right: Dr Johnson's statue at Lichfield, where he was born, shows him in the pose of a thinking man.

Below: An advert in an Edinburgh newspaper for chaises for hire at Kinghorn. The date – 3 June 1761 – was twelve years prior to Johnson and Boswell's tour.

THAT ALEXANDER BRUCE, vintner and chaise hirer in Kinghorn, being provided with three handsome new easy going four-wheel'd chaises, and several two wheel'd ones, he has the pleasure to inform the publick, that he is now enabled to furnish chaises at an easier rate than formerly, and therefore proposes to accomodate travellers for the future, at the following prices, viz. four wheel chaises at nine pence per mile, when the traveller maintains the horses and driver upon the journey, and one shilling per mile without such mantainance; and the two wheel'd chaises at two pence per mile lower. His drivers are experienced in all the roads and Ferries on the North side of Forth.

A late 1930s view of Dunvegan Castle, the home of the hereditary chiefs of Clan MacLeod. There has been a fortification on this spot for 800 years. It is open to the public from April to October. (© Judges of Hastings, www.judges.co.uk)

S.S. "GRENADIER" AT IONA

These tourists embarking for the PS *Grenadier* were among the countless numbers of visitors who followed in the footsteps of Johnson and Boswell.

Chapter Four

Picturesque and Romantic Tourism

'Perhaps no country in the world abounds more with grand situations, especially in the highland part, than Scotland.' (William Gilpin)

What had been a trickle of tourists became an ever expanding stream during the latter years of the eighteenth century and the first decades of the nineteenth century. This increased flow of tourists began to make a noticeable impact on Scottish life and society, coming as a consequence of new ideas and theories emanating from writers and artists. By the late eighteenth century the intelligentsia of the day were beginning to veer away from the accepted canons of taste in art and literature, and we see this in changes in attitudes to nature and landscape. The English poet Thomas Gray, after a brief tour in 1765, had waxed lyrical about the ecstatic mountains 'which ought to be visited once a year'. Not since he had been in the Alps had he seen anything so sublime. In this Gray foreshadowed the Romantic movement in poetry and the other arts that flowered in the later years of that century and the next. Neither Johnson nor Boswell, like most of their generation, had much feeling for scenery. Boswell had confessed to a 'wretched deficiency in expressing … visible objects'. As for Johnson, what to most people would have been an impressive mountain was but 'a considerable protuberance'. Their descriptions of place are bare and factual, except when expressing sentiments of gloom and horror. The hills along the shores of Loch Ness were, according to Johnson, 'Sometimes covered with verdure, and sometimes towering in horrid nakedness.' What pleased his eye was when every now and then, 'We espied a little corn-field, which served to impress more strongly the general barrenness.'

Attitudes were beginning to change, however. William Gilpin (1724–1804), an English clergyman-cum-headmaster, took a very different standpoint. His books, which defined a theory of the picturesque, were very influential. Nowadays picturesque is a catch-all adjective for bonnie scenery. For the devotees of the eighteenth-century cult, it necessitated a particular way of looking at landscapes. Thus a wild landscape composed of rocks, cliffs and mountains previously generally despised might now be admired. But even then there were conditions to be fulfilled for a specific landscape to be classified as 'picturesque' in Gilpin's terms. Gilpin, the 'Master of the Picturesque', defined these conditions – his particular way of looking at landscape – in a series of books. These books, illustrated by his own sketches, were, in effect, teaching aids for the educated classes of late Georgian Britain. His missionary-like zeal helped to bring about a wider appreciation of natural beauty and the more dramatic forms of landscape – the 'grand situations' mentioned in the quotation at the start of this chapter. The cult of the picturesque, and the later-to-be-developed Romantic movement, made a long-lasting impact, as is evident by the huge amount of tourist literature in the form of guidebooks, handbooks and histories with the words 'picturesque' or 'romantic' in their titles, and indeed in their content.

The features of a picturesque landscape were irregularity, roughness and variety. Medieval ruins could enhance the picturesque quality of a specific landscape. The same was true of people if sufficiently picturesque. For artists, kilted figures thus became almost essential for an illustration of a Highland scene. Animals too might qualify if shaggy looking. Highland cattle would have fitted the bill one would have thought, but Gilpin was disappointed with Scottish cattle as picturesque appurtenances: their horns were too wide and their countenances usually sour. Views, however, could also be improved by judicious tree planting. Gilpin's theories enjoyed considerable popularity for some years. His devotees, when travelling, searched for views and prospects that could be classified as picturesque and were therefore worth admiring or sketching. Hunting for picturesque views became something near an obsession for tourists, akin in a way to today's Munro-bagging. Some tourists viewed places of scenic beauty using a small mirror, known as a Claude Lorraine glass. With this slightly convex and usually coloured mirror, tourists saw a landscape that, like Claude Lorraine's paintings, was suffused with a mellow golden hue. By turning his back on the landscape, a tourist could then sketch or paint in the fashionable picturesque manner.

Gilpin, after touring England and Wales, came to Scotland in 1776, where he found many of the 'grand situations' that fitted his theories. He subsequently wrote a book with the cumbersome title *Observations, Relative to Picturesque Beauty, Made in the Year 1776, on Several Parts of Great Britain, Particularly the High-Lands of Scotland*. First printed in 1789, it ran to several editions.

Gilpin, like many other travellers before him and countless since, had found his way to the Duke of Atholl's estate at Dunkeld, on the fringe of the Highlands. Guided to the by now famous waterfalls on the River Braan, he visited the Duke's hermitage, whose main features were a simple man-made hermit's cave and the highly adorned Ossian's Hall viewpoint. According to Gilpin's canons, however, such artificial adornments to nature were an obstruction. Views that were picturesque had to be unimproved and untouched by manmade artefacts. Genuine ruins, especially abbeys, could qualify, but the artificial accessories at this hermitage tourist hotspot were an obstruction to an otherwise picturesque scene – 'All appearance of artificial ornament offends.' The Ossian's Hall folly so admired by Bishop Forbes was an unnecessary adornment. Its mirrors and other internal features were undignified tricks. 'Wherever man appears ... deformity follows his steps.' The waterfall, the Falls of Braan, viewed from the windows of Ossian's Hall folly was a very different matter; they were truly picturesque:

> Down the abrupt channel the whole stream is foaming violence ... [It] forms one of the grandest and most beautiful cascades we had ever seen ... This whole scene, and its accompaniments are not only grand; but picturesquely beautiful in the highest degree.

Gilpin's views were easily satirised, with William Coombe poking fun at the whole business with the publication of *The Tour of Doctor Syntax in Search of the Picturesque* by 'Dr Prosody'. It didn't matter, for other thinkers and artists were now focusing on the study and appreciation of nature for its own sake. This came as part of an artistic and intellectual movement that broke away from accepted rules and conventions in literature and the other arts. The individual's own emotions could come into play. Jagged, irregular crags and peaks that to the likes of Dr Johnson were horrid and ugly, were now sublime and awesome. Awesome is a word which is now overused, but to those with romantic sensibilities it was applied to something that inspired feelings of fear, horror and awe. Mountains, gorges and crags could even be construed as possessing a moral quality as the majestic creation of the Almighty.

Likewise, there was a stirring of interest in the medieval world. The castles and monasteries of that time were no longer the relics of a barbarous past but were seen as the symbols of an ideal world. In opposition to the industrial society that was beginning to emerge, the medieval world was idealised and romanticised. Romantic tales of chivalry and stirring deeds excited the imagination of the reading public. We see the expression of the romantic ideal in a letter written by Robert Burns in 1787. On the eve of two tours he made in that year – the first to the Highlands, the second to the Borders – Burns described his intention to make a 'leisurely pilgrimage through Caledonia.' Burns, in his poem 'The Twa Dogs,' had poked fun at the trendy young men of his day who rushed away on a Grand Tour of Europe: 'To mak a *tour* an' tak a whirl, To learn *bon ton* and see the worl'. The tours in Scotland that Burns had planned were more focused. He wished to see for himself Caledonia's battlefields and ancient relics, 'to wander on the romantic banks of her rivers and to muse by the stately tower or venerable ruins, once the honoured abodes of her heroes'. There were, in addition, more practical reasons for these tours. He hoped to meet patrons among the great magnates who might be of help in the future.

Burns' 'leisurely pilgrimage' brought him to places that were becoming established as wonders of nature and naturally, therefore, as places of tourist interest, such as the Moness Falls at Aberfeldy in Perthshire. The poem 'The Birks of Aberfeldy' well expresses Burns' love of nature:

The braes ascend like lofty wa's [walls]
The foamy stream deep-roaring fa's [falls]
O'erhung wi' fragrant-spreading shaws.

Not far away by Loch Tay there was another waterfall, the Falls of Acharn, its 'headlong tumbling floods' also seen and described in verse by Robert Burns. There was also a folly there, another hermitage. This kind of romantic folly, as we have seen at Dunkeld, was very much in vogue at this time. The Acharn folly must have been fairly well known, as, not long after Burns' visit, Elizabeth Diggle, an English tourist, went to see it. She was impressed, considering this folly to be 'more like a hermitage than most things of the kind … and has facing it a most stupendous waterfall of two hundred and twenty feet.' As hermit's cells go, the Acharn one is definitely a more upmarket habitation than the Duke of Atholl's tiny hermitage at Dunkeld. As for the Acharn waterfall, the flow of water as I saw it was far from being stupendous, but the amount of water in a fall always depends on the amount of rain there has been. The Falls of Bruar, near Blair Atholl, was another beauty spot seen by Burns. These he visited on his 1787 tour, when he was a guest of the Duke and Duchess of Atholl at Blair Castle. They were potential patrons and indeed welcomed Burns and his companion to Blair Castle. Although the poet admired the Falls of Bruar, he thought that the prospect could be improved by the planting of trees – 'lofty firs and ashes cool'. Burns later wrote a poem in the first tense addressed to the 'Noble Duke of Atholl' in the form of an imaginary petition to the Duke from the burn, the Bruar Water:

Would, then, my noble master please
To grant my highest wishes?
He'll shade my banks wi' tow'ring trees,
And bonnie spreading bushes.

Robert Burns was by no means the first to point out the deficiencies of the view. An earlier visitor considered the effort to reach the falls was hardly worth the bother: 'One of them indeed is a grand fall, but is so naked in its accompaniments that … it is of little value.' This particular tourist was no less a person than William Gilpin. Since they lacked suitable 'accompaniments', the Falls of Bruar were, in Gilpin's terms, not sufficiently picturesque to be worth visiting. Another notable visitor to the Bruar area was Mrs Sarah Murray, the widow of a Scottish naval captain and a celebrated guidebook author. She had seen the falls in 1796 when on a tour of Scotland. Though the sides were very bare, the falls she described as very pretty. Now Mrs Murray was a real aficionada of waterfalls, and indeed went out of her way to 'bag' as many as possible. Coming from her, the words 'very pretty' was, therefore, somewhat muted praise. She did add, nevertheless, that since she had been there, the Duke of Atholl had had an arch thrown over the topmost fall and the banks planted.

As we have seen, a number of tourists to Scotland, some of them ladies, kept a record of their travels, but few of their journals were meant for publication. The Hon. Mrs Sarah Murray's journal was, however, written with publication in mind. It was the basis for the book she published on her travels, *A Companion and Useful Guide to the Beauties of Scotland*. This book, first published in 1799, was an exceptional work in that it was written to be a practical handbook. It is the kind of guide that nowadays we take for granted, but a novel idea in a Scottish context. Her guide pointed to the places and things most worth seeing, gave distances from place to place, and gave advice about inns and the condition of the roads. No other publication, she claimed, gave such practical advice.

For some tourists her book would have been 'a companion' and 'useful guide' to Scotland. They would, however, have been mainly like her – wealthy and well-connected. When she toured Scotland in 1796, Mrs Murray was affluent enough to be travelling in her own specially designed and well-equipped carriage and to be able to pay for post-horses and drivers, and all this while covering nearly 2,000 miles. Since north of Perth post-horses were available only on the east coast route, she hired horses at Perth initially for a month. Her advice for other travellers was to go to Mr Millar at the Salutation Inn for good, steady horses. Sarah Murray had nothing but praise for the driver he provided for her, James Allen: 'For I verily believe he will drive you (and with perfect safety too) through roads that no other man can drive, without accident.' She had her own maid beside her in the carriage and a manservant perched on a dickey seat outside at the rear of the carriage. When she stayed at inns, she ate and drank there, as she felt it right and proper for the innkeepers to make some profit for the use of their beds. For her midday meals, however, she preferred to eat within her own carriage while the horses were being fed and watered, this being done at roadside inns. Those inns that supplied fodder were the equivalent of today's petrol stations. The laws of supply and demand were just as valid then as today, as she found in 1796 when she toured the Highlands. In that summer hay was scarce and, consequently, very expensive. Travellers had to eat too, so for tourists following her route north, she recommended purchasing enough bread, cold meat and wine in Perth to last until reaching Inverness. 'Good water,' she added, 'you may at all times, and in all places, procure.' Mrs Murray, ever prudent, had wine glasses, cutlery, bed linen, towels, napkins and other useful items with her. Her eye to detail included the carriage, as she provided a list of useful spare parts and tools to take as well.

As with most travellers at that time, it helped a great deal to be well-connected. As her late husband had been the Earl of Dunmore's brother, Mrs Murray certainly had the right connections. She was fortunate to have 'a good many kind friends and relations by marriage in Perthshire, and other parts of the Highlands, whose hospitality and kindness are stampt [*sic*] on my heart'. Although she had experience of some inns, the various letters of introduction she carried opened doors that would have been firmly shut for more humble tourists. Time after time she was offered help and hospitality, not just in the homes of lairds and ministers, but among the poor as well.

One thing is evident from both her 1796 tour and later short tours to the west coast and some of the islands – Mrs Murray embraced the spirit of adventure, and was always ready to take the rough with the smooth. Determined to visit Glencoe, she travelled north to the King's House Inn on the bare and lonely Rannoch Moor. Since her carriage-horses were exhausted, she had to travel the next 9 miles into the glen itself in a peat-cart. So, planked on a board placed across the body of the cart, she advanced into 'this solemn, sublime, gloomy, steep pass.' Passing by the spot where the Macdonald chieftain and the greatest part of his clan were massacred, she 'could not help paying the tribute of a sigh for their melancholy fate.' Mrs Murray then returned to the Kingshouse, an inn mainly used by drovers. Although she likened it to a pigsty, there was nowhere else to stay. At night, though she probably had the best room at this inn, she kept her petticoats tucked to her knees for fear of the dirt on the floor, which lay half an inch deep. Her maid slept on a shake-down made up of chairs. As to the accommodation for her manservant and the driver, she is silent. On the previous night, when they had stayed at the overcrowded but otherwise 'tolerable' Tyndrum Inn, her manservant, however, had no alternative but to sleep in the carriage. The inn that night was packed with Highland drovers returning from Falkirk Tryst – the great meeting place where huge numbers of cattle and sheep were sold.

Mrs Murray was prone to indulging her romantic sensibilities, sprinkling her pages with over-the-top descriptive words like 'fearsome', 'awesome' and 'sublime', particularly when she was indulging in her self-confessed 'great passion for water-falls'. Evidently afflicted with the cult of the picturesque, she rapturised on the Falls of Moness at Aberfeldy. There the 'goddess [of Nature] reigns in triumph, there not appearing the least trace of man, or his interference'. To climb to the best viewpoints for the Falls of Foyers near Fort Augustus was for a woman a bold adventure (her words) but left her 'in ecstasy with all around'. To see and experience these spectacular falls was for her an emotional experience. Deafened by the noise and drenched with spray, she was deprived of sight and breath, 'so that only, every now and then, by gulping and shutting my eyes for relief, I was by intervals enabled to look and breathe; to admire, and, I might say, almost adore.' Early on her tour, the Bracklinn Falls at Callander had drawn her like a moth to the light. On her first approach, she was disappointed because it was nothing like the romantic horror she had been told to expect. On closer view, however, she saw the falls as 'grand and beautiful; dashing in different directions, height and breadths, till the water roars and foams through the deep chasm under the bridge'. It needed 'some strength of head' to creep down to the crossing place but down she went. The bridge across the chasm was made of pine poles covered with branches and turf. It was extremely narrow and had no guard rails. It was, therefore, with a mixture of fear and pleasure that she viewed this flimsy structure:

> Before I ventured upon the bridge, I stood trembling to gaze and admire; for I could not help shuddering, though I was highly gratified by the whole scene ... The bridge appeared so light and the depth below so terrific, that I was in some doubt whether to cross it.

In the end the decision was made for her as her guide, a young boy, preceded her and stood on the bridge whistling nonchalantly. Mrs Murray then followed, skipping quickly across, looking neither to one side or the other.

From Callander Lady Murray set off 'to see the wonders of the Trossachs, around Loch Catherine (Loch Katrine)'. Unfortunately for her, heavy rain made her despair of seeing 'the surrounding scenes of Loch Catherine, which, I had been informed, were more romantic than any other in Scotland'. Interestingly, this desire to see the Trossachs came before Sir Walter Scott and his writings rendered Loch Katrine and the Trossachs famous. The rain did cease, however, and on she went, crossing the Finglas Water by a ford. Mrs Murray, of course, described the scene with her usual sense of drama:

> As I entered the ford, the scene was solemn, gloomy and awful ... my mind was perfectly free from all sensations but those produced by the extraordinary scenery around me. On the right a few scattered huts and the river roaring from the deep glen...

Further on past Loch Achray, the road to Loch Katrine became amazingly jumbled and wild with 'rent chasms, deep and dark on every side; no trace of man, or living thing to be seen; every sound reverberated from rock to rock, flying through the gloomy labyrinth, to announce the approach of unhallowed steps'. Once the road petered out, her only alternative was to proceed on foot through the defile. It was worth it, though: her first glimpse of Loch Katrine astonished and delighted her. A faint ray of sun penetrated the mist, tingeing the woodlands on the mountain slopes and gleaming on the islands of the loch. Mrs Murray was, of course, quite wrong as to there being no trace of man, as woodcutters were at work unloading logs from a boat they had brought from the head of the loch. This was fortunate for her, as she persuaded them to take her on an exploratory sail on the loch. There was still one final coda to be played. Returning to Callander in the near dark, she entered the inn to find the floor carpets had been removed from her rooms. They had been taken to cover new-made hay ricks to protect them from the rain. The needs of a precarious rural economy were more important than the comfort of a passing tourist.

It is clear from Sarah Murray's account that the Trossachs was already recognised as a beauty spot. Others had written about it previously, including the Church of Scotland minister at Callander. Six years before Mrs Murray's visit, he penned some remarks for the Statistical Account of Scotland entitled 'Romantic Prospects': 'The Trossachs are often visited by persons of taste, who are desirous of seeing nature in her rudest and most unpolished state.' There were even wicker-work shelters for the use of sightseers. It is likely that these, which had been provided by the Hon. Mrs Drummond of Perth, would have been situated at key viewing points. It had become general practice to assist 'picturesque' tourists by identifying the best spots, or 'stations' as they were called, for capturing the view. The Duke of Atholl had done the same at the Falls of Bruar, building 'view-houses' at strategic points on the path, as well as bridges to ease access.

Among the 'persons of taste' who came sightseeing to the Trossachs were the poet William Wordsworth and his no less talented younger sister Dorothy. They were accompanied for part of the time by another of the so-called 'Lake Poets', Samuel Taylor Coleridge. This trio were among the category of tourists who were moderately well-off. They certainly could not travel in the same style as Sarah Murray, but they had enough cash, and just as important, the leisure time, to spend on an extensive tour. Thanks to a legacy, William, for instance, had no real financial worries, which meant that he could devote his life to poetry and, at the same time, left him free to explore the wider world. Indeed the notion of travel for its own sake was an intrinsic component of the romantic ideal and this is reflected in the poetry of the poets of the Romantic era. The Wordsworths and Coleridge were at the forefront of the Romantic movement that sought to appreciate nature for its own sake. They were therefore, not surprisingly, drawn to visit Scotland and the Highlands in particular, as a land of romance and picturesque and dramatic beauty. The trio had travelled from the English Lake District through Southern Scotland to Glasgow and thence towards the Highlands. Although they walked much of the way, they had their own back-up transport in the form of an Irish jaunting car pulled by a single horse. Loch Lomond was one of the places they had to see and it was by its banks that they realised that they were in a strange and very different territory. They had been told that the Highlands started at the village of Luss. Two miles short of that loch-side village, however, they reached a group of cottages where Dorothy, who kept a journal of the tour, recorded: 'I would gladly have believed we were there [in the Highlands], for it was like a new region. The huts were after the Highland fashion, and the boys who were playing wore the Highland dress and philabeg.' As for Luss itself, they found the white and nice-looking inn to be 'clean for a Scotch inn'; the other dwellings were, Dorothy noted, the first they saw that were lacking in windows and with a hole in the roof serving as a chimney.

Determined to see the Trossachs, William, Dorothy and Coleridge left their horse and vehicle at the inn at Tarbet. They were then rowed across Loch Lomond from Tarbet to Inversnaid on the east side of the loch and then walked eastward to Loch Katrine. They had been informed that there was no inn on the way, so they just had to hope that some householder would take pity on them. Their first sight of Loch Katrine was a disappointment, with 'neither boats, islands or houses, no grandeur in the hill, nor any loveliness in the shores'. The scenery compared unfavourably with the Lake District, they decided. Closer inspection revealed a more pleasing scene, with rocky promontories and woody islands. While they were debating whether to go on or turn back, a man on horseback came into view. Dorothy seems to have been stage-struck:

> We should have been glad to have seen either man, woman or child at this time, but there was something uncommon and interesting in this man's appearance ... He was the complete Highlander in dress, figure, and face, and a very fine-looking man, hardy and vigorous, though past his prime. While he stood waiting for us in his bonnet and plaid ... I forgot my errand, and only felt glad that we were in the Highlands.

The Highlander was on his way to Callander, but he reassured them that there were two gentlemen's houses nearby where they might find shelter. Reaching the first house, they found the owner, a Mr Macfarlane, out in the fields with his servants gathering hay. William tried to explain what they were doing in this remote, out-of-the-way corner by saying that they had come to see the Trossachs. This, according to Dorothy, caused much amusement: 'A laugh was on every face when William said we were come to see the Trossachs'. Evidently tourists were not a common sight at the western end of Loch Katrine. The poet, accordingly, felt it expedient to explain that the Trossachs was a place much celebrated in England.

The farmer and his wife, 'a tall, fine-looking woman', received them hospitably, their hostess assuring them that they would sleep on blankets 'fresh from the fauld'. Their hosts told them tales of Rob Roy, a hero who defended the poor from oppression. They related stories of the hardships and oppressions endured by Highlanders 'further up'. To live in any degree of comfort, they were told, was virtually impossible, and all the more so since emigration had so many restraints laid on it. Next day the party continued on their way, fortunately finding a boatman who took them to the eastern end of the loch, which they found delightful – 'All that we beheld was the perfection of loveliness and beauty.' Unfortunately, we cannot see Loch Katrine and the Trossachs as the Wordsworths saw it. The Victorians used Loch Katrine to supply the City of Glasgow with fresh, clean water. The water level was raised, thus obliterating landmarks and beauty spots that our tourists would have seen.

Having gone out of their way to see the Trossachs, the three tourists returned the same way, back to Tarbet on Loch Lomond where they separated, with Coleridge going off on his own. Although allegedly suffering poor health, Coleridge was a strong walker, reaching Fort William before proceeding to Inverness. His solitary tour was not without adventures. At Fort Augustus he was suspected of being a French spy and was clapped into prison. Wars and suspicions of wars, it must be said, always bring spy mania. The fort governor made amends by giving him a good breakfast before sending him on his way. Coleridge's problems did not finish there. Going south from Inverness by post-chaise, he found himself in the hands of a dangerous driver – a 'mad, drunk Post Boy'.

Meantime, the Wordsworths had visited Glencoe, which was also becoming a magnet for tourists, the story of the Massacre of Glencoe featuring in the guidebooks. Although William and Dorothy Wordsworth described the Glencoe Mountains as majestic and the grandest they had ever seen, they were nonetheless disappointed, as they had expected something more terrifying. In September, on their way south, William and Dorothy were determined to see the Trossachs again, approaching this time from the Callander side. They travelled with their jaunting car to the head of Loch Achray. A boy accompanied them to take the horse and vehicle back to Callander. Once again they were delighted with the view – 'surprised with pleasure'. The track towards the head of the loch, Dorothy added, was the pleasantest she had ever travelled in her life. As sister and brother went on their way, they met two women coming towards them. One exclaimed, 'What! You are stepping westward?' This simple, friendly greeting left an indelible impression on the tourists. Long after, William recalled these simple words:

> I liked the greeting, 'twas a sound
> Of something without place or bound;
> And seem'd to give me spiritual right
> To travel through that region bright.

What the travellers of that period, and indeed almost all tourists thereafter, lacked was knowledge of the language spoken by the overwhelming majority of Highlanders. Mutual incomprehension was a barrier to any real understanding of Gaelic society and way of life. Consequently, William and Dorothy Wordsworth and Coleridge, like most other tourists, travelled through the Highlands quite oblivious to the Highlanders' own culture. They knew nothing of the Gaels' own bards and poets, like Duncan Ban MacIntyre (1724–1812) who also loved nature. Like many Gaels, Duncan Ban MacIntyre had left his beloved Highlands to find employment – in his case eventually to settle in Edinburgh where he served, from 1767 to 1806, as one of the city's guards. He never, though, forgot the parts of the Southern Highlands where he had once lived and worked. He was illiterate and needed others to record and translate his poems, in which he praised the beauty of his native heath and, also, as in his poem *Moladh Beinn Dobhrain* (In Praise of Beinn Dorain), to express regret for the coming of large-scale sheep farming.

The Last Farewell to the Hills

Yestreen I wandered in the glen; what thoughts were in my head!
There had I walked with friends of yore – where are those dear ones fled?
I looked and looked; where'er I looked was naught but sheep! sheep! sheep!
A woeful change was in the hill! World, thy deceit was deep!

From side to side I turn'd mine eyes – alas! my soul was sore –
The mountain bloom, the forest's pride, the old men were no more:
Nay, not one antler'd stag was there, nor doe so soft and slight,
No bird to fill the hunter's bag – all, all, were fled from sight!

Right: Displaying every possible visual cliché, this colour plate from an 1889 book entitled *Picturesque Scotland* exemplified the image of Scotland as later perpetuated by the Victorian tourist industry.

Below: The unrestored medieval ruins of Iona Abbey appealed not only to the romantic tourist but also to the practical-minded Dr Johnson, who revered Iona for its part in the historical development of Christianity.

Queen Victoria sailed on this steamship, the *Rob Roy*, on Loch Katrine, but for the earliest tourists rowing boats had to suffice.

Kilchurn Castle on Loch Awe was for Dorothy Wordsworth 'a most impressive scene'. The photographer seems to have inserted the Highland cattle to add to the picturesque quality of the view.

Tourists were expected to regard Glencoe as a fearful place, but that was not the case with Dorothy and William Wordsworth. For Dorothy the Glencoe hills were majestic – 'The grandest I had ever seen.' This postcard shows the 1930s new road.

Chapter Five

Travelling – Ways and Means

'Previous to the year 1742 the roads were merely the tracks of black cattle and horses intersected by numerous rapid streams which being frequently swollen into torrents by heavy rains rendered them dangerous or impassable.' (Thomas Telford, *A Survey and Report of the Coasts and Central Highlands of Scotland*, 1803)

Over large parts of the Highlands properly made roads were virtually non-existent until the building of military roads commenced after the '15 Jacobite Rising. As Telford shows in the above quotation many roads in the Highlands were mere tracks or ways, as Burt had put it. Not surprisingly therefore, as Dr Johnson and other travellers remarked, wheeled vehicles of any kind were rarely seen. Travellers had little option other than to go on foot or on horseback. Boswell reported that the doctor, while on the Isle of Inchkenneth, said how his heart was cheered to see the mark of cart-wheels, something they had not seen for a long time. For those on or near the coast, sea travel was as often as not the preferable option. In the far north-west, north of Ullapool, the situation was even worse. For Timothy Pont, who had surveyed much of the country around 1590, the far north was extreme wilderness. Even 200 years later it was little different. John Knox commented, 'It is a country where no man, who cannot climb like a goat and jump like a grasshopper, should attempt to travel, especially in the month of October.' The countryside northward from Assynt to Caithness was, he wrote, 'One continued wild or desart [*sic*], composed of almost impassable swamps and ridges of mountains, where I would find few inhabitants, no seats of gentlemen, no roads, inns, or conveniences of any kind except water.' Not surprisingly tourists stayed away. Even the hardy Thomas Pennant had to give up his attempt to travel overland to the utmost points of Sutherland and Caithness.

In the late eighteenth century, although Pennant and Knox had no accurate maps to guide them through the wild terrain of the north-west of Scotland, there were outline maps and charts that at least provided some guidance as to the direction of travel. When Pennant toured the West Highlands in 1772, the skipper of his cutter would have relied on the passed-on knowledge of local pilots as well as the elementary charts of that time. Pennant must have planned his route from whatever maps were available, as, for instance, when his vessel was at Dundonnell at the head of Little Loch Broom, he procured horses to ride to Loch Maree, but ordered his shipmaster to sail south to Loch Gairloch and await him there.

As we have seen, maps of varying quality were available for travellers. While Johnson and Boswell were at Cawdor Manse near Nairn, Boswell and Mr Macaulay, the minister, spread out the map of Scotland to plan the next stage of their route, but which map they used we do not know. With more travellers coming from England and other countries there was both need and demand for better information and guidance about the country, and the number of guidebooks and maps for travellers that were coming off the printing presses was a reflection of this demand. Robert Burns, we know, for his 1789 tour took Ainslie's Map of Scotland, which was one of the better maps available at that time. James Hogg mentions a pocket-map, but provides no details. However, pocket-maps like *Kirkwood's Travellers Map of Scotland* (1804), which was mounted in cloth and folded in a leather case, would have been an expensive item for the humble traveller. For those who could afford them, road-books, with the roads delineated in strip form, were another form of useful guide. Daniel Paterson's road-book of 1771, describing the direct and cross roads of Britain, included a section on Scotland. *Paterson's Roads* was very popular, going through many editions and revisions. For visitors to Scotland, George Taylor and Andrew Skinner's *Survey and Maps of the Roads of North Britain and Scotland* (1776) provided more detail. That it didn't sell very well is an indication of the limited market for such aids. There were just not enough tourists around in Scotland at that time, and that, to a considerable extent, was due to the inadequacies of the road system and other means of communication.

The Wade and Caulfeild roads shown on maps and guidebooks were an improvement on what had gone before, but roads built purely for military purposes were not always suitable for civilian use. They had other limitations, with winter storms and spates causing damage that was not always or easily repaired. Also, the islands and large parts of the Highland mainland had been excluded. Few rivers in the Highlands were bridged, with the result that burns and rivers that could be easily forded one day could be transformed into a dangerous, raging torrent on the next. It is not surprising that tales of kelpies and water bulls carrying away the unwary traveller were commonplace.

Where there was no bridge or ford, a ferry was the only alternative. Ferries and ferrymen both, however, were the source of constant complaints. The ferrymen could be dilatory or reluctant to cross and frequently overcharged strangers. Sarah Murray complained about the length of time it took to get her carriage across the River Conon in Ross-shire. Lord Cockburn, recalling his time travelling round Scotland as a circuit judge, described the hazards of crossing major fast-flowing rivers like the Tay and the Spey where wretched, pierless ferries were 'let to poor cottars who rowed or hauled or pushed a crazy boat across or more commonly got their wives to do it'. Crossing sea lochs was even more hazardous on small, unstable highland boats. The crossing at Ballachulish, part of an important artery, was reckoned by Thomas Telford to be highly dangerous. Writing in 1794, the minister of the parish of Assynt, north of Ullapool, described the communication problems that his parishioners had to endure. The nearest towns of any consequence were Thurso in Caithness and Dornoch in East Sutherland, the latter with three rivers and 'several considerable rivulets' separating it from Assynt. After heavy rain, these watercourses were tremendous torrents 'not to be forded, and when rashly attempted, the consequence seldom fails to prove fatal'. On this route there are no bridges, just 'one or two small boats … in which a stranger would think himself not safe, far less would he think of having his horse wasted in them, though both are often done by the adventurous natives'. On the east coast the great firths could also prove to be perilous. The boats at the Meikle Ferry on the Dornoch Firth were notoriously poorly equipped and maintained. In August 1809 ninety-nine lives were lost when an overcrowded ferry boat sank. This was a spur to the building of the new bridge at Bonar which was completed three years later.

The ferry at Dunkeld was another choke point. Though the Duke of Atholl had thwarted Wade's proposal to build a bridge across the Tay at Dunkeld, the need remained. The government, however, came forward with funds towards the cost, with the balance made up by the Duke. Built to Telford's design, the bridge was completed in 1809. To recompense the Duke for his outlay and loss of income from ferry dues, he was permitted to charge tolls (one half penny in 1826). This was highly unpopular with the locals who rioted, tossing the toll gates into the Tay. With the neighbouring village of Birnam growing in size with the coming of the railway in 1856, the inconvenience of the tolls for those making frequent crossings caused trouble. In 1878 one local merchant ended up in Edinburgh's Calton Jail for refusing to pay the Duke's toll. One year later the bridge was taken over by Perthshire County Council. There may have been no connection with the toll bridge riots, but in 1869 the Dunkeld hermitage was destroyed by gunpowder by persons unknown and had to be rebuilt.

While the government took responsibility for military roads, elsewhere road and bridge building and maintenance were the responsibility of the landowners. They had the right to push through improvements using statute labour. This meant that their tenants and their servants were required to work, unpaid of course, on local roads and bridges for six days a year. It was a method that was both inefficient and greatly resented by the ordinary folk conscripted for this service. The solution was to levy tolls and the money then raised used for road and bridge construction. Having your right of passage barred by toll gates until the toll charge was handed over was also unpopular, but in general it did lead to better roads. Where, as in the Inverness and Easter Ross areas, there was a substantial and comparatively prosperous population, turnpike roads could pay, especially where they used John Macadam's improved methods of road construction. Macadam's 'macadamised' road system was even more efficient than Telford's, his roads having better draining and being cheaper. Even so, in more remote areas with an impoverished population and few visitors from outside, the turnpike system could not pay.

For tourists and other travellers, even where the roads were comparatively good, the coaches were inadequate. Inverness, the principal town in the Highlands, was badly served. One coach sardonically nicknamed the 'God-permit' was claimed to be able to reach Perth in four days 'if God permits'. This failed but in 1806 a new coach, *The Caledonian*, went on the road and was able to maintain a service of sorts. Even then, for the journey from Inverness to Perth (114 miles) three overnight stops were required – at Carrbridge, Dalwhinnie and Blair Atholl. Slow it may have been, but with drivers quite prepared to diverge to show tourists a historic building or scenic viewpoint, it was at least tourist-friendly.

New bridges, better roads, horses and vehicles eventually brought the stagecoach time on that route down to sixteen hours. Carriages like the Inverness–Perth coach described by Lord Cockburn as 'an ark of a vehicle' were replaced by lighter coaches with better springs. Except for time allocated for changing horses and for feeding passengers and horses, there was no stopping, which meant there were no longer any overnight halts. Even more revolutionary was the establishment in 1819 of a mail-coach service to Thurso, about as far north as one could go. Leaving Inverness at 6 a.m. on a Monday, you could expect to reach Thurso around noon on Wednesday. This was possible only because a series of road improvements and other advances finished in that same year. The most notable of these improvements was the bridge completed in 1812 over the Kyle of Sutherland at the place that now bears the name of Bonar Bridge. The drawback to this route was that in the less civilised parts of Sutherland and Caithness the bright red Royal Mail coach attracted attacks, not by highwaymen but by stone-throwing youths. In the danger areas the interior passengers cowered down away from the glass windows. The unfortunates on the top had to use umbrellas as shields.

A plaque at Bonar Bridge celebrates the construction of Telford's new bridge crossing the Kyle of Sutherland. Those crossing the bridge were implored:

Traveller, Stop and Read with gratitude the names of the Parliamentary Commissioners appointed in the Year 1803 to direct the making of above Five Hundred Miles of Roads through the Highlands of Scotland and of numerous Bridges, particularly those at Beauly, Scuddel [for the River Conon], Bonar, Fleet and Helmsdale, connecting those roads.

The commissioners referred to above had been appointed by the government to help solve the emigration problem that Dr Johnson had commented on thirty years earlier. At that time Napoleonic France was a constant threat, so the Highlands was valued as an important reservoir of men for the army and navy. Better communications, the theory went, would benefit the Highland economy and thus help keep the Highlanders at home. Two commissions were appointed – the one already mentioned to supervise the construction of roads and bridges; the other to supervise the building of a major canal along the length of the Great Glen from Inverness to Fort William – the Caledonian Canal. The outstanding engineer of the day, Thomas Telford, was appointed to draw up plans and carry out the necessary work for both projects. Half the cost of the roads was to be met by the state, the rest by the local landowners. The cost of the canal, which was regarded as of strategic importance, was met wholly by the government.

Government intervention certainly worked. A total of 920 new roads – Parliamentary roads as they were termed – were built in the Highlands as well as 1,117 bridges, including over some major rivers. No wonder, with his accomplishments in Shropshire, North Wales and elsewhere, the workaholic Telford was nicknamed the Colossus of Roads. We can illustrate the nature of Telford's achievements by following him on an inspection tour of some of the various building works for which he was responsible. On this tour made in 1819 he was accompanied by the Secretary to the Commission for Highland Roads and Bridges, John Rickman, and a number of Telford's friends, including the Poet Laureate Robert Southey who, fortunately for us, kept a detailed private journal. Southey came to Scotland by the Carlisle mail coach, joining the rest of the party in Edinburgh. On 20 August 1819, they departed from Edinburgh, travelling in a postilion-driven coach hired for a trip that lasted six weeks.

On the east coast they went as far as Loch Fleet, on the east side of Sutherland. Until 1816 the tidal lagoon at the mouth of the River Fleet had meant taking a ferry boat that was often delayed because of fast currents. Telford's solution to this barrier had been to construct an embankment, christened the Mound by Southey and still bearing that name. Four arches allowed the water to pass through, with river water coming downstream and seawater going up and sluice gates controlling the flow. Here, as for all of Telford's undertakings, Southey was full of praise, commending not just the simplicity and utility of this great work but also its beauty. It is doubtful, however, if many of today's travellers give this crossing a second thought.

Loch Fleet is not far from Dunrobin Castle. This was the seat of the Marquess of Stafford and his wife the Countess of Sutherland, whose factors at that time were carrying out brutal clearances on a massive scale – the notorious Sutherland Clearances. A few decades earlier the landowning elite had been concerned by the exodus of their tenants. Now, since sheep farming was the new fashion, many of them were getting rid of what they now saw as their mainly impoverished, surplus population. Southey was well aware of the controversy created by expelling the smallholders on parts of the Sutherland estates – an estimated 6–10,000 – and creating enormous sheep farms in their place. While he saw an economic rationale and admitted the legality of it, he queried both the humanity and advisability of the process. The dispossessed Highlanders, he wrote, were not wild and turbulent; they were quiet, thoughtful and religious people. To transfer mainly pastoral farmers to the coast, as was happening, and expect them to suddenly and totally change their whole mode of life and work was, for him, indefensible.

Returning south to Dingwall, the group then separated. While the ladies and children of the party went back to Inverness, the males continued the inspection tour by journeying westward by chaise. Leaving Dingwall at 6 a.m. they breakfasted at the little inn at Garve built by the laird, 'one of the innumerable Mackenzies' in this area. Southey commented on the books on view in the sitting room, presumably, like Dr Johnson before him, regarding this as a surprising mark of civilization. The next stop at Auchnault was pronounced to be a miserable place, but the whisky 'unexcised by Kings' was of the very best. As for the inn at Luip, at least it was clean and they dined very well 'on good mutton chops, excellent potatoes and fresh soft curds and cream' and of course the 'right' Highland whisky, presumably also smuggled. They spent the night at Lochcarron, then called Jeantown, where, once again, they enjoyed their dinner – delicious herring this time. Strome Ferry on Loch Carron was their next destination to inspect piers built by Telford's men. Reaching it they had achieved their goal of driving a vehicle from sea to sea. It was a historic visit as their coach was the very first to reach the Strome Ferry. Southey reports on how it aroused great excitement and curiosity among the people of the area.

Looking around at the wild Western Highlands, Southey wondered at the value of the Commissioners' new roads, such as the one they were on. 100 miles of new road had been built between Dingwall and Skye's 'Kyle Haken Ferry' (Kyleakin). If it had not been for the landowners contributing half the cost, such 'lavish expenditure' on the government's part would not have been justified. It was a good deal for the lairds, he considered, since the new roads and bridges were of great benefit to their estates. Nor did they need to provide much in the way of hard cash, as Southey pointed out, since they got their tenants (those who hadn't been cleared) to work on the roads. As most of the crofters had been in arrears with their rent, the pay they got went back to the landlords. The new roads, though, did benefit trade and commerce, as well as the steadily increasing number of tourists. Inverness, in particular, became a transport hub, with numerous coaches arriving and departing.

Once the funds for the Parliamentary roads had run out, it was up to the landowners to carry out any necessary improvements. By 1837 the then parish minister of Assynt, the Revd Charles Gordon, was able to praise the excellent roads in his district:

> Nothing has so much contributed to the external improvement of the country as these, by which this interesting district has been opened up to the public; and thus, advantage secured to the inhabitants, which our ancestors would have deemed impossible.

The advantages included a twice-weekly mail delivery, with letters and newspapers from London arriving within five days. This was largely due, he asserted, to the noble proprietors, most notably 'the late excellent Duke of Sutherland'. A significant development was the decision in 1839 to place signposts at road junctions. It was only the increase in the number of tourists, many of them anglers, that made this necessary. In Assynt the Inchnadamph and Aultnacealgach Inns, both adjacent to popular fishing lochs, were enlarged (*see Chapter 9*). When the Potato Famine hit the Highlands in the 1840s, other new roads were built to relieve hunger and poverty. This resulted in a number of 'Destitution Roads' being built in, for example, the Loch Maree and Gairloch areas. As a result of these programmes of road-building, the famine in the Highlands, bad as it was, didn't have the same devastating effect as in Ireland.

By the 1830s the coming of the steamboat, road improvements and faster, slicker stagecoach services, although still very costly, had made tourist travel from the south much easier. *Leigh's New Pocket Road-Book of Scotland* (1836 edition) listed the different ways of travels to Scotland from London to Glasgow, Edinburgh and other destinations. There were steamers to the major cities, as well as sailing smacks, including a weekly one to Inverness. In the 1830s the prestigious Royal Mail coach from London to Edinburgh was achieving very fast times, averaging 9–10 mph. That required its four-horse team to be changed twenty-eight times, with only three halts allowed for refreshment. Once in Edinburgh there were other coaches that could then take the tourist onward to Aberdeen, Inverness and other towns. By 1836 travellers to Inverness could leave Edinburgh at 4 p.m. and be in the Highland capital by 10.30 a.m. the following day. To those not accustomed to such high speed the rapidity of travel was alarming. One foreign visitor, Christian Ployen, was initially frightened by the furious speed of the mail coach when he travelled from Aberdeen to Arbroath in 1840. But then, he had come to Scotland from the Faroe Isles. Pedestrians too often had good reason to curse the stagecoach. Fast-moving coaches created dust clouds and could leave the foot traveller coughing.

Success in improving communications had to be matched by improvements in inns and other hostelries. In tourists' accounts, dissatisfaction with the quality of Scottish inns is a recurrent complaint. Among the litany of charges, we have seen Johnson and Boswell roughing it at Glenelg, and Southey likewise in a variety of miserable establishments but having the consolation of fine 'unexcised whisky'. As we have seen, General Wade was responsible for building a number of inns, the best known being the Kingshouse on Rannoch Moor. But a building was not enough in itself. As this inn on a bare and isolated spot with few moneyed travellers was uneconomic, the innkeeper received government support. Nevertheless, a constant refrain from travellers was how poor it was for provisions and beds alike. Dorothy Wordsworth in 1803 described it as 'a wretched place'. Strangely, James Hogg, a poet in his own right, who passed this way in that same year, had little to say on that inn. On the other hand, he certainly had a night to remember at the inn of Invershiel, with all the guests packed into the one room. Though Hogg got the best bed, it was hard, full of bedbugs, and the bedclothes 'had not the smell of roses'. Even worse, he was disturbed by an unsavoury band of Gaels, both male and female, drinking whisky and creating a disturbance. Worse still, after they had all gone in the morning, Hogg found that he had been robbed of a packet of six letters of introduction to gentlemen in Sutherland. Worthless though the letters were to the thief, they were a great loss to James. Without them he was unable to travel on to Sutherland as he had hoped. Someone who was obviously a gentleman might have been able to get by, but not this outspoken and roughly dressed Border shepherd. Hogg doesn't say who his sponsors were. Though of humble birth, his talents as a writer of prose and poetry had earned him the friendship of important people, most notably his fellow Borderer and Sheriff of Selkirk, Walter Scott.

If the upper echelons seldom used inns or the much more basic change houses, there was no incentive to improve them. In the Highlands, where wealthy strangers were few and far between, there was no incentive to improve standards. Always an astute observer, Lord Cockburn remarked how few vehicles were to be seen on Highland roads, even on a major artery like the Great North Road. Travelling between Dunkeld and Aviemore in 1839, he saw only 'two gigs, one mail coach and not a dozen carts'. Innkeepers' usual customers were humble cattle drovers and packmen. Hardy drovers, accustomed to sleeping in the open, wrapped in their plaids, were used to roughing it, so rough-and-ready quarters were all they needed or could afford. In Assynt in 1794, according to the parish minister, there were no alehouses, let alone inns. Travellers there could, however, find accommodation in 'honest tenants' houses'.

It was increasingly in the interest of landowners to build hostelries in strategic locations for the convenience of strangers and for their own benefit too.

In the late 1770s the 4th Duke of Gordon had an inn built at Garvamore on the Wade road from Dalwhinnie to Fort Augustus via the dreaded Corrieyairack Pass. The same Duke was persuaded by an enterprising farmer, John Maclean of Pitmain, near Kingussie, to build an inn there. Pitmain was, Maclean judged, a suitable location since the military road had been realigned on the north side of the Spey. The Menzies family provided the Weem Inn, near Aberfeldy, a village which grew in importance following the construction of General Wade's bridge across the Tay. The Earl of Breadalbane built a new inn and a bridge as well at Kenmore, where the River Tay debouched from the loch of the same name. The Earl also transformed the old burgh of barony, creating a new village that was greatly admired by visitors. In the nineteenth century, Kenmore, like Aberfeldy, became popular with summer visitors. This was only possible because communications and standards of accommodation had been vastly improved. Further west at Inverary, the Duke of Argyll, like the Earl of Breadalbane at Kenmore, reconstructed the old burgh, transforming it into an architectural showpiece. The new Inverary included a new inn with an impressive frontage. Elizabeth Grant of Rothiemurchus bore witness to the process of improvement. She had seen, she wrote in her journal, the best and the worst of Highland inns.

In 1812 Dalwhinnie Inn on what is now the A9 was reckoned to be good, but as for Pitmain:

> We never see such inns nowadays; no carpets on the floors, no cushions on the chairs, no curtains to the windows. Of course polished tables, or even clean ones, were unknown. All the accessories of the dinner were wretched…

To compensate, she went on to add that the dinner was excellent. A new coaching inn was built in 1838 at Kingussie, presumably replacing Pitmain Inn. Part of that inn was incorporated in the present-day Duke of Gordon Hotel.

As the number of tourists and other travellers continued to rise, so the pressure mounted to provide better facilities and service for visitors, especially with the increasing number of coaches on the road. On a long journey, horses had to be changed frequently at inns or change-houses. Coaching inns on a main route, therefore, had to be well stocked with relief horses and that also meant roomy stables and plentiful supplies of fodder for the beasts and fast food for the passengers. Only large and well-staffed inns could provide that kind of service and, in the remoter Highland districts, that was difficult to achieve. In the larger towns and tourist traps though, standards had gone up. Touring Scotland in 1826, John E. Bowman found hotels in Inverness, Dunkeld and Perth, making no adverse comments. By the mid-nineteenth century, Danish poet and writer Hans Christian Anderson was able to write:

> Travel is dear in England and Scotland, but one receives value for one's money. Everything is excellent; guests are looked after, and even the smallest village is comfortable; thus at least I found it. Callander is not much more than a hamlet, but I felt as if I were staying at a count's residence; there were soft carpets on the stairs and in the passages…

It was always possible for visitors to find something to criticise – prices compared with those in England most notably – or alternatively something to poke fun at. John E. Bowman went from Dunkeld to Perth in a new coach *The Duchess of Atholl*. Waiting in the inn, the Atholl Arms, from which the coach departed, he claimed he saw a 'ludicrous' handbill reading 'The Duchess of Atholl starts from the Duke's arms every lawful evening at six o'clock.' It is probable, though, that Bowman changed the wording from Atholl Arms to Duke's arms to entertain the readers of his journal, who would have been family and friends. 'Lawful', incidentally, in this context was normal usage – it meant every day except Sunday.

There are plenty of instances where tourists had justifiable complaints, as with Theodor Fontane and Bernhard von Keppel at Oban. In August 1858 the German tourists Fontane and von Keppel arrived at Oban by steamer. This was peak time for visitors, though, and there was strong competition for scarce accommodation. When the tourists came off the boat, it was every man for himself. Once ashore a crowd of them rushed off to the main hotel. Not to be left behind the two Germans joined in, and with true German competitiveness 'trotted along the quay in a sort of race with a number of Scots' to secure accommodation in the hotel. The Germans won the race, but to no avail as the Caledonian Hotel was already full. With no room at the inn, all they could find was a room above a stable. They were not long installed when the stable smells 'soon became unpleasantly noticeable', but neither the smells nor the snorting and stamping of the horses below kept them from sleeping. On the morning of their departure, their landlady delayed their morning call until the steamer was about to sail. Hurriedly packing they had to go without breakfast and, when settling up, were dreadfully overcharged. Nor was that the end of their losses. The landlady, of course, had no change and, as they had to rush off to the boat, they were obliged to leave an involuntary tip. When at their next stop they came to unpack, they realised that in their haste to pack they had left an assortment of items behind, thus further adding to her loot. These German tourists had to admit, rather reluctantly, that they had been the victims of a well-rehearsed confidence trick.

Many once famous hostelries, both good and bad, lost their trade with the coming of the railways. The inn at Pitmain, between Newtonmore and Kingussie, had been a key stop in the stagecoach era, but there is no trace of it now. Pitmain lost out to the comparatively new village of Kingussie, which was boosted by the arrival of the Highland Railway in 1863. At Aviemore, with a new, big hotel being planned, the once greatly lauded Aviemore Inn closed its doors to travellers, the building being converted into a shooting lodge for well-heeled sportsmen. Some stagecoach inns survived long enough to enjoy a revival once new, exciting means of locomotion came into vogue towards the end of the nineteenth century. First came the bicycle and then the automobile, bringing some tourists away from the railways and back on to roads that had for years been bereft of through traffic. Since cyclists in those early days were, like tricyclist Commander C. E. Reade, usually well-off, even large, prestigious hotels like the Atholl Hydropathic in Pitlochry competed for their custom, publicising accommodation for bicycles. The arrival of a cycling club at a former coaching inn – say the Royal Hotel at Dunkeld – did not, however, have the same excitement and drama as when the old-time *Caledonian* and *Duke of Wellington* coaches used to thunder up the highway. In the heyday of coaching, the arrival of a stagecoach brought quiet towns and villages into a bustle of activity, as travel-weary passengers rushed into the inn for a bite to eat and ostlers hurried to change the lathered and sweating horses for a fresh team of four straight from the stable.

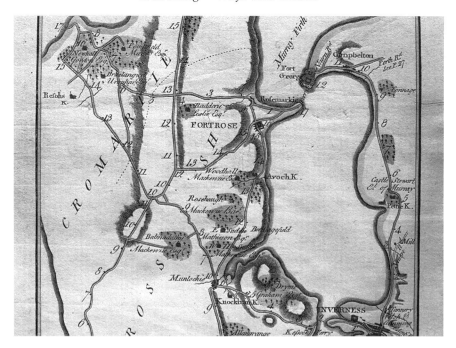

Important crossings like the Kessock Ferry from Inverness to the Black Isle and the ferry from Fort George to the Black Isle are marked on this 1776 Taylor and Skinner road-book map.

Fast flowing rivers like the River Spey provided a challenge for travellers and had to be crossed by primitive ferry boats.

The original Bonar Bridge was built by Telford in 1812, but was destroyed in a flood in 1892. This commemorative plaque to the Parliamentary Commissioners of the time survives, however.

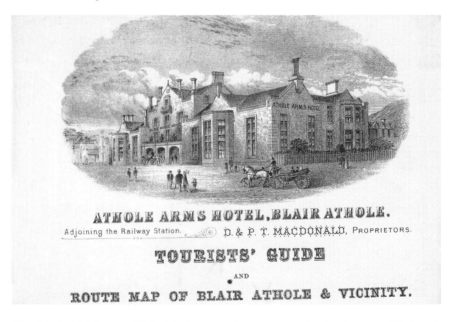

The Athole (*sic*) Arms at Blair Atholl was an important staging inn between Edinburgh and Perth. Carriages could be hired for visits to local beauty spots and likewise ponies and guide for the trek via Glen Tilt to Braemar.

FOR ISLAY AND STRANRAER,
With Goods and Passengers,
THE WELL KNOWN STEAM PACKET
MAID OF ISLAY,

WILL continue to Sail from the BROOMIELAW, for ISLAY, every TUESDAY Morning, calling at the intermediate ports, returning on Wednesday, and will SAIL for STRANRAER every Thursday Morning, calling at LARGS and GIRVAN, and returning on Saturday.
Apply to
ALEX. GRAHAM, Maxwell Street;
and to
ALEX. LAIRD & CO.
8, York Street.
Glasgow, 12th Oct. 1826.

Steamboat travel to Islay was in existence at least as early as 1826.

The bridge across the River Helmsdale was built in 1811 as one of a chain of Telford bridges on the road from Inverness to Thurso.

"OVER THE SEA TO SKYE"

Travel to the Hebrides had its travails as well as its pleasures.

Chapter Six

The Land of Romance
and Scientific Mysteries

'Immediately beyond Callander we come to a stretch of road ... along which there begins that beautiful stretch of country, adorned by lakes and mountains, which the Scots, in thankful homage to the poet who has here made every inch of earth glorious, have called the country of *The Lady of the Lake*.'

The above is an extract from a book published in Germany in 1860. The author was the poet Theodor Fontane who, with a companion, had travelled in Scotland two years earlier. In this book, translated into English as *Across the Tweed*, the author describes, and justifies, their travels in search of a Scotland that to these two Germans was a 'Land of Romance'. Their main inspiration was the poet whose name is alluded to in the above extract – Sir Walter Scott. For much of the time, the two Germans were on what would now be called a Sir Walter Scott trail. They had travelled through the Borders, seen Edinburgh and then toured the Trossachs, before heading to Inverness and then west to Staffa and Iona. It was the publication in 1810 of Scott's poem that brought tourists flocking to Loch Katrine and the wider Trossachs area. The Trossachs were, as we have already seen, not exactly unknown, but the spell cast by Scott's pen had rendered the area internationally famous. It was, accordingly, thanks to that verse-drama that Theodor Fontane and his artistic friend Bernhard von Keppel were rattling towards Loch Katrine, perched precariously on the top of a grossly overladen coach. Loch Katrine was, of course, right at the heart of the Trossachs, which to these German visitors was the 'country of *The Lady of the Lake*'.

By 1858 these German tourists were travelling an already well-trodden trail. Nearly two decades earlier Lord Cockburn, a Scottish law lord, was amazed by the number of tourists coming to Scotland: 'The number of foreign, but chiefly English travellers, is extraordinary. They fill every conveyance, and every inn, attracted by scenery, curiosity, superfluous time and wealth, and the fascination of Scott.' Cockburn made this observation following a round trip from Oban to Iona and Staffa on a steamboat. It was the advent of the steamship that had made this kind of excursion feasible. By the time Fontane and von Keppel arrived on their Scottish pilgrimage, their journey had been made even simpler by the spread of the railway system. Even when they opted for travel by coach, their journey was eased by roads, inns and hotels that for the most part were greatly improved from Cockburn's time.

Scott not only popularised the Trossachs, but through his writings, both poetry and prose, made Scotland a tourist destination not just for a small elite but for a much wider public. Scott's career as a poet had started with the publication of a long narrative poem, *The Lay of the Last Minstrel*, which was followed three years later by another medieval romance, *Marmion*. These poetic dramas sold very well and helped to reawaken the interest of the reading public in Scotland and its history. Scott had visited the Trossachs several times between 1790 and 1809, and was friendly with the parish minister, the Revd Patrick Graham. Graham had already drawn attention to the picturesque nature of the local scenery in a book published in 1806. Scott's visits to the Trossachs inspired him to describe the area in a dramatic poem, which was published to great acclaim in the following year. This long narrative epic poem, *The Lady of the Lake*, was an immediate success, selling 25,000 copies in eight months – a record for any poetic work. *The Lady of the Lake* was the catalyst for a major rise in public awareness of, and interest in, the history and heritage of the Highlands. Its publication brought tourists flocking in unparalleled numbers to the Southern Highlands to visit the scene of the action, Loch Katrine and the Trossachs. Loch Katrine may have seen a surge in visitor numbers, but not everyone welcomed that. Four years after the poem's publication, a Highlander who had been a Ben Lomond guide for many years complained how 'a Walter Scott' had affected his business. Everybody, he lamented, was now going to Loch Katrine: 'The devil confound his ladies and his lakes.'

People now wanted to see for themselves the actual 'lake' [Loch Katrine] and other places so vividly brought to life in Scott's poem. In consequence, there was a rush of visitors to the Trossachs, an area that did not then have the accommodation and facilities to cater for large numbers. Mrs Grant of Laggan visiting Callander in September 1810 (the book first appeared in May) remarked that there had been 500 chaises in the village that summer – 'the "annus mirabilis" of romance'. As we have seen, the Trossachs had long been recognised as a beauty spot. Nevertheless, tourists then and for much of the nineteenth century viewed the Trossachs through the prism of *The Lady of the Lake*. Nearly fifty years after its first publication, Theodor Fontane observed 'considerable quantities' of copies of the poem lying on the breakfast tables of Stirling hotels, alongside the latest newspapers. Even if they had not read the poem themselves, tourists would certainly have had the story and its associations continually brought to their attention.

In 1869 Queen Victoria made a return visit to the Trossachs. As she had been there ten years earlier when Albert was still alive, it was for her a place full of memories. While at her holiday home at Invertrossachs, she made a number of short trips. On one of these, while returning from a sail on Loch Katrine on the steamer *Rob Roy*, she had the carriage halted at Loch Achray for a sketch. 'A lovelier picture could not be seen,' she wrote. On this visit she made constant allusions to Scott's novel *Rob Roy*, much of which is set in the area. She quoted from *The Lady of the Lake* Scott's description of the view from Loch Achray:

> The western waves of ebbing day
> Rolled o'er the glen the level way
> Each purple peak, each flinty spire
> Was bathed in floods of living fire.

As influential as Scott's verse was, his fiction made an even greater impact. The anonymously published *Waverley* – a historical novel set in the Highlands at the time of the 1745 Jacobite Rising – made a sensational impact when published in 1814. In this novel, the fictional and eponymous Waverley was a hapless English officer, who became deeply involved in the Forty-Five. This work, arguably the first ever historical novel, was just the first of many novels by Scott which became enormously popular not just in Scotland but also in Europe and North America. The time was right since romantic fiction – so-called Gothic novels – had been in vogue for some time. Sir Walter Scott tapped into this vein of myth and romance with his popular epic poems and even more so with his historical novels. The 'Wizard of the North', as he was known, imbued Scotland and its people, more particularly the landscape and people of the Highlands, with an aura of romance.

The impact of Scott's works is illustrated by the way his book titles and the names of leading characters were exploited by Scottish entrepreneurs who used the names of some of Scott's fictional characters for coaches, excursion steamers and hotels. The name *Waverley*, for instance, was given to numerous hotels and most prominently to Edinburgh's principal railway station. The popularity of his novel *Rob Roy*, published in 1818, is reflected in the way the name Rob Roy appears in many different places and contexts. As with Bonnie Prince Charlie, Rob Roy's name is associated with innumerable caves and hiding places. Just as Scott was not the first to describe the Trossachs, so others had preceded him by writing about Rob Roy. Thomas Pennant knew all about Rob Roy, as did Dorothy and William Wordsworth. When the Wordsworths came to Loch Katrine on their 1803 tour they received hospitality from a local farmer who saw Rob Roy as a hero – 'a good man'. This, of course, was Macgregor clan territory, the neighbouring farm having belonged to Rob Roy.

Dorothy Wordsworth, on a return visit to Scotland in 1822, witnessed the Rob Roy mania at first hand while on a Loch Lomond steamer. When the steamer reached the so-called Rob Roy's caves near Inversnaid, every passenger left the boat to see the caves. 'They profess to have no other motive,' she wrote, 'but to say they have been in Rob Roy's caves because Sir

Walter Scott has made them so much talked about.' Musical and dramatic adaptations furthered the popularity of his works. Scott's magic transcended frontiers, with his work translated into many different languages and formats. It is said that Sir Walter Scott's writings are second only to Shakespeare's as a source for operas and other musical adaptations. A stage version of *Rob Roy* was performed in Edinburgh just a year after the novel's first publication. Many who had not read any of his poems or novels became acquainted with the characters in this way. Scots in general became more interested and involved in their country's Highland inheritance. Whereas Lowland Scots had once seen the kilt as the dress of outlanders and cattle thieves, they now began to adopt Highland dress as part of their culture too. You might almost say that it is thanks to Sir Walter Scott that Scottish football fans wear kilts for international matches.

There is no question that Sir Walter Scott played a significant part in making Scotland a tourist destination of major importance. There was luck, though, on the side of those who profited from this initial influx. The Napoleonic Wars meant that from 1803 to 1815 the Continent was virtually closed to British travellers and this undoubtedly boosted the domestic market. However, once Napoleon was finally vanquished at the Battle of Waterloo in 1815, the Continent was re-opened to British tourists. The immediate impact for Scotland was dramatic, as *The Scotsman* newspaper observed. Until late July 1816 the number of travellers, in comparison with the previous years, had been very low: 'Many of the post horses stand inactive in their stables for days, while about the same period of the last and previous seasons, every worn out hack and cart nag had been in requisition.' The flow of tourists did resume, nevertheless. In 1818 Keats found the Trossachs 'vexatiously full of visitors'.

As the number of tourists to the Trossachs increased, so facilities were improved, including a dedicated cruise-boat on Loch Katrine – an eight-oared galley called *Water Witch*. When, however, a competitor arrived in 1843 in the shape of a small steamboat, the *Gipsy*, the *Water Witch* boatmen were greatly displeased. Just over a week later, the *Gipsy* mysteriously disappeared – scuttled to the bottom of the loch. Suspicion fell on the local boatmen, but there was no proof. The new technology was not to be denied, however, and another steamer was placed on the loch – the *Rob Roy*, the first of two to bear that very appropriate name (Rob Roy, after all, was born and lived for many years at Glen Gyle near the head of the loch). Their present-day successor, the *Sir Walter Scott*, dates back to 1899, but is still going strong with its original engine now burning an eco-friendly fuel.

Unsurprisingly, some commentators made the obvious connection with Scott's surname and his native country, the term 'Scott-land' first entering print in 1836. No country showed more enthusiasm for Scott than Germany. His romantic poetry and fiction accorded with the mood of the time and, in consequence, translations of his books were widely read. So many sought to read his books in their original language that one German publisher even printed a *Pocket Dictionary of the Scottish Idiom*. Goethe said that *Waverley* could be 'set besides the best works that have ever been written in this world.' As the following quotation shows, Scotland was for many Germans truly the land of romance. Art critic Titus Ullrich, who visited Scotland in 1857, wrote: 'Scotland's name is poetry to our ears. It awakens memories of Walter Scott's most interesting characters, of the most beautiful ancient ballads, of the spirited morning-fresh songs of Robert Burns and, above all, of the melancholy songs of Ossian.'

Clearly there was a mixture of ingredients in this image, with the poems of Ossian still appealing to the romantic mind. For another German author, the Trossachs brought not Scott to mind but Ossian:

> Everywhere one sees the bold and the terrible mixed with the mild and the melancholy. Everywhere the severe and the grand, the lofty and the heaven-reaching. Such was the world of the ancient bard, Ossian, and so it is still.

French novelist Charles Nodier admired both Ossian and Scott. Sir Walter Scott was for him *'le brilliant Ossian de l'Ecosse moderne.'*

King George IV was another Scott devotee. When he visited Scotland in 1822, the whole event was orchestrated by Scott, who turned it into a tartan jamboree, complete with Highland dress, bagpipes and weapons. This Celtic extravaganza repelled some Lowlanders. For Henry Lord Cockburn the whole affair was 'absurd and nauseous'. Probably the most ludicrous part of the display came when the overweight King appeared wearing a shortie kilt. When some onlookers criticised his kilt for being immodestly short, Lady Hamilton-Dalrymple came up with the perfect one-liner: 'Since he is to be with us for so short a time, the more we see of him the better.' There was a long-term impact from the King's visit. Tartan adornments became fashionable in Lowland Scotland and long-standing local sporting events were rebranded as Highland Games. In the Highlands, ironically, the kilt as an adult garment had gone out of use, except for children and the gentry. Gaelic, however, remained the predominant language for much longer. Thomas Pennant on his 1772 tour, found that in Arran, whereas the male population had entirely abandoned their ancient dress, they 'all spoke the Erse language'.

Undoubtedly the image of Scotland and the Scots that Scott helped to create was over-romanticised and bogus in many ways. However, there are worse images to have, especially considering the bad press that Scotland and its people had endured in the past. Scott, by depicting the landscape in vivid language, by bringing the nation's past to life and by rendering it dramatic and exciting, did more than any individual to bring Scotland to the attention of the wider world and in a generally favourable way. Artists and book engravers produced images that reinforced this romantic view of Scotland. They depicted the Highland way of life and culture in a stereotyped way, showing Scotland as tourists wanted it to be. Commercial postcard artists and photographers followed suit. The wide distribution of cheap postcards helped to perpetuate the popular image of the Highlands as a place of romance and picturesque beauty.

Tales of clan warfare, treachery and bloody deeds, and tragic stories from the past also appealed to the romantic imagination. Glencoe, so closely associated with the tragedy of the Massacre in 1692, and Culloden, where the clans and the Stewart dream alike were shattered, became, as they remain today, 'must-sees' on the tourist itinerary. The battlefield of Culloden made an indelible impression on Theodor Fontane:

> This piece of moorland which has become so famous stretches for miles … and could not fail, alone through its stillness and loneliness, to make an impression on the traveller, even if such a one did not know that it was a battlefield and the cemetery of so many brave men.

When he arrived at the clan graves, he knelt down to pick a sprig of broom from the grave of the Frasers and a bunch of heather from that of the Macphersons. Fontane then plaited a wreath from both these plants to take home in memory of Culloden Moor.

Glencoe, too, was a place for sad thoughts and reflection. Queen Victoria, when passing through Glencoe, saw heaps of stones, the 'remains of what once were homes, which tell the bloody, fearful tale of woe.' She asked how such a thing could have been done to innocent, sleeping people. Fearing for the reputation of her royal predecessors, she expressed her hope that William III knew nothing of it. Catherine Sinclair, when leaving Glencoe, let her imagination run riot. Her mind was 'filled with recollection of murder, massacre, and banditti'. Turning a sharp bend, she was alarmed to see a party of men advancing, armed with pistols. Fortunately for her purse and peace of mind, they were not banditti but a troop of excisemen on the hunt for whisky smugglers.

For many tourists it was the mountains, lochs, rushing rivers and spectacular ruins that made a Highland tour so memorable – always provided that the weather was not too unfavourable. There were, too, the wonders of nature, most notably the Isle of Staffa. Seen at close quarters this island with its huge basalt columns and spectacular caves is an astonishing sight. The columns are so regular in shape and form that one might think that they could have been made by man. Staffa's basalt-column-lined caves have been described as nature's temples. Ever since this little island had been drawn to the attention of the wider world it has been a magnet for tourists. Pennant was the first to provide a written account of the wonders of the Isle of Staffa, not that he saw them himself. The distinguished scientist and traveller Sir Joseph Banks had visited the island in 1772 en route to Newfoundland and passed on a description of it to Pennant, who included it in an appendix to his tour account. Awestruck by the magnificent caves and cliffs formed of regular columns of basalt, Banks exclaimed: 'Compared to this what are the cathedrals and palaces built by man – mere models or playthings.' Chauncy Townshend was likewise astounded:

> With all my hate of having raptures dictated to me, I actually did what the guide-book declares to be done, on first beholding this stupendous sight,

namely, uttered an exclamation of delight and astonishment. Nothing I had as yet seen had prepared me for the surprising grandeur of this face of rock.

Sir Joseph Banks is usually given the credit for 'discovering' Staffa. It was, however, another English traveller, a Mr Leach, who had alerted Banks to this remarkable phenomenon. The people of the area, of course, knew it well. When Banks entered the most impressive of all the island's caves, he asked his guide what it was called. Banks seems to have misunderstood his answer. Taking the response to be the cave of Finn, Banks, well conversant with Macpherson's *Ossian*, gave this very special cavern the name of Fingal's Cave. It would seem in fact that the guide's answer was 'an-ua-vine' meaning the melodious cave. Nevertheless, the name Fingal's Cave was soon in print and that it has remained. Staffa with Fingal's Cave as the highlight was speedily recognised as one of the wonders of the natural world. Many distinguished visitors visited the cave and many of them left accounts of their visit, but none so memorably as Felix Mendelssohn.

Felix Mendelssohn-Bartholdy, to give him his full name, sailed to England in April 1829 on the first stage of what was to be an extended tour of Europe. He was, however, determined that Scotland was one place that he had to visit. A fortnight earlier, he had urged his friend Carl Klingemann, who at that time was based in London, to join him: 'Next August I am going to Scotland … Klingemann, you must join me … Demolish obstacles and fly to Scotland.' During a three-week tour, the two young men visited Edinburgh, then made the by now obligatory trip to Scott's home at Abbotsford before embarking on a Highland tour. Their circular tour included the standard tourist hotspots like the Dunkeld Hermitage, Blair Atholl, Killin, Glencoe, Oban, Inverary and Loch Katrine. Since the steamboat had made Staffa and Iona easier to reach, these islands were now almost mandatory destinations for the ambitious tourist. We have an account of their voyage and description of Staffa from Klingemann, but for Mendelssohn's impressions we turn to his Hebridean overture. It was actually the view from Oban towards the Hebrides that was the inspiration for the first few bars of his overture *The Hebrides*, otherwise known as *Fingal's Cave*. Nevertheless, there is no question that Mendelssohn was inspired by his visit to Staffa, and that overture along with his later 'Scottish' symphony are two of his most popular works. Unfortunately, Mendelssohn, along with many other travellers, was violently seasick. His companion Carl Klingemann described how passengers, male and female, 'fell down like flies', and added that he wished his 'travelling fellow sufferer had not been among them, but he is on better terms with the sea as a musician than as an individual or a stomach.'

The very name, Fingal's Cave, shows how the Ossianic legends impinged on the musicians, artists and writers of the Romantic movement. Though no longer so widely read, Macpherson's epics fitted the mood of romanticism. As there were plenty of Fingalian stories and legends in the Gaels' oral tradition, tourists were regaled with tales and legends of Ossianic heroes. These traditions had helped to give Macpherson's writings an appearance of verisimilitude. Although not directly part of Macpherson's epic, the story of the romance between the legendary warrior Diarmaid and Queen Grainne, Fingal's wife, was reflected in the oral culture of Glenshee in Perthshire. This ancient tale is commemorated at Spittal of Glenshee by a small stone circle, which local legend says is the grave of Diarmaid. Great hero though he was, Diarmaid died of a poisonous wound incurred as a result of a fight with a wild boar. Fingal, the legend goes, could have saved his life with a magical antidote, but the jealous king let the warrior die. Clan Campbell claim to be the descendants of Diarmaid and a boar's head is one of the clan symbols. Legends can indeed have a long life.

While legends and tales of romance influenced many tourists in their choice of holiday destination, visitors to the Highlands had many and varied interests and pursuits. There were antiquarians like Bishop Pococke, valetudinarians, and artists like Joseph Turner, William Daniell and Horatio McCulloch. Some tourists collected folklore and others, like Robert Burns and Alexander Campbell, sought out Scottish music and song. Men of science too found much in the Highlands to interest them. Thomas Pennant, like quite a few of the early tourists, had an interest in natural history and his books on zoology were highly regarded. One of his companions on his second 1771 tour, the Revd John Lightfoot, an amateur botanist, wrote *Flora Scotica* on his return to England.

One mystery that exercised the scientific mind of the day was the question of the density of the earth. To find an answer to this problem, in 1774 the Astronomer Royal Nevil Maskelyne led an expedition to Perthshire where they set up camp on the slopes of Schiehallion (3,547 feet). From some angles Schiehallion, the 'Fairy Hill of the Caledonians', appears to be a perfect cone, and it was this regularity that seemed ideal for experiments on the earth's mass. Measurements were made over a period of years to test the validity of Newton's theory of gravity and to measure the density and volume of the earth. To help with this process, the mathematician Charles Hutton devised a system of contour lines, a method of measurement that cartographers were to find invaluable.

Geologists also found the Highlands an especially fruitful area for their investigations. French geologist Barthélemy Faujas de Saint-Fond (1741–1819), as part of a tour of Britain, visited Staffa in 1777. It was Sir Joseph Banks' description of Staffa that inspired him to go there. Saint-Fond was enthused by Fingal's Cave: 'I have seen many ancient volcanoes; I have described and made known some superb basaltic causeways and fine caverns in the midst of lavas; but I have never found anything which comes near this one, or can be compared to it.' As a good scientist, Saint-Fond made many measurements and collected a number of specimens. Another geologist, James Hutton (1726–1797), searched the length of Scotland for traces of rock intrusion. In 1785, in Glen Tilt in Perthshire, Hutton spotted where granite had intruded the area's dominant schist rocks. What had been molten granite had penetrated the older schist before cooling. Though this was only one of the sites where he found a comparable phenomenon, this spot on the River

Tilt bears the name Hutton's Locality. Arran is another of the places where he identified an example of what came to be called Hutton's Unconformity. This was the kind of evidence that helped this Edinburgh scientist, 'the father of modern geology', to formulate his revolutionary ideas on the immensity of geological time, which had 'no vestige of a beginning, no prospect of an end.'

In the Lochaber district of Inverness-shire there are geological features – the so-called Parallel Roads of Glen Roy – which over a long period of time aroused the curiosity of tourists and scientists. These three straight, parallel terraces, like contour lines, can be traced on both sides of the glen. Once thought to be the work of Fingalian giants, scientists came up with different answers. Charles Darwin thought them to be the remains of ancient shorelines. It was the Swiss glaciologist Louis Agassiz who provided the solution: they were shorelines not of the sea, but of a lake that had been dammed up by ice as a result of glacial action.

Further north at Knockan Crag in Assynt, north of Ullapool, there are also features that long puzzled geologists. The landscape round Knockan Crag has some of the oldest rocks in the world, and yet younger rocks lay under the old rock formation. The riddle was solved by two British geologists, Ben Peach and John Horne, who put forward a theory that many million years ago it was movement beneath the earth's crust that forced these older rocks up and over the younger rocks. The result was a fault line, the Moine Thrust, which can be seen to very good effect at Knockan Crag National Nature Reserve, where you can follow geological trails and where there are also statues to commemorate the pioneering work of this remarkable double act. A little distance to the north, the geology of the Inchnadamph area is a magnet for serious cavers and the Grampian Speleological Club has a club hut there for members and visiting cavers. Walkers can see some of the caves by following the trail to the Crag Allt nan Uamh (the Crag of the Burn of the Caves). Some of the caves are for serious cavers only. These include the Uamh an Claonite, which gives entrance to the longest cave system in Scotland. In certain caves, now known as the Bone Caves, fragments of brown bears, Arctic fox, reindeer, lynx and human artefacts have been discovered. Appropriately, it was Peach and Horne who made the first discoveries there. However, there is undoubtedly more yet to be discovered in the cave systems of Inchnadamph. In the land of romance, there are still scientific questions to be answered and puzzles to be solved.

Following publication of Scott's verse-drama *The Lady of the Lake*, the bridge at Brig o'Turk and the Trossachs Hotel became must-sees on the Trossachs tourist trail. The artist depicts a crowded Stirling, Callander and Loch Katrine coach approaching the Trossachs Hotel.

Four-in-hand coaches like this one outside the Bailie Nicol Jarvie Hotel, Aberfoyle, were operated on the Trossachs tour as late as 1937. This tour would have taken them to Stronachlachar at the west end of Loch Katrine via Lochs Ard and Chon. Then it was by steamer to the east end of the loch, where coaches would have taken them to the Trossachs Hotel or further on to Callander.

Above: A rare German Staffa plate souvenir with music from the 'Hebridean Overture' inscribed round the edge. (Plate copied with the permission of Martin Mills)

Left: Cavers continue to follow the geologists Ben Peach and John Horne by exploring the Assynt caves. This 'secret' section of the Uamh an Claonaite cave system, photographed here by the author's son Fraser, is accessible only to experienced cave divers.

These sculptures of the geologists Peach and Horne are located at Knockan Crag National Nature Reserve in Assynt.

Chapter Seven

Rod, Gun and Royalty

'At that time (*c*.1840) the people were cleared off the land [Morvern] by that ruthless evictor Sellar they owed not a penny of Rent. The land held by so many families is now inhabited by three or four shepherds. The greater part of the estate has lately been turned into a deer forest by the proprietor T.V. Smith of Ardtornish ... today it is of no use to anyone unless it affords a few months sport to Mr Smith and his party during the shooting season.' (Letter to the Editor on 'Land Allocation' in Morvern, *Oban Times*, 3 March 1883 in *Source Book of Scottish Economic and Social History* by R.H. Campbell and J.B.A. Dow)

The proprietor of the estate described above was a wealthy English industrialist, but long before wealthy English industrialists and other outsiders gobbled up Highland estates, hunting had been a hobby of the Scottish elite, with little in the way of commercial exploitation. Success in hunting conveyed social standing and the harder the chase the greater the prestige. Sir Walter Scott's friend MacDonell of Glengarry sought to emulate the chiefs of old by pursuing the deer day after day. At nightfall, as Scott recorded in his journal, Glengarry slept in the open with his plaid wrapped round him. On Deeside, at the other side of the country, the Earl of Fife manifested a similar enthusiasm for the thrill of pursuit. James Duff, 2nd Earl of Fife (1729–1809) spent much of the first part of the year pursuing Parliamentary duties, but when the stalking season commenced he was off to his Deeside shooting estate. Lord Fife, like Glengarry, was passionate about his sport. On a typical day he would leave Mar Lodge (not the present building) at 3 a.m., not returning until past 11 o'clock at night. Writing on 21 August 1779, he described how his efforts were rewarded 'with pleasure, glory and success, and do figure me at one o'clock in the heat of the day on the Cairngorum hill [*sic*] stripping off my shirt, to dry in the sun'. Such was his enthusiasm for the hunt that he extended his deer forest by purchasing the neighbouring estates of Inverey and Balmoral, with the latter being leased to Sir Robert Gordon. After Sir Robert's death in 1847, his trustees sold the remaining twenty-six years of the lease to Prince Albert, a purchase which had significant repercussions for Deeside and indeed the Highlands in general.

The abundance of fish and game in the Highlands had lured a few wealthy sportsmen northward. Prominent among them was Colonel Thornton, an extremely wealthy Yorkshireman who on his first visit in 1789 rented a house near Kingussie in the upper reaches of the River Spey. While the Colonel and some friends travelled to Scotland by land, his servants and dogs and a huge amount of equipment, including a portable kitchen stove and two boats, were despatched by sea to the Moray port of Findhorn. Forty-nine carts were employed to carry his gear from Findhorn to the lodge, which he had rented. His own boats, which he had brought for loch fishing, were too large for the carts, so horse-drawn sledges were used instead. The Colonel's reward for all this effort and expense were game bags of enormous size. Perhaps not surprisingly his favourite guns were named Death and Destruction.

Not many could or would have wanted to emulate the scale of Colonel Thornton's expeditions. The lure of fishing for salmon and trout, however, drew many 'fishing gentlemen' into the Highlands. Game sportsmen – anglers mostly – explored the remote Highlands and were often content to rough it in a simple Highland inn or farmhouse, from which base they would wander the hills with rod or gun in hand. Catherine Sinclair, writing in the 1830s, was disappointed to find the best accommodation at the Arisaig Inn was taken. The parlour and three best bedrooms, she was told, had been 'continually occupied during the last twelve summers by a trio of gentlemen from Oxford.' Game sports were evidently their preoccupation, for the sitting room, as well as being adorned with a great variety of flies, was 'an armoury of guns and fishing-rods'. Gentlemen like the Oxford trio would have had little difficulty in securing permission to fish for trout from the local laird, whereas any of his tenants caught poaching would have been given short shrift.

Colonel Thornton had described his exploits in a book with the kind of long-winded title then in vogue: *A Sporting Tour Through the Northern Parts of England and Great Parts of the Highlands of Scotland*, which was published in 1804. Although this kind of expedition brought financial rewards to a few, more probably suffered from the clearances that ensued. When Colonel Thornton first arrived at Badenoch, he insisted that the tenant farmers in the immediate vicinity be removed. This early example of 'clearance' for the benefit of 'sportsmen' was one that was to be followed in the next century, including in Morvern (as mentioned in the introductory quotation). Books like Colonel Thornton's and a later one by Charles St John, *Wild Sports and Natural History of the Highlands*, published in 1845, were influential in attracting more wealthy incomers to Scotland, who were keen to lease or purchase shooting estates.

The failure of the 1745 Jacobite Rising and the subsequent disarming of the Highlands had meant that the chieftains had ceased to be the military leaders of their clan. The chieftains, no longer needing large numbers of fighting men, were now more interested in getting as much money as possible to sustain new, extravagant lifestyles. John Knox, writing in 1786, saw a major problem for the Highlands in that its wealth was overwhelmingly absorbed by the great landowners and spent by many of them in cities like Edinburgh, London and Bath. The result was that the people were left more or less at the mercy of stewards and tacksmen. With the landowners gleaning 'these wilds of the last shilling', the Highlanders lacked the opportunities and powers to raise themselves to a higher standard of living. The Highlands was a cattle economy, and money raised by selling their cattle enabled ordinary Highlanders to pay rent to their landlords. The introduction of hardy blackface sheep brought long-term change to the Highlands. Many landowners and the men who ran their estates found that sheep farming produced more profit. First of all, though, they had to evict the small tenants. Clearances of people started in the 1760s with the conversion of the traditional multi-tenancy farms into large single-tenancy farms. The parish of Aberfoyle was cleared by 1780, and Sutherland in the early 1800s. The ruthlessness of the Sutherland Clearances engendered much bitterness, with repercussions right up to the present day. Accusations of brutality led to the Duke's factor, Patrick Sellar, being put on trial, but he was acquitted. Duncan Ban MacIntyre's verse neatly encapsulates the sadness and loss felt by many: 'Yestreen I wandered in the glen … where'er I looked there was naught but sheep! sheep! sheep!' Clearances continued throughout the nineteenth century first for sheep ranching, then, as the value of sheep declined, land was turned into deer forest or grouse moor.

It was not just sheep that were on the increase. Flocks of tourists were coming north as well. As already noted, Lord Cockburn, returning from Staffa to Oban in 1840, had been surprised to see so many foreign travellers – most of them English. He noted too that the attraction of wild sports was one of the major factors in this growth. The attraction of the grouse moors ensured that 'the mansion-houses of half of our poor devils of Highland lairds are occupied by rich and titled southrons.' If he had been writing a decade later, Cockburn would have been bound to note the impact of royalty on the tourist stream. The visits by Queen Victoria and Prince Albert to the Highlands in the 1840s and their subsequent purchase of Balmoral Estate brought more sightseers and visitors to the Highlands and to 'Royal Deeside' in particular. The rich with, as Cockburn put it, 'superfluous time and wealth' also began to emulate the royal family by purchasing their own Highland estates. As Highland landowners had tended to live beyond their means, the Highlands were in a ferment of change once more.

With faltering incomes, Lord Cockburn's 'poor devils of Highland lairds' were now leasing or selling land to 'southrons' – wealthy incomers whose primary interest was to create a shooting estate. Since ownership of the land bestowed quasi-feudal powers, the consequence was more clearances, with crofters being evicted to make space for the better paying 'deer forests'. Land devoted to grouse or deer now brought more profit than sheep. Hill lands that had previously been turned into sheep runs were now converted into grouse moors or deer forests. An empty landscape was just what too many landowners and shooting tenants sought to achieve. Grouse to shoot and deer to stalk were more important than people and the ideal estate was a manmade wilderness with no crofters to bother the sporting tenants. While sporting tourism meant, for some individuals and some communities, economic gain and profit, for others it brought nothing but degradation and loss. Much of the Highlands was on the way to being a mere playground for the rich. In 1790 there were nine deer forests, by 1883 they totalled 99 and by 1912 there were no fewer than 203. Certainly there were new jobs available for those fortunate to be hired to work on the estates in different capacities, and generally they had better housing.

Some of the new owners came from the English aristocracy. More were wealthy industrialists and other members of the new greatly enriched middle-class. For example, Octavius Smith, who bought the Achranich Estate in Morvern in 1845 and fifteen years later added the neighbouring Ardtornish Estate, owned the largest distillery in England. It was the wealth thus engendered that paid for these purchases and the subsequent building of a family holiday home, Ardtornish Tower. The philosopher Herbert Spencer, a friend of Octavius Smith, allows us a glimpse of how he spent his time at Achranich in August 1856: 'I am enjoying myself much here … The days slip by very quickly … Fishing and rambling and boating form the staple occupations; varied, occasionally, with making artificial flies and mending fishing rods.' During his six-week stay, he and his hosts enjoyed excursions in the neighbourhood by boat and carriage, picnicking and hill walking. Spencer made no mention of shooting, however, which was unusual for a Highland sporting estate. Octavius Smith had kept the flocks of sheep that were on the estate when he purchased it, because angling was his hobby and he had no interest in shooting. His son, Thomas Valentine Smith (the T. V. Smith of the introductory quotation), who followed him, took the opposite course, and, since his hobby was deer stalking, he sold all the sheep and turned Ardtornish into a deer forest.

Grouse shooting, like angling for salmon, was another prestigious, and very expensive, sporting pursuit. These sports were only for the elite, since only the very rich could afford to purchase or rent a grouse moor. That kind of shoot was for family and friends. To be invited to a Highland shooting lodge was a sure sign that you had made it and was thus fertile territory for social climbers. Improvements in weapon design and technology included lighter and more accurate guns, and that too made shooting less complicated and more accessible. Women could now join the shooting parties on the grouse moors and not just as spectators. Such innovations helped ensure that 'going to the moors' was a must for the aspiring and fashion-conscious Victorian leisured class. Although Charles Macintosh's invention of rubberised fabric waterproofs had been on the market since 1824, tweeds were *de rigueur* for sportsmen, shooters and anglers alike, and for estate employees also. Some of the new owners, however, wore the kilt, although unfortunately not always to their best advantage, and that was a fertile subject for cartoonists. Members of the female sex were more dress conscious. This extract from a Victorian novel gives us an idea of what might have been appropriate costume for a day on the hills. The girls 'were suitably dressed in serviceable tweeds. They wore gaiters over their thick boots, and any unprejudiced observer must agree that a well-made shooting costume was really becoming.' Thick boots were all-important the novelist and aptly named Mrs Tweedie informs us: 'Thin boots mean bad colds, and bad colds mean no fun.'

Fishing for salmon was another prestigious sport, but, as with grouse shooting, it was some years before it attained widespread popularity. The older generation of lairds, like the 2nd Earl of Fife, were well aware that salmon was a valuable product worth catching, not by rod but netted for commercial gain. For the older generation of landowners, salmon fisheries produced a very valuable cash crop. Thomas Pennant in his 1769 tour was informed that about 1,700 barrelfuls were caught on the River Spey each year. Gradually, with industrialisation polluting many English rivers, more and more anglers sought out the clean, unpolluted lochs, rivers and burns of the Highlands and Islands. Landowners saw that more money could be raised by letting instead of netting. Likewise with shooting rights, once landowners realised that money could be made from wealthy southerners and foreigners, they adopted a more businesslike approach.

The new sporting tenants and lairds sought a better class of accommodation than had hitherto been available. An impoverished laird might make his own residence available, as with Castle Grant in Speyside. In the 1840s it was advertised as 'completely & splendidly furnished and a fit residence for a nobleman's family.' In addition, new shooting lodges were built all over the Highlands. For example, the Earl of Southesk in about 1865 had a shooting lodge, Glendoll Lodge, built at the head of Glen Clova in the Angus Glens. In the 1880s Glendoll Lodge was occupied by one Duncan Macpherson, who stopped anyone crossing his land. This blocked access to a traditional route, the Tolmount, which ran from Glen Clova to Braemar. The Scottish Rights of Way Society fought this ban in a case that went all the way to the House of Lords. The Tolmount, popularly known as Jock's Road, was a traditional drove road, and that historic usage was the clinching argument in the Scottish Right of Way Society's victory in 1888. Unfortunately, it was a Pyrrhic victory, as the Society ended up bankrupt. The members were no doubt consoled to know that Duncan Macpherson was likewise bankrupt. This proprietor's hostile attitude to pedestrians was not untypical. For most landowners, their estates with their hunting, shooting and fishing rights were for themselves or a few favoured guests or their lessees. Ironically, between 1950 and 2002 Glendoll Lodge was a Youth Hostel. It has now reverted to private ownership.

Further impetus to the shooting craze came when Queen Victoria and Albert, the Prince Consort, opted for a holiday home in the Highlands. They had visited Scotland in 1842 and 1844, and in 1847 they sampled the Loch

Laggan area in the Western Highlands, but had to endure bad weather. The Queen's physician, Sir James Clark, however, was able to point her in another direction. Clark, author of an influential work, *The Sanative Influence of Climate*, and perhaps significantly an Aberdeen graduate, advised Deeside. Following Clark's advice, in the following year Victoria and Albert headed for the drier east, leasing the old castle of Balmoral. Their first impressions in September 1848 were very favourable. The air, they found, was pure and dry, and the scenery reminded Albert of his German homeland, resembling, he claimed, the Thuringian Forest. In addition, for this enthusiastic, but not very skilful, hunter there were deer and other kinds of game in abundance. Balmoral Estate had already been converted to a deer forest when it was cleared in the 1830s by Sir Robert Gordon, the leaseholder at that time. For Victoria: 'It was all so calm and so solitary. All seemed to breathe freedom and peace, and to make one forget the world and its sad turmoils.'

Initially Balmoral was leased, then, four years later, in 1852, the house and estate were purchased by Albert. Following his death in 1861, the estate became the property of the Queen, with the castle remaining a private residence to this day. Since the existing property was small and inconvenient, it was demolished. William Smith, an Aberdeen architect, was commissioned to design a new building using local granite and in the fashionable Scottish baronial style. By 1855 the new Balmoral was ready. The interior too reflected the royal couple's fascination with all things Scottish. Victoria and Albert were both avid Scott readers and this influenced the design within and without the house, and indeed their whole mode of life while at their Highland retreat. For the internal decoration Highland motifs were favoured. Their enthusiasm for the romantic Highlands was certainly reflected in their choice of furnishings. Tartan was everywhere – carpets, curtains, upholstery. The Queen's devotion to the Highlands and Deeside in particular was not confined to the physical environment. 'Every year,' she wrote in 1856, 'my heart becomes more fixed in this dear paradise.' It was not just the climate and scenery. It was also 'the atmosphere of loving affection and hearty attachment of the people … which warms the heart and does one good'. Away from the constraints and formalities of Court life in London and Windsor, the Queen and her consort could live a comparatively simple life.

Queen Victoria's annual pilgrimages to the Highlands were a potent factor in turning the Highlands into a playground for the rich. The visitors to Balmoral included the high and mighty of the United Kingdom and of much of Europe. Balmoral hosted monarchs and princes plus their wives, offspring and other kin – many of them Victoria's blood relatives. Among the potentates were Prince Frederick William of Prussia (the future German Emperor who courted and won Vicky, the Queen's firstborn) and Tsar Nicholas II of Russia. Then there were regular visits from British Prime Ministers and statesmen of many nations.

Royal approval had consequences for the immediate area. The royal presence on an annual basis brought fame and prosperity to an area that could truly claim to be Royal Deeside. Quiet villages became tourist meccas and householders caught on to the bounty that could be realised by letting rooms to strangers. The Highland clachan, Castleton of Braemar, was one of these miniscule settlements. In 1800 all John Stoddart saw were the ruins of the castle and a few huts. The Braemar the Revd Thomas Grierson found on his first visit consisted of 'low smoky cottages, overgrown with grass and noisome weeds'. Even the best inn was 'more suitable for drovers and excise-officers than any higher description of travellers.' However, by 1837, with two good inns, it was already attracting more attention – being, according to Robert Chambers, 'A place where two days may be very agreeably spent.' Guides, he wrote, were available to take strangers to places of interest, including the high tops of the Cairngorms and even as far as remote Loch Avon. 'Another object of the same kind frequently visited by enterprising young men,' he noted, 'is the source of the Dee.' Like the mountains he listed, ascending to the Pools of the Dee, as they were called, involved considerable physical effort, climbing as they did to over 4,000 feet.

The village really began to flourish once the royal family opted for Deeside for their holiday home. When the Revd Grierson revisited Braemar in 1850, he found the old thatched cottages gone, replaced with solid, well-roofed stone houses. There were now, he found, two elegant hotels suitable for the poshest of the posh (not his terminology, I hasten to add). When the hotels were full, the overflow, as in Grierson's case, was accommodated in private homes but given their meals at the hotels. A clergyman himself, Grierson was pleased to find that the villagers and its visitors were well served with respect to its churches and clergymen – both Protestant and Catholic.

The high altitude of the village meant that it was thought to be very healthy, which also helped to boost the village population. Between 1842 and 1895 the population had doubled to around 600. In the summer season there were sometimes nearly 2,000 people living in or near Braemar. With no Gaelic taught in schools, fewer and fewer people were speaking the language. Writing in 1895, Deeside historian John Mackintosh observed: 'Not many years ago, most of the natives of Braemar, spoke Gaelic. But it is not now spoken, although the older inhabitants can speak it; the children and the rising generation are not learning Gaelic, and it is rapidly becoming extinct in the district.'

One thing missing was a railway link, with the 18 miles from the rail head at Ballater to Braemar being served by coach. The railway line from Aberdeen, the Deeside Line, had reached Ballater by October 1866. There were plans to extend it to Braemar but that proposal was dropped, even though a part of the line had already been constructed. While its cancellation may have been due to the cost of the works, there is a body of opinion that says that the Queen would not have approved. The solitude that the Queen valued meant that her privacy was jealously guarded. While the locals in the main respected her wishes, outsiders were not always so respectful. Few, though, would have followed the example of prolific writer and clergyman Charles Rogers. Given a commission to write a Deeside guidebook, he travelled north where, in 1852, he witnessed the laying of the foundation stone of the new Balmoral. However, Rogers, who was certainly no shrinking violet, abandoned the whole project, fearing that publicity would adversely affect the Queen's privacy. With or without a guidebook, visitors nevertheless found ways of satisfying their curiosity. Close access to Balmoral had been blocked when a historic road on the south side of the River Dee was closed. With access to Balmoral shut off, tourists had to be content with a distant view from the North Deeside Road. Consequently, assiduous sightseers targeted places and buildings closely associated with the monarch. With the Queen attending the Presbyterian kirk at Crathie, that church soon became a rubberneckers' target.

One tourist published an account of his monarch-spotting expedition to Deeside in October 1856 in the *Dunfermline Journal*. It took him eight and a half hours to reach Crathie from Aberdeen, most of the journey by coach. He and three companions found lodgings near Balmoral. Their endeavours were soon rewarded when two open carriages passed, each carrying members of the royal family including 'our beloved Sovereign'. On the Sunday they went to a 'very plain-looking' Crathie Kirk, the forerunner of the present church, for a service that lasted for four hours. Our nosey tourist must have had inside information, since, as on the first spotting mission, he was able to name every notability present, including the Prince of Hohenlohe. The celebrities, as we would now term them, included a Miss Florence Nightingale, by then famous after her nursing reforms during the Crimean War (1854–56). The number of inquisitive onlookers increased to such an extent that Victoria was eventually obliged to cease regular attendance at Crathie Kirk. This was, as local author Alex Inkson McConnochie wrote in 1891, because of the behaviour of 'tourists from a distance'. Although she had been crowned head of the Church of England, Queen Victoria continued to attend this Presbyterian kirk's October Communion, much to the displeasure of both the Archbishop of Canterbury and Prime Minister Gladstone, the latter of whom was never a royal favourite.

For late Victorian tourists, the grave of John Brown was another must-see. It was the custom for coaches en route from Ballater to Braemar to stop for ten minutes at Crathie kirkyard. Even the then Prime Minister William Ewart Gladstone was curious enough to have a look at the grave. This was in 1884, a year after Brown died. The inscription on John Brown's tombstone testifies to her feeling for the man who, after the death of Albert in 1861, was her steadfast support and companion. 'Friend more than Servant. Loyal. Truthful. Brave. Self less than Duty, even to the Grave.' Brown's tombstone is only one of a clutch of memorials erected to commemorate the Queen's employees and his is far from the most impressive. Today tourists still stop at Crathie kirkyard to see Brown's grave, though a film starring Billy Connolly as John Brown and Judy Dench as Queen Victoria has probably played a part in this.

Queen Victoria did what no other monarch had done – namely, publish an account of her and her family's mode of life while on holiday in

Scotland. *Leaves from the Journal of Our Life in the Highlands*, published in 1868, covered the years from 1848 to 1861. A follow-up volume, *More Leaves from the Journal of a Life in the Highlands*, took in the years from 1862 to 1882, a time when Victoria was spending up to four months in the year at Balmoral. Her account of life in her Deeside 'dear paradise' and descriptions of her travels within Scotland undoubtedly meant more tourists heading north.

As for Braemar's neighbouring villages, the Royal Deeside tag, proximity to the booming city of Aberdeen and the arrival of the railway helped other Deeside communities to blossom, most notably Banchory, Aboyne and Ballater. Banchory in the 1890s, according to local historian John Mackintosh, had expanded, with many fine new dwellings erected following the arrival of the railway in 1853. It enjoyed a fine site, sheltered from cold north winds by the Hill of Fare, and thus had 'long been a favourite resort of visitors in the summer months.' Ballater had developed in the first instance as a spa town (a topic which will be examined in detail in a later chapter), but like the other towns and villages had thrived as a result of the Victorian tourist boom. Railway companies tried to increase the number of passengers by promoting tourism and the Great North of Scotland Railway Company was no exception. It promoted its Deeside and Speyside lines by advertising a 'Three Rivers Tour' – embracing the rivers Dee, Don and Spey – but this was only feasible by combining its railway and charabanc services. On this two-day tour (there was an overnight stay at Tomintoul) motor buses were used on the section of the route where there was no railway. Even then horse-drawn vehicles were needed for the very difficult section from Cockbridge over the Lecht to Tomintoul.

The number of guidebooks to the Deeside villages being published was testimony to the area's increasing popularity. According to local writer Alex Inkson McConnachie, Braemar was more fashionable than the other resorts, its visitors being of a more select class. James G. Kyd, writing in 1958, was of the same opinion:

> Sixty years ago the influence of its proximity to Balmoral and to the residences of the great families of Farquharson and Fife, with their magnificent houses of Invercauld and Mar Lodge, cast a strange, almost feudal, spell over the lives of the people. This influence ... had a marked effect in determining the type of visitor in the summer season. The two hotels catered for such of the shooting tenants of the two estates who did not themselves occupy one or other of the many shooting lodges then standing. The hotels drew their clientele also from the dignitaries of the Church and State, from the ranks of the international financiers, and from the social class which fluttered around the brilliance of the lights of the Court.

Not surprisingly, these circumstances engendered a deferential attitude. According to twentieth-century writer Edwin Muir, deference was a factor in what he saw as the destruction of Highland life. Scott and Queen Victoria, quite innocently, had helped to turn the Highlands, Muir wrote, into a huge fenced-off game preserve where pedestrians were not welcome. While the Highlanders retained their dignity, they had, he asserted, become dependent for their livelihood 'on their obsequious skill in rendering the slaughter of wild animals more easy or convenient to the foreign owners of the shooting lodges, and in performing whatever other menial services these people may require'. Edwin Muir's contemporary, Alasdair Alpin MacGregor, went even further. Turning the Highlands into a game reserve, he argued rather sourly, had a deleterious effect not only on the countryside, but also on the Highlander himself, 'who has now become a mere cap-touching flunkey to "the gentry" in the "Big House"'.

The present Mar Lodge was built in 1895 for Alexander Duff, 1st Duke of Fife. The lodge and estate are now the property of the National Trust for Scotland.

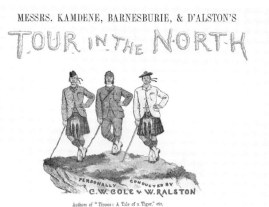

MESSRS. KAMDENE, BARNESBURIE, & D'ALSTON'S

TOUR IN THE NORTH

PERSONALLY CONDUCTED BY
C. W. COLE & W. RALSTON

Authors of " Tippoo: A Tale of a Tiger," etc.

EDINBURGH: ANDREW ELLIOT. 17 PRINCES STREET
LONDON: SIMPKIN MARSHALL, HAMILTON, KENT & CO., Limited

Sassenach 'shooting guests' dressed for the moors.

FALLS OF GARR-VALT, BRAEMAR.

Right: The Falls of Garbh Allt (Gaelic for rough burn) are in the royal-owned Ballochbuie Estate near Braemar. Queen Victoria described a favourite walk here: 'The rocks are very grand, and the view from the little bridge ... is very pretty.'

Below: Gillies – no kilts for them – are bringing the deer carcasses down from the hill after a successful shoot.

BRINGING HOME THE KILL, GLENISLA, BY KIRRIEMUIR

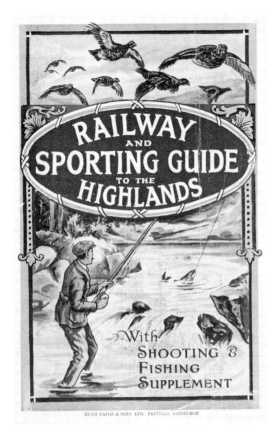

Left: Sport in the context of this guide meant shooting and fishing. Ready access by rail meant that owning a shooting estate or renting one was popular with the newly rich from home and abroad.

Below: These fishermen and a gillie – or half of one – are having a rest.

Chapter Eight

Gatherings, Games and Sacraments

In 1848 Victoria and Albert attended the local Braemar sports day, starting a tradition of royal attendance. Though legend gives it a long history, the Braemar Games only date back to 1832. It was then a simple and essentially local affair, little resembling the elaborate Games of more recent times. Simple it may have been but, organised as it was by the Braemar Highland Society, it was an event with the support of the local elite. While their positions as patrons and presidents may only have been honorary, there is no doubt that the lairds played a significant part in directing and restructuring an event that had started as a charity walk for carpenters. In class-conscious and socially deferential communities, the patronage of the gentry and nobility was regarded as both right and proper. The dates when the Braemar Games were held were not infrequently rearranged to suit the convenience not only of the royal family but of other important locals. In the nineteenth century the death of one of the royals or of one of the Deeside elite meant that, out of respect, the Braemar Games were cancelled for that year. Queen Victoria's patronage of the Braemar Games even extended to hosting the Games at Balmoral on five occasions. Her support encouraged others to start up their own Games – at Ballater in 1864 and Aboyne in 1867, both with the encouragement of the local gentry and other prominent figures. Likewise, over on the west it was the members of the Argyll Gathering who founded the Oban Games. This was clearly an elite society. According to its rules, as laid down in 1871, the membership of this Gathering was 'restricted generally to landowners of Argyllshire, their sons and brothers'.

Even before Victoria evinced an interest in the local Deeside culture, the revival of Highland traditional sports was already under way. A revival was necessary because a lot of customary practices had been suppressed in the Highlands following the evangelical revival of the early nineteenth century. For example, the parishioners of Kilmory in Arran, we are told, had come to regard old pastimes as 'profane and superstitious'. To add to the weight of Calvinist gloom, traditional customs were further discredited by their association with 'the vices of drinking, swearing, etc.' This religious revival, as we shall see, reinforced and in some places indeed restored the sanctity and rigidity of the Scottish Sabbath.

Coincidentally, however, revivalists of another kind were trying to restore Celtic traditional values and other outmoded ways. Unlike the religious 'awakening', this movement sprang not from the lower ranks of society, but, in the main, from the upper. In 1826, for instance, the Highland Society of St Fillans, in Perthshire, established its Highland Games. The first Games proving popular, it became an annual event, thus setting a pattern that was followed by similar groups and societies. Judging by the programme for the 1826 Games, the Perthshire gentlemen of the St Fillans Highland Society gave prizes to 'best tosser of the bar' and 'best thrower of the putting stone'. They also presented awards for Highland dancing, piping, singing and for 'the best essay, or song in Gaelic'. The prizes too were evidently potent symbols of cultural regeneration. There were artefacts such as quaichs and dirks and five copies of Ossian's poems in the original Gaelic. The cultural revival was extended to dress, with attempts to revive the wearing of traditional Highland costume. Some landowners supplied their gamekeepers and other retainers with kilts in what was supposed to be the correct clan tartan. Queen Victoria followed suit by having her staff dress in Royal Stuart tartan.

This was the age of Romanticism and in trying to recreate and glorify Celtic traditions, the members of the St Fillans Highland Society exemplified the spirit of the age. It was, after all, but a few years since Sir Walter Scott had fascinated the reading public by the description, in his novel *Waverley*, of the old pre-1745 society of the Highlands. There is little doubt that the Highland Society of London, who gave prizes for the St Fillans 'best shot' and 'Highland broad sword' competitions, would have read Scott's account of the military exercises of the clansmen of the pre-Culloden era. This restoration of traditional ways and customs, limited though it was, had incidental consequences. The revival of Highland Games, and in the course of time their expansion, was tailor-made for the Victorian tourist industry. The wearing of the kilt and other traditional dress seemed to most tourists to be the exemplification of Highland culture and also of what Victoria termed the Scottish national spirit. Though tourists expected to see tartan and the kilt, they were more often than not disappointed. The Revd Chauncy Hare Townsend on his 1846 tour was near to Lochearnhead in the Highlands before he saw anyone in the genuine Highland garb, and he had already been to Loch Lomond and the Trossachs. By and large, ordinary Highlanders did not wear the kilt. At the Highland Games and other social occasions, it was the gentry and aristocracy and their retainers who sported the tartan.

With any kind of revival, accretions of dubious historical provenance creep in, with legends taken as proven fact. The success of the great jamboree celebrating George IV's visit to Edinburgh in 1822 inspired the Celtic revivalists to even greater enthusiasm for traditional ways. One Highlander who did not need much encouragement was MacDonell of Glengarry. As his friend Scott put it, he endeavoured to rule his clan like a Glengarry of old.

This idiosyncratic, and ruthless, chieftain included in his Glengarry Games a contest that involved the competitors twisting the four legs off a dead cow.

During the 1820s and '30s other Games were started at, for instance, Strathdon (the Lonach Gathering), Tomintoul and Inverness. In small towns and rural communities the gatherings offered the chance of a holiday and a welcome diversion. With Highland dancing, kilted pipe-bands and a variety of sports and stunts, they provided a spectacle that appealed to a wider public. This was the case in 1850, when the Revd Thomas Grierson diverted from his pedestrian journey through the Grampians to attend the Clova Gathering. This he described as a grand annual event treated by the folk of nearby Kirriemuir and district as an excuse for a holiday. On the day of the event, the roads were packed with carriages of all descriptions. The kilt was widely worn, though more as a dress item, he thought, than for everyday wear. Grierson noted the presence of aristocrats of both sexes; also, in addition to the numerous locals, a number of tourists. The contests he witnessed – including caber tossing – were similar to those at Braemar. The Highland reels with the dancers all in kilts, he applauded. This was, he thought, a savage-looking display. The gathering was wrapped up with a grand ball in the evening.

Following the extension of the railway system during the latter part of the nineteenth century, sizeable crowds travelled from towns and cities to enjoy the Games. Contests like foot races, throwing the hammer and the other 'heavy events' conformed to the Victorians' enthusiasm for healthy, manly sports. When in 1890 Queen Victoria permitted the Braemar Gathering to be held at Balmoral, special trains carried thousands of spectators to the railway terminus at Ballater. The railways also allowed 'big name' competitors to tour and further boost attendances. Leading figures such as 'heavy event' specialist Donald Dinnie (1837–1916) rose to considerable fame and renown. To make their trouble worthwhile, Games organisers had to raise the prize money and thus hastened the trend towards more commercialism and professionalism. Although those behind the first of the revived Games do not seem to have been aiming at tourists, the latter-day organisers were not oblivious to financial returns. Indeed, critics like M. E. M. Donaldson saw them for the most part as 'merely fancy dress shows, got up for the entertainment of visitors who don't know the difference between a philabeg and a pibroch'. The Victorian tourists and other visitors may have patronised Highland Games but participation was left largely to the locals. The toffs, be they natives, incomers or tourists, had their sports, with the most significant being the blood sports – hunting and fishing. The royal family have continued their patronage of the Braemar Games, with their arrival during the event being the highlight of the day.

There was another kind of gathering that aroused visitors' curiosity and interest. These were the open-air religious meetings or Sacraments that were a feature of the Protestant parts of the Highlands. Arriving at Ardhill in Lochalsh in June 1803, James Hogg found the inn packed with Presbyterian ministers and kirk elders. This was because the following day, a Saturday, was a Sacrament Day – an open-air communion on a large scale. This form of service had begun in the seventeenth century when devout Protestants gathered from far and wide to hear their favourite preachers and to participate in what was, for the committed, a deeply moving experience. The popularity of these 'Great Occasions' or 'Great Events', as they were solemnly titled, owed a great deal to the fact that in those days communion services in the Presbyterian Church were rather rare. It was not unusual for communions to be held at intervals of two, three or more years. Calvinistic Presbyterians may have abolished Roman Catholic pilgrimages and holy days but the 'Great Occasions' were, in a way, their substitute. People came from far and wide, often from distant parishes, to attend these communions. These large-scale gatherings or tent preachings were often on such a considerable scale that no country kirk could hold all the potential participants. This was exactly what Hogg encountered at Ardhill – an 'extraordinary multitude', with far too many to be contained in the kirk. Accordingly, while one clergyman held forth in the church, another minister outside preached from the 'tent' – a narrow box-like stand like a Punch and Judy tent.

Other visitors commented on this phenomenon. Further north in Wick, Beriah Botfield observed a clergyman on a mound with a large congregation around him, while on the opposite side of the river a preacher in the parish kirkyard had the benefit of a tent, or moveable pulpit, as he termed it. Botfield was favourably impressed with the communicants' piety. Sixty years earlier Thomas Pennant, on his 1769 tour, was more critical. In addition to those taking communion, which could sometimes number as many as 3,000, there could be just as many 'idle' spectators. In some places, he added, before the day was out there could be fighting and other 'indecencies'. The indecencies, and hypocrisy too, of one particular Ayrshire parish sacrament were satirised by Robert Burns in his poem *The Holy Fair*. Burns' account was far from the kind of sacrament observed by William Howitt in 1836 at the Kilmorac Sacrament. Howitt had attended because he wished to see the celebrated Falls of Kilmorac (now Kilmorack). It was a Sunday and he had asked his landlady how far they were. It was a bare 2 miles, she replied, and, 'You will just be there in the nick of time to see the sacrament administered to the Gaelic population in the open air.' English speakers, however, had their own service inside the kirk. What impressed Howitt and his companions was how well dressed the folk were, especially the young women. On the weekdays they scarcely saw a woman with shoes or stockings on, but on that Sunday none were without. Howitt was surprised to find that most of the young people attending did not actually take the communion. Such was the sense of the sacredness of the occasion that few of them felt they were worthy enough. The whole scene certainly made a deep impression on this particular tourist:

> Just where the river [the Beauly] issues from the cliffs, and overlooking
> the salmon leap, juts out a piece of tableland. That is the burial-ground of

Kilmorac; and there, as we approached, we beheld upwards of a thousand people collected, conspicuous in the bright and varied hues of Highland costume The sound of their hymn – a sound, wild, pensive, and peculiar, as if it were modulated by the mountain breeze, came mingled with the solemn roar of the waters. We stood, and for a moment saw … Nothing but the pencil could convey to an English mind how different to anything seen in England was the scene.

Many of the Kilmorac folk had travelled long distances, most probably on foot, and that was generally the same with other great sacramental occasions. The Revd A. M. Houston, a Fife clergyman, attending a Communion Sunday in Iona, was impressed with the number of boats arriving from Mull, Gometra and other islands. Another Presbyterian minister, the Revd Thomas Grierson, saw communicants who had travelled even further. At a Free Church Sacrament he attended in Skye in 1849, the participants, estimated at around 7,000, travelled not just from the mainland but even from the Outer Hebrides and other islands. The communicants, he observed, were calm and paid attention to the sermons. The psalm singing – in Gaelic, like the sermons – was particularly impressive. A visit to another Free Church Sacrament at Brora in the Eastern Highlands was viewed in a less favourable light, with some of the leading lay figures striking him as sanctimonious 'Holy Willies'. As a clergyman in the established Church of Scotland, Grierson was, it must be said, not a friend to the Free Kirk. Overindulgence in alcohol at a sacrament was not uncommon, as Dr Edward Charlton discovered when he arrived at an Ullapool inn in June 1853. A number of intoxicated people, all well dressed nevertheless, were wandering about; the landlord was drunk and in bed and the landlady 'not sober'. The only sober individuals were some young ministers. On asking the serving maid the cause of all this drunkenness, she replied, 'Ow, it's only the Sacrament, they'll be a'reet the morn.' By this time, the form of giving communion in much of Scotland had changed and large religious gatherings were a thing of the past. Still, in the Highlands, where the Free Kirk and other secession churches were strong, the sacramental occasions were being observed in the old way well into the nineteenth century. Indeed, twentieth-century postcards depicting a Highland Sacrament show that it was still regarded as a typical feature of Highland life.

The dourness of the Scottish Sabbath was a source of complaint with quite a few visitors who thought that religious ordinances and piety could be carried too far. German visitor Theodor Fontane found it depressing:

A Sunday in Scotland is for the traveller like a thunderstorm at a picnic. You get wet, you can't go on and all your good humour vanishes. We had seen all the sights of Stirling and were horrified at the thought that for the next twenty-four hours we should have nothing to entertain us but an old copy of The Times and a silent table d'hote.

However, they did get a train to Perth, though there were no Sunday trains in Scotland (this one had started in London on the Saturday evening, so that was alright). A Scot making use of this train once it touched Scottish soil would have been breaking the Sabbath, 'but there is no limit to the licence accorded to foreigners'. Once in Perth, Fontane's companion von Lepel murmured, 'Sunday in Perth seems worse than a Sunday in Stirling.' Some travellers took the contrary view. Staying at Golspie in 1829, Beriah Botfield expressed his respect and admiration for the Sabbath Day devoutness of the Highland peasantry. Others poured scorn on what they regarded as cant and hypocrisy. Botfield's French contemporary, Stendhal, decried the 'terrible Scotch Sunday' as, 'The nearest thing to hell that I have ever seen on earth.'

If the Sabbath was strictly observed in Lowland Scotland, in the Highlands it was, or seemed to be, doubly so. The new and strongly evangelical Free Church (formed in 1843 following the break away from the established Church of Scotland) ensured that Sabbatarianism remained strong in the Hebrides and Highland mainland, while its hold began to be weakened in the rest of Scotland. Though the main Presbyterian Kirks eventually reunited, the rump Free Kirk (the Wee Frees) and Free Presbyterians upheld a dogmatic form of Calvinism. Consequently, in their strongholds in Lewis and Harris Sabbath observance remained the norm.

Religious issues that aroused fierce debate and controversy in Scotland came as a surprise to most English visitors. The 'Disruption' of 1843 that saw the breakup of the Established Church of Scotland was, for Scots people, an almost earth-shattering event. It was an event, however, that attracted little attention, and less understanding, south of the border. Dr Charlton, an English visitor to the north-west Highlands, admitted as much: 'In England we have little or no idea of the intense interest excited by the question of ecclesiastical polity in remote Highland districts.' In Assynt, as in most of the Highlands, congregations followed the clergy who gave up their stipends and manses to join the new Free Kirk. Some of the seceding clergy suffered great hardship. It would have been difficult for tourists, however, not to notice the proliferation of new Free Church of Scotland buildings that were being built, or had been newly erected, to cope with the mass exodus from the Established Church. The later divisions in the Free Church meant even more new kirks. Guidebook authors and editors tended to gloss over the ins and outs of the Disruption and later secessions. Even the Revd John M. Wilson, who compiled *Nelson's Hand-Book for Tourists in Scotland* (1860), didn't make the attempt. Although he wrote an outline of the early religious history of Scotland in his introduction, the Reformation and subsequent events were, he claimed, too complex to be contained in a paragraph.

Regular worshippers coming to the Highlands from England were faced with a dilemma when it came to the Sabbath. In some parts of the Highlands and Islands, Roman Catholicism was the main faith, so visiting Catholics were well served. The majority of English visitors were Church of England, and again they could be catered for where the Scottish Episcopalian Church was strong. However, over most of the Highlands and Islands the only option was to attend one or other of the Presbyterian kirks. Some visitors from other denominations did attend services in Presbyterian places of worship, even though it was just out of curiosity. To most tourists from south of the border, Gaelic services with no organs and unaccompanied psalm-singing was just too strange.

By 1843, most landowners were Episcopalians, due in part to intermarriage with the English aristocracy. Some lairds either paid for, or contributed to, the building of a church that could be used by adherents of the Church of England. The Grants of Rothiemurchus helped to provide one for visitors to their area. In Grantown in Speyside, Episcopalian services were provided in the summer for southern visitors. In Killin, the 7th Earl of Breadbalane had a small corrugated iron kirk built for his shooting guests. The villagers accordingly nicknamed it the 'Grouse Chapel'.

Large-scale secular gatherings like the fairs for selling cattle and sheep also attracted attention. Broadford Fair was a great event for Skye's crofters and farmers and is vividly described by Alexander Smith:

> In a little while the road was filled with cattle, driven forward with oath and shout. Every now and then a dog-car came skirring along, and infinite was the confusion, and dire the clangour of tongues, when it plunged into a herd of sheep or skittish 'three-year-olds'. .. On either side of the road stood hordes of cattle, the wildest-looking creatures, with fells of hair hanging over their eyes, and tossing horns of preposterous dimensions. On knolls, a little apart, women with white caps and wrapped in scarlet tartan plaids, sat beside a staked cow or pony … Down in the hollow tents had been knocked up since dawn; there potatoes were being cooked for drovers who had been travelling all night; there also liquor could be had. To these places, I observed, contracting parties invariably repaired to solemnise a bargain.

After a time, Smith wandered off. His companion was engaged in wheeling and dealing, so he set off to the ruins of Corachatachin. That had been the tenant's dwelling where Johnson and Boswell had, in Boswell's words, for the first time experienced, 'A specimen of the joyous social manners of the inhabitants of the Highlands.' Now in the 1860s, what had been a two-storey house was now just a confused pile of stones. To Alexander Smith it was a kind of shrine and he was there, like others before and after him, to pay honour to the memory of these erudite and intrepid tourists James Boswell and Dr Samuel Johnson: 'I wandered around it more reverently than if it had been the cairn of a chief.'

THE ROYAL FAMILY IN THE HIGHLANDS: TUG OF WAR–BALMORAL v ABERGELDIE.

In this tug-of-war the servants of Abergeldie Estate were competing against those from Balmoral.

A BIRD'S-EYE VIEW OF BRAEMAR GATHERING

An early twentieth-century image of the Braemar Games.

SACRAMENT SUNDAY AT KILMORAC.

The gathering for the Sacrament Day at Kilmorac (now Kilmorack). The waterfalls were greatly reduced when a hydro-electric dam and power station were built in 1962.

Highland Sacraments aroused the curiosity of visitors so this kind of postcard was aimed at tourists.

The Episcopal Church of St Fillan in Killin was built in 1876 by the Earl of Breadalbane for his shooting guests.

A postcard skit on an inappropriately dressed tourist.

An Unspeakable Scot?

Chapter Nine

New Ways by Land and Sea

Conveyance by steam ... has been as signal in its effects in our northern localities as elsewhere annihilating, and pouring a tide of living energies through scenes heretofore secluded. (George and Peter Anderson, *Guide to the Highlands and Islands of Scotland*, 1834)

The adoption of steam power for travel by sea and land was a revolutionary step in the history of the Highlands. Usually the railways take first place in describing the transport revolution, but the railways were late in reaching the Highlands. In the Highlands, in an area with numerous sea lochs and countless islands, it was the steamboat that was the main driver of change. It was on the Clyde that this travel revolution started. In 1812 Henry Bell of Helensburgh brought the *Comet* into service – the first successful steam-propelled vessel to sail in British waters. The *Comet* and its successors opened up the Western Highlands and Islands to tourists. Southey saw the impact of this new mode of transport when he arrived at Inverary in late September 1819: 'The steam boat which has lately started to ply between Glasgow and Fort William, and touch at the interjacent [*sic*] places, brings a great number of visitors to Inverary.' Probably few of the visitors he saw in Inverary were through travellers, since Southey's reference to these visitors idling away their time points to most being excursionists. It also hints perhaps at the sense of superiority that 'travellers' felt over mere day-trippers. Wordsworth too had his reservations. Sailing down the Firth of Clyde in 1833, he was enthralled by Arran's 'crowded peaks and ridges blue', but he evidently had some doubts about travelling by steamboat – 'This dull Monster and her sooty crew.' Wordsworth, of course, also opposed the coming of the railway to his beloved Lake District; it would bring the wrong kind of person, people who would not appreciate the mountains and lakes for their aesthetic quality.

'Dull monster' it may have been, but tourists were taking advantage of this new kind of vessel to go to places hitherto difficult to reach. In the summer of 1822, for instance, parties were sailing from Glasgow once a fortnight, by the steamboat *Highlander*, to visit Fingal's Cave on Staffa – an island that until then had been but rarely visited. By the late 1820s there was a twice-weekly steamboat service from Oban to Iona and Staffa. With its 'constant and animating communication by steam-vessels', Oban blossomed as a service centre for the islands. Once the Caledonian Canal was opened to traffic in 1822, the town also became an intermediary stop on the tourist route by sea to Fort William and Inverness. With Staffa and Iona becoming favourite tourist destinations, Oban, the 'Charing Cross of the Highlands', developed into an important resort.

Different individuals and companies had been involved in developing steam navigation in western waters, but in the middle years of the nineteenth century one man stood out. From 1851 until 1876, David Hutcheson's fleet of ships was the West Highlanders' lifeline. Theodor Fontane wrote appreciatively of the improvements wrought by David Hutcheson. The Highlands and the west coast of Scotland, he wrote, have Mr Hutcheson to thank for 'the improvement in their circumstances which has taken place over the last few years'. Oban he recognised as a major beneficiary, a creation of the network of steamship lines with which Mr Hutcheson has surrounded the west coast. While on a steamboat cruise to Staffa and Iona, Fontane was pleased to note that the estimable Mr Hutcheson himself was on board, as he often was, 'to look after the comfort and wellbeing of his passengers as best he can'.

When David Hutcheson and his brother Alexander retired, David's son-in-law David MacBrayne took over the business. The MacBrayne name, in its turn, was to become a byword for marine transport in the West Highlands. MacBrayne's hegemony seemed to be threatened when the railway reached Oban in 1880, Fort William in 1898, and Mallaig three years later. Good publicity and astute marketing and the fact that they reached parts that the railway never did meant that MacBrayne's retained a share of the traffic. Naming the steamboat service from the Clyde to Fort William and Inverness the 'Royal Route' was a nifty piece of business; certainly the Queen had only sailed on the two canal sections of the so-called Royal Route, but that was enough for David MacBrayne.

On the west coast MacBrayne's name was praised in mock reverence. As a local rhyme went:

The earth belongs unto the Lord
And all that it contains
Except the Western Islands
And they are David MacBrayne's.

Other vessels served the commercial and other needs of the Inner and Outer Hebrides and also the more remote parts of the north-west Highlands. From the 1840s, a steamer called at Lochinver in Assynt once a fortnight en route to Stornoway. A large number of remote settlements had no pier or, if there was one, a pier large enough for a steamer to dock. In that case a small boat had to come out to the steamer to be loaded with goods and passengers, which then had to be ferried ashore. When large numbers of sheep or cattle were being delivered to southern markets, their shipment was certainly an interesting spectacle. It meant that boats were often late, however, and that, with some passengers, was a source of complaint.

There is a lovely diary account by two young women, the Astley sisters, who were reluctantly departing after a holiday at Ardtornish House on the Morvern peninsula. The date was 12 November 1872 when the steamer (possibly Hutcheson's *Clansman* from Stornoway) arrived at Lochaline in the Sound of Mull. The diary, which is written in the third person, tells how the sisters with their maid were rowed out to the boat where 'their melancholy thoughts are much aggravated by finding the whole steamer crammed with steerage passengers, cows, sheep, horses, etc'. More sheep were taken on at Craignure in Mull and this meant that the steamer was late in arriving at Oban, with the consequent knock-on effect on their transport arrangements. For the overnight part of the journey from Oban to the south, they enjoyed the benefit of a comfortable state cabin. The steerage passengers, not buttressed by great wealth, would have been far less comfortable, especially when rounding the Mull of Kintyre. Next morning, when the Astley sisters appeared on deck, a bitter wind was blowing and 'everybody look[ed] miserable'. They arrived at Greenock at 10.30 a.m. and two hours later they were on the train to Edinburgh. There they were met by Alexander Craig Sellar, MP, and his wife, who had been their hosts at Ardtornish House. Alexander Craig Sellar was the son of the late Patrick Sellar of Sutherland Clearances notoriety.

For those who did not fancy a potentially stormy sea journey up the exposed west coast, there were alternatives. According to *Murray's Hand-Book for Scotland* (1868), a tourist's coach left Ardrishaig daily during the season after the arrival of the steamer *Iona* from Glasgow. This coach connected with another steamer at Ford on Loch Awe, which took the tourists halfway up the loch to Cladich. From there coaches carried them through the Pass of Brander to Oban. Murray warns that if it is wet it could be an unpleasant trip, 'as the tourist has sometimes an hour or more to wait for steamer or coach', and that was at places with no shelter, not even a shed.

While the steamer was the product of Clydeside ingenuity and engineering skills, it was not long before steamboats were providing an acceptable means of travel on the east coast in the summer months, if not the winter. By 1834, according to *The Scottish Tourist* (fifth edition), there was a weekly sailing from Newhaven by Edinburgh to Inverness, and from thence to Wick and Kirkwall, calling at intermediate towns. When in June 1853 Dr Edward Charlton went from the north of England in the Western Highlands to fish, he elected to travel to the North by the east coast route from Newcastle to Aberdeen. From Aberdeen he boarded the mail coach for an overnight journey to Inverness. 'It was something novel to me,' he wrote, 'in these railway days to be reduced to coach travelling again, but the mail was well appointed quite in the old style, and the horses were excellent.' Bowling along an excellent road 'as is generally the case in Scotland', he observed railway works in progress. In another year or two, he reckoned, the old coaches would be laid off. After breakfasting in Inverness, he continued in the mail coach northward to Dingwall. To his great joy, there was a mail gig about to start for the west coast. At Garve Inn, Charlton changed vehicles to a primitive little mail car 'drawn by one lazy horse'. The 37 miles from Garve to Ullapool took seven hours, changing horses three times on the way. Before descending to Loch Broom, the driver halted the coach to take his passenger to a deep gorge with a spectacular waterfall. There is no name mentioned in the diary but it has to be the Corrieshalloch Gorge, now a National Nature Reserve and a must-see stop on the road to Ullapool.

Having slept in the stagecoach from Aberdeen to Inverness and on the boat from Newcastle the previous night, the Ullapool Inn was Charlton's first overnight stop. Procuring a guide and a horse for his luggage, he was off early the next morning, heading north with his angling gear to the Altnacealgach Inn at Loch Borralan. Tempted by a series of small lochs by the wayside, Dr Charlton sent the guide on ahead with horse and luggage while he continued on foot. Walking cross-country, he tried his luck at a whole succession of lochs. Losing his way, he arrived late at the inn utterly exhausted, but a draught of whisky and milk soon revived him. After two days fishing around the inn, he headed off on foot again. Since the doctor was looking for places to cast his rod, he only took his fishing rod and landing net. His luggage, or 'things', as he called them, he left for the mail coach to drop off at the next inn at Inchnadamph. This coaching inn was, and still is, a favourite with anglers. Since he had last stayed there twenty years earlier, it had been transformed out of all recognition. On that occasion Charlton had been one of a large party of twenty-one from Edinburgh that had been squashed into the then tiny inn. Since the party had been 'botanising', they were probably a university group.

In writing his journal Dr Charlton describes in great detail his fishing exploits – the fish he caught and how he played them – but he had an eye too for the plants and wildlife he observed as he wandered from loch to loch. He noted the absence of the eyrie on the top of old Ardvreck Castle, where ospreys had built their nests since time immemorial. For the past three years, he wrote, none had bred here. To the 'sportsmen' who came to the Highlands to shoot and fish, ospreys, like other birds of prey, were 'vermin' to be blasted from the sky. Though he was on holiday, his medical skill was brought into play when the landlord, Mr Macgregor, asked if he could visit a poor boy lying seriously ill. The doctor diagnosed a bad case of pleurisy with little hope of a cure unless he could be got to an infirmary, and the nearest was in Inverness: 'The poor people were very grateful for my visit, and I only wish I could have done more for them.' By chance, some days later the local doctor turned up at the inn – a Dr Mackenzie from Lochalsh in Ross-shire. Since Dr Mackenzie's practice extended from Oban in Argyle-shire to Cape Wrath, a distance of about 200 miles, the word 'local' is used advisedly.

On his return journey, Dr Charlton took a different route across the Highlands. Instead of going south to Ullapool, he headed west with Mr Macgregor driving a dogcart, a horse borrowed from the minister in harness. The first stop was at Oykel Inn, another anglers' haunt, where,

'The landlord … solicited my advice about his ailments, and in return plied me with the best French brandy.' Parting with 'my good friend Macgregor', Dr Charlton carried on towards Bonar Bridge in a gig and driver supplied by the Oykel's landlord. It was 11.30 p.m. and pouring in torrents before they arrived at the next halt, Ardgay Inn, near Bonar Bridge: 'We roused the inmates and I ordered a horse and gig to convey me at once to Invergordon. Mr Kinghorn, the worthy landlord, supplied me with an excellent supper, and at half past twelve I resumed my journey through the rain.' The sun was rising as they neared Invergordon, where they saw two rival steamers both getting up steam. The one he boarded was the *Queen*, on which he had sailed to Shetland the preceding year. At 6 a.m. both vessels started and steamed down the Dornoch Firth at full speed. Next day, 26 June, the *Queen* docked at Edinburgh's Granton Pier at 10.30 a.m.

> At 12 I seated myself in the railway train and by half past four pm I arrived at Newcastle, exactly half an hour less than the fortnight I had allotted to myself for my tour. I have never, thank God, enjoyed an excursion more, no accident, no disappointment marred the pleasure of my tour.

The doctor was fortunate that his voyage passed without incident, as four years later the *Queen*, which was owned by the Aberdeen, Leith & Clyde Shipping Company, was wrecked on the notorious North Carr reef, 1½ miles off the East Fife coast.

The major west coast canals were also a boon to tourists. The John Rennie-designed Crinan Canal ensured that travellers sailing to Oban could avoid the treacherous waters of the Mull of Kintyre. In the 1840s, a track-boat pulled by horses, their riders splendidly dressed in scarlet, provided a regular passenger service. The Crinan route received the royal imprimatur when, in 1847, Queen Victoria was a passenger. For the Queen's benefit a new vessel was commissioned. Though just 8½ miles long, the canal had eleven locks and the Queen found the journey tedious. However, its magnificent decorations at least met with her approval. Many tourists preferred to walk at least part of the way, leaving their luggage on board. Enterprising locals saw the canal boats as a retail opportunity and set up stalls by the towpath selling milk, souvenirs and other items. Following the Queen's visit tourist numbers grew and even more so when, in 1866, a small steamboat, the *Linnet*, replaced the track-boat. A popular vessel, the *Linnet* remained in service for over sixty years.

The 62 miles of the Caledonian Canal from Banavie Locks to Inverness also saw a lot of tourist traffic. This canal, the work of William Jessop and Thomas Telford, was built along the line of the Great Glen, a geological fault line, and linked three natural waterways. Going south-west from Inverness to Fort William, steamers sailed down Loch Ness, then by a canal link to Loch Oich. There was another canal stretch to Loch Lochy, then another link to Banavie Locks, otherwise known as Neptune's Staircase. These eight successive locks led to Loch Linnhe – a sea loch. Southey had seen it under course of construction and was hugely impressed with the scale of the work. The *Inverness Courier* celebrated its completion in 1822 in trenchant terms: 'The doubters, the prophets and the sneerers were all put to shame: for the 24th of October was at length to witness the Western joined to the Eastern Sea.' Although the ever-increasing size of ocean-going vessels ensured that as an artery of trade it was soon outmoded, the Caledonian Canal now enabled tourists to travel by a succession of steamers from Glasgow and the Clyde via the Crinan Canal to Fort William, where another steamer took them via the Caledonian Canal to Inverness. As we have seen before, Queen Victoria's patronage of the route allowed MacBrayne's to cash in on the royal name and so 'The Royal Route' it became. This was justified on the grounds that the Queen had passed through the Crinan Canal in 1847 and then the Caledonian Canal in 1873 on board the paddle-steamer *Gondolier*. Victoria admired the Caledonian Canal as a wonderful piece of engineering. What did not amuse her, however, was being in the canal sections, where she was too close to the crowds of curious onlookers. The 38 miles of sailing in the three lochs, the largest being Loch Ness, gave more privacy.

Loch Lomond was an obvious place to place a steamer and in 1818 'the elegantly and commodiously fitted out' paddle steamer *Marion* was transferred from the Clyde to Loch Lomond, the most visited of all the lochs. That same year the poet John Keats, while on a walking tour, saw the steamer as taking 'something of the romance of the loch'. Francis Jeffrey, likewise, was not enamoured: 'It rather vulgarises the scene too much.' The Loch Lomond steamers may have been unpleasing to the eye of the romantically minded, but they were of inestimable benefit to those who actually lived there and for travellers going further north. Indeed, in the 1840s a canal was built from the head of Loch Lomond to Inverarnan Inn, thus enabling the loch steamers to connect with the coaches that left the inn for Fort William.

For some years David Napier, who had put the first steamer on Loch Lomond, also had a small steamer operating on Loch Eck, north of Dunoon. Tourists could go to Inverary this way, with steam carriages providing the overland link. Felix Mendelssohn and Karl Klingemann travelled from Inverary in 1829 by this route. By then the steam-coach had been replaced by a conventional carriage. Klingemann observed the steam-coach standing idly by the roadside, 'Having already been used but not found quite practicable yet, and looking very ridiculous with a high funnel and a rudder.' In the course of time, steamers were placed on other major lochs, benefiting not just tourists but the loch-side communities as well. The loch steamer services on Loch Awe and Loch Tay formed part of an integrated transport system. At 22 miles long, Loch Awe was another obvious place for a steamer service, and steamers were operating on this loch from 1861. This allowed the Loch Eck sailing to be revived and this service was renewed in 1878.

The Loch Tay steamer service was the brainchild of the Marquis of Breadalbane, who formed the Loch Tay Steamboat Company in 1882. During the tourist season the steamer, the *Lady of the Lake*, sailed between Kenmore at the east end of the loch to Killin at the west. Killin was an angling resort and, with the spectacular falls of Dochart and, as one gazetteer put it 'girt with magnificent scenery', it made an attractive excursion destination. Loch Tay railway station was built in 1866 at the terminus of the Killin branch on the same Callander to Oban line. With four-in-hand coaches running between the railhead at Aberfeldy to Kenmore, Loch Tay circular tours were feasible.

The advance of the railways into the Highlands was late compared with the rest of the country. The line from Perth to Inverness was built in stages, with formerly quiet villages gaining new life with the increase in the number of tourists. Birnam, the gateway to the Central Highlands, was reached in 1856 and remained the railway terminus for seven years, with stagecoaches taking over for the rest of the way. These years were a boost to the development of the village, with the 'spacious Saxon-Gothic Birnam Hotel' acquiring an excellent reputation. Just as well-to-do families had been accustomed to spend weeks and sometimes months in one favoured seaside resort, so too many middle-class southerners sought out quiet country places. There the paterfamilias could indulge in golf or fishing and other rural sports, while the womenfolk and children could wander about in safety untroubled by the plebeian hordes that were invading their former seaside sanctums. The railways provided the means of transport not just for the families, but could in addition cope with the massive amounts of luggage required for an extended stay. Dalguise House near Birnam was from 1871 to 1881 the holiday home of the wealthy Potter family from London. During their annual three-month-long vacation Mr Potter fished for salmon. His daughter, Beatrix, loved the rural life, and the Perthshire countryside and people provided the inspiration for many of her later books. The local postman, Charles Macintosh, shared her interest in the local fauna and flora, and for years they exchanged correspondence on their common fascination with fungi. Today Birnam hosts a permanent Beatrix Potter Exhibition and Garden.

It was 1863 before Inverness was connected to Perth. Then the line went the long way round via Boat of Garten, Forres and Nairn. The direct route via Aviemore had to wait until 1898. For five of these years the Highland Railway Company's works were stalled at Carrbridge, bringing, as at Birnam, extra visitors to that village. For a good part of its route the line to Inverness ran along the valley of the River Spey. Following the completion of that line in 1863, the villages of Badenoch and Strathspey, built on or close to that great salmon river, became increasingly popular with seasonal visitors. In the late nineteenth century, hotels and villas for letting were built in villages like Kingussie, the 'capital' of Badenoch district, and Aviemore in Strathspey, though the latter in its early years had been little more than a railway village. As these villages came to be seen as desirable places to stay for a holiday, sporting and other facilities for tourists were provided. A bowling club was founded at Kingussie in 1877 and a golf club in 1890. Seventeen years later the course was extended to eighteen holes. By the early twentieth century the growing Strathspey village of Aviemore possessed tennis courts and two nine-hole golf courses. Newtonmore in Badenoch also made rapid progress in this regard. According to an early 1930s guidebook, Newtonmore – with an estimated population of 800 in 1931 – had no fewer than seventy furnished houses and apartments to let. With four tennis courts and a first-class golf course, sporting visitors to Newtonmore were well catered for.

There was population growth further down the River Spey where, also from 1863, the Great North of Scotland Railway Company's Speyside Line served villages like Nethybridge, Grantown-on-Spey and Craigellachie. By the end of the nineteenth century, the village of Craigellachie had increased its population fivefold. Like other Speyside villages, it grew on the twin motors of tourism and whisky distilling. As with their counterparts on Deeside, all the Badenoch, Strathspey and Speyside villages laid claim to be health resorts. Tourist literature for Grantown-on-Spey stated that convalescents 'requiring rest and quiet on account of nervous overstrain and debility are greatly benefited by the stillness of the woods and the privileges extended to visitors who can roam about the country without hindrance'. It must be added that game-conscious Highland landlords were more noted for restricting rights to roam than permitting them.

At that time, the holidaymakers in their rented villas and the customers of the new big hotels were not tourists in the same way as Wordsworth and Southey had been. Like the Potter family at Birnam in Perthshire, they stayed in their chosen resort for weeks or months at a time. The better-off holidaymakers, or summer visitors as they were now called, went to places like Aviemore or Aberfeldy in Perthshire or Edzell in Angus for a change of scene, for fresh mountain air or, if on the coast, for sea air and to view the scenic delights of their chosen place of resort. For the wealthy, leisured classes, they were places where they could indulge in the most prestigious of holiday pastimes – the 'country sports' of fishing and shooting. Not surprisingly, therefore, the railways were especially busy when the grouse-shooting season started on 12 August ('The Glorious Twelfth'). The rich and the famous, their servants and even their carriages, were whisked north by train to Strathspey and other favoured Highland locations. Kingussie station, opened in 1863, was during the shooting season one of the busiest stations, it being, among other things, a toilet stop. Many carriages had no toilets, so the station had no fewer than forty urinals. Fortunately, the Victorians were also producing patent India rubber urinating devices that could be fitted to one's person. Both sexes were able to urinate discretely and, hopefully, silently while aboard the train (for interested readers, modern equivalents are available). With no refreshment cars available on trains either, refreshment rooms were installed at key railway stations. At Kingussie station there were refreshment rooms on both platforms, and passengers could order meals or food baskets in advance by sending a telegram. When the train halted, food baskets were handed into the train for passengers who had pre-ordered. In 1912, breakfast baskets comprising tea and bread with butter and jam and a plate of bacon and eggs cost two shillings and sixpence. Lunch and dinner baskets included a small bottle of claret or mineral water. On busy days up to 500 baskets could be supplied to hungry train travellers at Kingussie and in July and August travellers consumed around 8,000 cups of tea. To the

Highland Railway Company's annoyance, a huge number of cups and saucers went missing. Although vacuum flasks for keeping drinks hot had been on the market since 1904, they were a luxury item at that time. During the shooting season, because some trains had so many carriages and wagons, the platforms at stations like Kingussie and Nairn were much longer than the average.

The growth of the steamer and rail networks greatly increased the number of tourists and therefore brought an expansion in the number of hotels and other forms of accommodation and facilities. The newly affluent middle-class demanded comfort when travelling and could afford to pay for it. New, better-furnished hotels were built to meet their demands. The splendid Trossachs Hotel, built in 1849, was one of the earliest. In the stagecoach era, Pitlochry, a staging point on the Great North Road with whisky distilling and weaving as the main industries, had one large hotel, Fisher's, which was built around 1839. In 1863 the railway arrived and Pitlochry's growth as a holiday resort was ensured. It was already recommended as a healthy area. Sir James Clarke, Queen Victoria's physician, in addition to boosting Deeside, had bestowed a similar cachet on Pitlochry. Thirty years after the first trains arrived, the population had quadrupled and six major hotels, two of them hydropathics, were listed in the guidebooks. Numerous new villas were also being built; most, as in other resorts, with a 'back house', which could be used as a summer retreat for the owners, who could then let the main house to summer visitors. Without the arrival of the railway, this kind of growth would have been impossible. For developers, however, it was not all plain sailing. Some entrepreneurs overreached themselves. Over in the west a grandiose hydropathic in Oban was never completed. With two bankruptcies, even the now hugely successful Athol Palace Hotel in Pitlochry had problems in its early days. The railway companies, nevertheless, saw advantage in having their own hotels in the places that were becoming tourist hotspots. The Highland Railway Company had hotels on the west coast at Kyle of Lochalsh (1897), the golf resort of Dornoch on the east coast (1904) and at the spa resort of Strathpeffer (1911). Aviemore had its large and highly profitable Station Hotel, but this palatial building was owned by an independent company. Not long after it was completed, the Cairngorm Hotel, a near neighbour, opened for business in 1903. Although both hotels were popular, by this time visitors to Aviemore had a great choice of alternative accommodation – from basic rural cottage to magnificent private villa. You could even rent a manse.

Grantown-on-Spey, originally planned to be an industrial centre, also found its niche as a holiday town. It too expanded once it was connected to the railway system. As well as a first-class hotel, the Grant Arms, and an excellent inn, the *Highland Railway Handbook* of 1892 tells us that in the holiday season 'every house in the town and every farmhouse … readily find tenants'. The town's open tennis tournament was a notable event, drawing competitors from far and wide. The village of Boat of Garten, 'The Boat', was a creation of the railway. As with the other villages in the region, the River Spey was popular with anglers. A tiny inn was rebuilt in the 1890s and renamed the Boat Hotel. A golf course was opened in 1898, which is now one of Britain's top courses. New life came to 'The Boat' in the last quarter of the twentieth century with the return of the railway – namely the opening in 1978 of the Strathspey Steam Railway, operating on the old Highland Railway line from the village to Aviemore.

With the continued expansion of the Victorian railways, the crack mail coach thundering through market towns and villages soon became for most people but a sentimental memory. Though the disappearance of the mail coach, as with the more recent demise of the steam locomotive, was regretted by some, the less romantically inclined recalled instead how expensive it was. They remembered too the discomfort and precarious nature of outside travel, with passengers exposed to the worst that the elements could throw at them. Coaches still ran in those parts of the Highlands the railway didn't reach, but one by one the coaches were withdrawn. In 1874 it was farewell to the Thurso mail, the last long-distance coach in Britain. A stagecoach, the handsome black and yellow 'Duchess of Gordon', however, still ran from Kingussie to Fort William via Laggan and Spean Bridge. With the railway from the south reaching Fort William in 1894, the coach run was restricted to the intermediary station at Tulloch, and then eventually it went only as far as Laggan. The final indignity came when, in July 1914, the stagecoach was replaced by a motor bus.

David MacBrayne Ltd steamships were the Western Islanders' lifeline over a long period of time, and the tourists they brought helped boost the local economy.

MacBrayne's PS *Gondolier* is shown here at the Fort Augustus locks. When war broke out in 1939, the *Gondolier* was withdrawn from service but then served the national wartime interest by being used as one of the Scapa Flow block ships.

Once arrived at the Muirtown Locks on the outskirts of Inverness, hotel buses wait ready for the arrival of the steamer.

Railway Station, Killiecrankie

R. H. Stewart, The Arcade, Pitlochry   434

With the famous Killiecrankie Gorge and battle site nearby, the Highland Railway Company's station at Killiecrankie was a popular tourist stop.

"IN THE PULLMAN"
LET ME SEE,- WHICH IS THE FRONT?

Sporting tourists in the sleeping car on their way to the Highlands. 'Let me see,' says one, 'which is the front?'

Chapter Ten

Tourists All

'What is this life, if it be not mixed with some delight? And what delight is more pleasing than to see the fashions and manners of unknown places?' (Sir Walter Scott)

As we have seen, Sir Walter Scott brought the romance of the Trossachs and the Highlands in general to the reading public through the magic of his poetry and prose. Artists, through paintings and prints, gave added emphasis to Scotland and the Highlands in particular as a land of dramatic mountains and flood, picturesque ruins and romantically costumed people. What Scott achieved for the Trossachs through poetic description was reciprocated by popular artists like Horatio McCulloch and Edwin Landseer. Reproductions and imitations of paintings like Landseer's 'Stag at Bay' adorned countless walls – castle and cottage alike – and also featured in guidebooks. People who had never read Scott's *The Lady of the Lake* could be inspired by McCulloch's painting of Loch Katrine, dominated by a dramatic Ben Venue. Where McCulloch led, lesser artists followed – witness the plethora of 'Art Postcards' bought by tourists from the early 1900s onward.

Of all the artists who featured Highland scenery and subjects in their work, it was Edwin Landseer who made the greatest impact. His paintings of Highland scenes, incidents and animals proved to be widely popular. Landseer had first come to Scotland in 1824 and had fallen in love with the country. If Landseer had a favourite place in the Highlands, it was Glen Feshie in the Cairngorms, which he visited frequently. In 1825 part of Glen Feshie had been leased by the Duke and Duchess of Bedford. Georgiana, 6th Duchess of Bedford (1781–1853), had been brought up not too far away at Kinrara near Kingussie by her mother Jane, the estranged wife of the 4th Duke of Gordon. While there Duchess Jane and her family had lived in what was for people of their rank a comparatively simple style. Georgiana, following in her mother's tradition, had a cluster of backwoods-style cabins built as a holiday retreat fairly far up Glen Feshie. For Georgiana, her hut-settlement provided a refuge from family troubles; it was a place where she could entertain her high society friends and at the same time embrace what they conceived to be a simple, natural way of living. It was also a place where she could entertain Landseer, who had become her lover. Landseer's visits to Glen Feshie, where he had the use of one of the 'huts', allowed him to study the wildlife of the Highlands at close hand and in naturalistic surroundings and thus to perfect paintings such as his famous *Monarch of the Glen.*

Remote though it was, the hut that Landseer lived in became a kind of early visitor attraction. To Queen Victoria on her and Albert's first great expedition in 1860, this lovely part of the glen was 'the scene of all Landseer's glory'. The Duchess of Bedford's huts by then were falling into decay. The royal couple were back again in the glen in the following year. Victoria gushed: 'I felt what a delightful encampment it must have been, and how enchanting to live in such a spot as this beautiful solitary wood in a glen surrounded by the high hills.' The Queen and Albert entered Landseer's hut to see a fresco of stags painted by the artist on a plaster wall over a chimneypiece. Over the years visitors noted further gradual decay, and today the only thing left is the fireplace and chimney standing incongruously alone.

Whereas Landseer favoured Glen Feshie, two other important figures in the Victorian art world, John Ruskin and John Everett Millais, chose the Trossachs. They based themselves at Brig o'Turk, a small village between Callander and Loch Katrine, which is on the Scott tourist trail. Scott in *The Lady of the Lake* described a fictional hunt in which the hero, a disguised King James V, is chasing after a stag, outstripping his followers:

Few were the stragglers, following far,
That reached the Lake of Vennachar;

And when the Brigg of Turk was won,
The headmost horseman rode alone.

It was these last two lines that ensured that, as Theodor Fontane noted in 1858, the Brig o'Turk was a stop-to-look-at point on the Trossachs trail. The bridge crosses the Water of Finglas, which flows down from Glen Finglas – a favourite location for Ruskin and Millais. The artists arrived at this Highland clachan in 1853 for the serious purpose of painting, but they were also prepared to enjoy themselves. 'We have immense enjoyment,' wrote Millais, 'painting out on the rocks, and having our dinner brought to us here, and in the evening climbing up steep mountains for exercise, Mrs Ruskin accompanying us …' Ruskin, the best-known art critic of the day, wanted his younger fellow artist and protégé to combine in a single painting the disparate skills of both landscape and portrait painting. The intention was to have Millais paint his portrait not as was usual in a studio or other indoor setting, but with a wild Highland scene as background. Ruskin rejected imaginary landscapes and insisted that nature had to be treated honestly. Although the spot Millais selected for this work has been described as 'the most important site in the history of British landscape painting', it is only in recent years that the site has been positively identified. In consequence, 'Ruskin Rock' now features in the Art and Literature trail of the Trossachs. Signposts point to the site where a waterfall provided the background to the portrait and an explanatory plaque includes a reproduction of Millais' painting.

The Ruskin-Millais partnership soon foundered, however. During their sojourn at Brig o'Turk, Millais and Mrs Ruskin (Effie) fell in love. Effie, unhappy with her marriage, sued for divorce from Ruskin on the grounds that, despite their having been married for seven years, the marriage was not consummated. Her petition was successful and the marriage was annulled. These events and her subsequent marriage to Millais caused a Victorian sensation. As Effie gave birth to eight children, her second marriage was certainly consummated. The couple's sensationally dramatic story has been told in books, in an opera and in films – the first in 1912 and the most recent in 2014. For the latter film the title is *Effie Gray* – Gray being her maiden name. Other artists to come to Brig o'Turk included the Glasgow Boys, the avant-garde painters of their day who established an artists' colony in the clachan. All this attention meant that holiday accommodation in Brig o'Turk was in demand. The mainly working-class cottagers profited from this demand by letting their homes to summer visitors. As in other tourist hotspots, many of the cottages are today second homes.

Artistic talent can be shown in different ways, as a young lady demonstrated by the sketches she made in the journal she kept while on tour in Scotland with her family in 1863. This young woman – unfortunately we don't know her first name – wrote with verve and sketched with no little skill. Her humorous sketches provide a delightful accompaniment to her text. She commenced her journal at midnight on 5 August on the night express from London to Edinburgh and concluded on 31 August, when 'our Scotch tour' ended. While the original journal is in the possession of Viscount Strathallan, the Viscount's late father, the Earl of Perth, gave permission for a facsimile to be printed for the Roxburghe Society. Very little can be gleaned from the journal about this young girl or her family. Her surname was Parker and she was accompanied by her two sisters and parents, her father being duly described as 'Paterfamilias'. This was a cultured family. They knew their Scott and could quote Burns. For this journey, *Black's Guide to Scotland* was their bible. They used a variety of means of travel including trains and steamers; at other times they travelled independently, hiring vehicles of varying quality at a succession of inns.

The Highland part of their tour commenced with the family's arrival at Callander, the gateway to the Trossachs. After having enjoyed fine weather in Edinburgh they found the rain falling in torrents – an experience unfortunately too frequently repeated during the Highland part of their tour. The Trossachs part of their holiday did not go too well. Travelling in a leaking coach, they arrived at the Trossachs Hotel 'in a crumpled and streaming state' only to find that there were no vacancies. The Parkers, like most travellers in those days, had made no prior arrangements and had to trust to luck that their preferred choice of residence had rooms for them. If not, they might be offered a shakedown or have to move on. On this occasion, they ended up in pokey rooms in an annexe, which our young diarist unflatteringly compared to a House of Correction. With no improvement in the weather and miserable accommodation the family abandoned the idea of seeing Loch Katrine and returned to Callander. Having to spend the Sunday at Callander they went to the morning service in the 'Scotch Free Church', which they enjoyed very much, the sermon being 'most beautiful'. The sermon at the afternoon service, which they also attended, was not nearly so good. Both sermons lasted nearly an hour. Miss Parker further lamented that, 'Scotch Churches would be much nicer if old gentlemen didn't take snuff with a spoon, and circulate their boxes so sociably in all the seats adjacent to them, and if large families of young ladies could be induced not to eat peppermint lozenges immediately behind one's head during the whole service.' The Scottish tradition of sucking peppermint drops during sermons evidently goes back a long way!

From Callander the family proceeded by the 'wild and beautiful' Pass of Leny to Lochearnhead, thence by Killin and Loch Tay to Kenmore. Before leaving Kenmore, they were given a guided tour of the grounds of Taymouth Castle, which greatly pleased them. Then they headed for Dunkeld, going by Aberfeldy. Miss Parker thought the views beautiful and the town of Aberfeldy quite different from what she had expected: 'We were rather surprised to find a clean smart little town, with "fleshers" [butchers] and linen drapers' shops, near a turnpike.' The River Tay accompanied them nearly all the way. She commented on the number of people fishing on the river banks 'and pines [logs] floating down it in large quantities, tied together and steered by a boat'. Nearing Dunkeld they found themselves in shooting country. Their driver pointed to a distant 'dark heath-covered mountain' where the shooting rights belonged to the Maharajah Dulup Singh. The Maharajah (1836–1893), it must be explained, was the last ruler of the Sikh Empire. The Sikhs had been defeated by the army of the British East India Company and the young Maharajah was sent into exile. Taken to Britain at the age of thirteen he was a favourite of Queen Victoria and Albert and was given a pension. He spent many years in Perthshire, where he enjoyed shooting and gained the affectionate nickname of the Black Prince of Perthshire. An infant son of his is buried in the kirkyard of Kenmore and this has become a place of pilgrimage for Scottish Sikhs.

Reaching Dunkeld, the family found accommodation at the Birnam Hotel. The hermitage was by then on virtually every tourist's itinerary, so naturally the Parkers went to see the edifice that their guide called 'Ossian's Hall'. Their escort was delighted to demonstrate the various tricks and marvels in the building, all designed to impress visitors. To the Parker family, however, it was all just too absurd – hardly the expected response. Then it was on to another tourist hotspot, Killiecrankie, where in 1689 Viscount Dundee – 'Bonnie Dundee' – led a Highland Jacobite army to victory against the forces of William III. He, however, was killed at the moment of victory, and without their charismatic leader the Highlanders were repelled at Dunkeld. Thus, this first attempt by the Scottish followers of James VII and II to regain the throne lost to the Protestant William III was thwarted. The Parkers' guide at Killiecrankie they at first thought to be very amusing, but by the end of his spiel they condemned him as a total humbug. He claimed to be well acquainted with such prominent visitors as Mr Gladstone (then Chancellor of the Exchequer) and Queen Victoria, even taking them to the stone that the Queen had sat on while sketching.

The Parkers, like many other tourists at that time, had the benefit of waterproof cloaks, which were essential as some of the vehicles they travelled in were open to the elements. That was the case when they headed north from Pitlochry. They were blasted by a cold wind and at the same time suffered heavy rain. Being jolted over an atrocious road didn't help either: 'We all shook and swayed about, and bumped and wiggled in our big cloaks, like sacks of flour set on end.' The standard of the inns varied greatly. While they found the people at Spittal of Glenshee inhospitable and unfriendly, they were well treated at the Invercauld Arms Hotel at Braemar, where they arrived exceedingly wet. Driving from Braemar to Ballater, they were 'in a state of intense excitement' as they had hoped to spot the Prince and Princess of Wales, who were then staying at Balmoral. They had no luck, she light-heartedly confessed, despite 'straining our eyes in every direction'.

From Deeside the Parkers went first to Aberdeen and then to Inverness. Most visitors making an extensive tour of Scotland travelled by steamer at some stage and when the Parker family headed west, they took a steamer down the Caledonian Canal. Loch Ness they did not find very interesting. Of course, in those days there was no monster to strain their eyes for (Nessie wasn't 'discovered' until 1933). Miss Parker thought the next loch, Loch Oich, a decided improvement on Loch Ness and the next, Loch Lochy, very beautiful, and there was the added excitement of being passed by a blockade runner – a Confederate steamer returning from the Southern States of America. This was at the height of the American Civil War when the rebel Confederacy of Southern States was blockaded by the North's powerful navy. When the North's blockade commenced, Confederate agents had purchased a number of Scotland's fastest steamers as blockade runners and this would have been one of them returning for a fresh load of weapons and munitions. David Hutcheson was one of the owners who disposed of his crack steamers in this way.

Glencoe was another 'must-see' for the Parkers. Visitors to Glencoe, usually came with preconceptions. If they didn't already know about the infamous massacre, they were sure to be told all about it by coach-drivers and guides. Guidebooks usually went into some detail about how King William had authorised a punitive expedition against the Macdonalds of Glencoe, which was carried out on 13 February 1692 by a force led by Campbell of Glenlyon. What made the massacre all the more abhorrent was the fact that the Macdonalds had treated the government troops with traditional Highland hospitality. Visitors to the glen were expected to react with appropriate feelings of horror exacerbated by what writers insisted were the 'gloomy confines' of the glen itself – the Gaelic name for Glencoe supposedly translating as the Glen of Weeping. The Parker family once again did not conform to the tourist norm, taking it all very lightly.

After visiting Glencoe, they returned north to Corran Ferry on Loch Linnhe, near Fort William. There they boarded a steamer for Oban, most likely David Hutcheson's *Mountaineer*. The Parker family were delighted with their cabin, which was large and magnificent in crimson, gold and white, and with 'plenty of windows'. From Oban they went by stagecoach to Inverary, then by a private hire carriage to Arrochar on Loch Long and from there by steamer to Bowling on the Firth of Clyde, and thence by train to Edinburgh via Glasgow and finally from there to their home in London. The Parker family made their tour of Scotland on their own, using only their invaluable Black's guidebook and with the sometimes dubious assistance of local guides at popular spots like Glencoe. By the time they travelled to Scotland, there was, however, an ever-increasing stream of tourists coming by rail and sea, many of them travelling in organised parties.

An enterprising Derbyshire man, Thomas Cook, was the pacesetter in this, bringing large groups of tourists to Scotland – his famous Tartan Tours. Cook, who had been organising temperance excursions in England and Wales for a number of years, took his first party north to Scotland in 1846. As there was no rail connection to Scotland in those days Thomas Cook's first tour north required his clients to travel by steamer for part of the way – namely from Fleetwood to Ardrossan in Ayrshire and from there to Edinburgh and Glasgow. With a sail on Loch Lomond included in the excursion, his group at least got to the edge of the Highlands. By all accounts, however, this first venture to Scotland was pretty much a disaster. For instance, on the steamer from Fleetwood there wasn't enough food to go round, nor were there enough cabins, so those on deck were thoroughly soaked when a storm developed. One excursionist sarcastically complained, 'I had the *pleasure* of passing the night with a wet plank for my bed and a carpet bag for my pillow.' Nevertheless, Thomas Cook was self-confident and adaptable and he resumed excursions to Scotland in 1849 and, with rail connections steadily improving, he expanded his business to include organised trips to more distant places like Balmoral, Skye, Staffa and Iona. Escorted tours like those organised by Cook's firm proved to be attractive to women, and those single no less than married.

While Cook provided background notes for his customers, he also suggested that they do some homework. As preparation for the visit to Skye, Cook's excursionists were encouraged to read Scott's verse-drama *The Lord of the Isles*. Sir Walter Scott's various works were evidently still regarded as essential reading. They were treated almost as guidebooks, but they were guides to a Scotland that was distant in time and which bore little or no relation to the Scotland of Cook's day. Thomas Cook, however, was not blind to the social problems of the day. Appalled by the poverty of the people of Iona, he did something about it by helping them to help themselves by the purchase of fishing boats and the necessary equipment. Through his own donations and with the help of his excursionists, he provided twenty-four boats by 1861.

Thomas Cook was not alone in the field of package holidays. John Bradbury wrote guides for people who sought an economical holiday. His 1868 guidebook

Scotland: How to See It for Five Guineas was designed to allow the tourist to 'travel through some of its finest scenery visiting places celebrated in history, or rendered famous by the poetical genius of Scott, Burns, and other distinguished men (a guinea was worth £1 1s). Bradbury didn't operate tours himself, but assumed that the tourists he wrote for would be going on tours operated by one or the other of two North of England travel firms. The excursions to Scotland that both companies ran started from Manchester and lasted nine days. Alternatively, northern tourists could sail from Liverpool to Glasgow and London excursionists to Granton or Leith. The prospective tourist was advised to order 'Murray's Timetables' for the month when he proposed to travel (Murray's Timetables provided Scottish train times and other travel information.) He should also take as little luggage as possible – a knapsack being the most suitable for his needs. The tourist, Bradbury further recommended, should wear a tweed suit and also carry a light mackintosh.

Reaching Edinburgh on the first day, Bradbury's guidebook describes the main sights of the city where the second day was also spent and also itemises all hotel and other charges. The third day is dedicated to Stirling and Callander, the train departing at 6.15 a.m. Just half an hour was allowed for breakfast and walking to the station. After a morning in Stirling, tourists had to take the train to Callander, making sure they took seats on the right for the best views. On changing carriages at Dunblane they were advised to switch to the left side. As on every journey, the landmarks and historical buildings on the route were described. Reaching Callander, the Dreadnought Hotel was specially recommended. Bradbury's readers were also told to ignore what all the other guidebooks said and not to bother visiting the Bracklinn Falls: 'I assure you it will be a disappointment and little better than wasting your time. You will see a much better fall … at Inversnaid.' Instead, a walk or coach drive to Loch Lubnaig and Balquidder was recommended, the latter containing the graves of Rob Roy, his wife and son.

The Trossachs was the choice of destination for the fourth day. Get to the coach as early as possible, John Bradbury advised, to get a place on the front seat to 'look upon places rendered famous by the poetical creations of one of the most graphic writers and ablest poets this country produced'. Then the tourists followed the by now well-established route from Callander to Loch Katrine, boarding the steamer to Stronachlachar Pier at the west end of the loch, followed by a horse-drawn coach to Inversnaid on Loch Lomond. Here is an example of the kind of precise directions provided:

> At Stronachlachar Pier, coaches will be waiting to convey tourists to Inversnaid, five miles distant; fare, 2s.; driver's fee, 6d. The pedestrian may walk, and by starting immediately, arrive almost as quickly as the coach. A moderate walker may reach Inversnaid easily in time for the steamer down Loch Lomond.

Lunch, the tourist was further advised, should be taken at the Inversnaid Hotel and not on the steamboat, because while dinner is being served on the boat you will miss some very important scenery. There was still time after lunch to see the picturesque Inversnaid Waterfall, the best view 'being from the stones at the edge of the lake'. The party were then advised to depart for Balloch at the foot of the loch on the 1.45 p.m. boat. This would cost 2*d* for pier dues and 2*s* 6*d* for the steamboat.

Following their trip down Loch Lomond to Balloch, the tourists were to take the train to Glasgow and thence to Ayr. Ayr, with its Robert Burns associations, was judged a suitable place to spend the next day, a Sunday, as, except for some mail trains, no trains ran on the Sabbath. The sail on Loch Lomond concluded the Highland part of the nine-day tour, except for a Clyde steamer trip, at a later stage, to Ardrishaig on Loch Fyne.

The increase in package tours of the kind described above brought a new class of tourist to Scotland and other hitherto secluded parts of Britain. Better-off shopkeepers, clerks and other members of the aspiring lower middle-class, the 'Charles Pooters' of Victorian England, began to penetrate parts of the country that were previously the preserve of the upper classes. Some popular resorts were described as becoming 'Cockneyfied', and that was not meant as a compliment. This invasion was often resented by those of the 'superior' class. The Revd Francis Kilvert's opinion of tourists, as expressed in his diaries, was not untypical: 'Of all noxious animals, the most noxious is a tourist. And of all tourists the most vulgar, ill-bred, offensive and loathsome is the British tourist.' The fact that this English clergyman and others like him were tourists too did not seem to have occurred to them. Bradbury's tourists were very different from the norm of a few decades earlier when most tourists were from the elite of society, like the members of a so-called 'reading party' spotted by Cuthbert Bede at Balloch Pier in 1863, who came 'with their necessary paraphernalia of fishing-rods, gun-cases, and riding whips'.

Not all tourists were happy with their visit to Scotland. In the book they wrote about their tour, American visitors Joseph Pennell and his wife Elizabeth Robins Pennell stated that their trip to Scotland in 1888 was the most miserable they had ever undertaken. In fact, they did not really want to go to Scotland at all. Despite being London-based, or maybe because of that, they admitted: 'It was a country about which we cared little, and knew less.' It was only on the urging of an American magazine editor that they went there at all. The Pennells' account of their experiences first appeared in *Harper's Magazine*. The story of their journey was then published in America in 1889 with the title *Our Journey to the Hebrides*. Elizabeth Robins Pennell seemingly did the writing for the articles and book that followed, with her husband providing the sketches used as book illustrations. One major problem for the Pennells was that they elected to tour Scotland on foot, and they were not normally walkers. They had toured France and other parts of Europe and England, but on these occasions they were on bicycles. As they themselves acknowledged, they would have been better to stick to cycling rather than walking. This meant that, 'Day after day we were dispirited, disheartened, and only happy when we were not walking. We went to bed in the evening and got up in the morning wearied and exhausted.' Their intention was to follow the route that Dr Johnson and Boswell took in 1773, but in reverse and, in the end, with major deviations. The Pennells had bad luck with the weather and confidently stated, 'That the weather in the Western Highlands and Islands is vile is a fact which cannot be denied.'

The Pennells' magazine articles had been criticised for dwelling too much on the miserable state of the Highlanders and for their often vituperative condemnation of the Highland landlords. In the book's preface they defended themselves against their critics. Miserable though their experience was, they conceded in their book that Scotland was beautiful and 'full of the most wonderful effects'. Otherwise they stuck to their guns, asserting that the country 'is the most abominable to travel through, and its people are the most down-trodden on God's earth'. It was the poverty of the ordinary Highlanders, and the crofters in particular, that shocked them. Some tourists had criticised the Highlanders as lazy, saying that they could at least have improved their squalid dwellings. The Pennells, however, quoted evidence given by a Raasay doctor to a Royal Commission in 1883: 'The prevailing disease is poverty, and the chief remedy is food.' In other words, the Pennells concluded, the people were unable to work hard because they did not have enough to eat. Nor, lacking the materials and the money to buy them, could they do much to improve their homes, Even if they improved their homes or their land, the landlord immediately increased their rents. Often, too, the crofters had lost much of their best land for the creation of sporting estates. It was not until the passing of the Crofters' Act in 1886 that crofters enjoyed security of tenure.

The 1880s, when the Pennells went to Scotland, was a time of social and political unrest among the crofting population in the Highlands, which was sparked off in part by events in Ireland. The Highland crofters, angry at unfair rent rises and widespread evictions, followed the Irish example by direct action. During the so-called Crofters' War, there were riots in Skye, Lewis and Tiree. Arriving as they did at a time of hardship and discontent in the Highlands, the Pennells were clear as to whose side they were on. The Pennells' book *Our Journey to the Hebrides* is rather too acerbic and at times superficial. Nevertheless, at least they were sympathetic to the plight of the Highland crofters and fishermen and gave publicity to their cause. The condition of the crofters was comparable, they declared, to that of the slaves in the Southern States of pre-Civil War America. Indeed they went further by asserting that, 'The bondage in which they are held today is more cruel than was that of slaves in the slave States of America or of serfs in Russia.' To the Pennells it was the landlords who bore the responsibility for the Highlanders' poverty and lack of both means and opportunity to better themselves. The obduracy of the land-owning classes and their factors, they wrote, had brought tension, hatred and riots. Their warning to the landowners was couched in near revolutionary terms: 'Let the laird make hay while the sun shines, for the day is coming when the storms, forever brooding over the Isle of Mists [Skye], will break forth with a violence he has never felt before, and he and his kind will be swept off the face of the land.'

In their writing, the Pennells presented a portrait of Scotland that was at variance with the by then accepted image of the country as a land of romance and picturesque beauty. They were antipathetic to the picture of Scotland as presented in guidebooks like Black's. The tartan-hued image of Scotland with its 'stupid romance' created by Scott left them cold – likewise 'the sickly sentiment of Landseer'. The consequence was that most tourists, they maintained, averted their eyes from the real Scotland, whether it was the factories of the industrial Lowlands or the maltreated crofters of the Highlands and Islands. They themselves were enthused, however, when they chanced to see Highland Games at Ballachulish. The bagpipes, they thought, made a cheerful sound and the tartans 'a bright picture'. While some young men vaulted with poles, others in full tartan regalia danced Highland flings and the sword dance. While they watched, they heard only Gaelic spoken. 'We were in a foreign country,' they admitted. Did they realise, however, that without the spell cast by Scott's 'stupid romance' there might have been no Highland Games like these for them to watch?

The Pennells did not walk all the time, but made use of trains, boats and coaches at different points, which took them in due course to the east coast to the fishing port of Buckie, where they restarted the walking part of their tour. There and in the other small, picturesque fishing communities of the Banffshire coast, there was plenty of material for Joseph's sketchpad. The walking proved too much for them, however. The hike along the coast from Cullen to the tiny fishing village of Sandend was the last straw. Exhausted and, for a change, complaining of the heat, they headed for the nearest railway station. By train and coach they continued along the east coast, stopping overnight at a number of towns for sightseeing. Like Dr Johnson on his 1773 tour, the Pennells had started in Edinburgh and they intended to follow his example and conclude their tour there also.

In Fraserburgh they once more encountered people from the Western Isles. They saw men who had been hired by the east coast fishermen to bolster the large crews needed for the herring fishing drifters. Women, too, had also travelled east to toil, along with their east coast counterparts, as herring gutters. The money they earned helped to pay the laird's rent. The Pennells were probably unaware that, since 1884, the staple herring fishing industry was going through a downturn. This reduced the demand for migrant workers and many Highlanders had to return home with little or nothing to show for their long journey east. Of the women who did secure employment, Elizabeth Robins Pennell wrote, 'I have never seen women work so hard or so fast.' The 'Western Islanders' at Fraserburgh, working incessantly by day and by night, were, 'The people who, we are told, are so slovenly and lazy. No one who comes with them to the east coast for the fishing season will ever again believe in the oft-repeated lies about their idleness.'

Left: Glen Feshie in the Cairngorms was where Landseer painted his famous 'The Stag at Bay'. The author stands by all that remains of his hut – namely, the fireplace and chimney. There is a hikers' bothy nearby.

Below: The Parker family from London, as sketched by one of the daughters, had some uncomfortable moments on their tour of the Highlands.

The Parkers preferred to face the rigours of an 'evil stretch' of road in the wind and rain to staying longer in a dirty, smelly Kirkmichael inn.

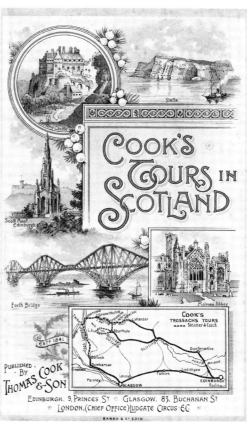

A brochure issued in 1893 advertising Cook's Tours in Scotland.

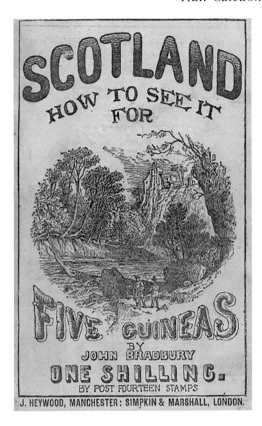

This 1868 guidebook, *Scotland for Five Guineas*, demonstrated how one could enjoy a cheap holiday in Scotland for just over £5.

American couple Joseph and Elizabeth Robins Pennell had a miserable time on their tour of Scotland in 1888.

Chapter Eleven

The Great Outdoors

'No one knows a country till he has walked through it; he then tastes the sweets and the bitters of it. He beholds its grand and important points, and all the subtler and concealed beauties that lie out of the beaten track.' (Alexander Smith, *A Summer in Skye*, 1865)

Getting back to nature was a factor in the vogue for walking – walking for pleasure, that is – that began in the eighteenth century. The native Highlanders, unless they were rich enough to afford a horse, were already well accustomed to walking long distances out of necessity. In the days when there were few or no shops, packmen – pedlars and gypsies – travelled the glens, bringing their wares to outlying farms. Bands of shearers followed the harvests, cutting crops in the south where they ripened early and then working their way north to the places where the harvests came later. In late September 1861, Queen Victoria, on her 'Second Great Expedition' from Deeside to Glenesk in Angus, met a party of reapers: 'We crossed the burn at the bottom, where a picturesque group of "shearers" were seated, chiefly women, the older ones smoking. They were returning from south to the north whence they came.'

As already noted, there were drovers too, driving cattle and sheep from the remotest glens to the major trysts (markets) at Crieff and Falkirk. The Revd Chauncy Hare Townshend encountered flock after flock of sheep passing through Kenmore. It was early September 1846, so the flocks would have been destined for the second of the three Falkirk Trysts, which was held in that month. By 1846 Falkirk had replaced Crieff as the main market for cattle and sheep. On the following day Townshend and his companion, now travelling towards Dunkeld, were half-stifled by the dust kicked up by many thousands of sheep. 'Every drove,' he wrote, 'was attended by two shepherds – picturesque figures in kilt and plaid ... and two dogs, the sagacity and cleverness of which were something astounding.' Drovers, as with other itinerant workers, had to be hardy and self-reliant. As often as not, they slept in the open and in all kinds of weather, a plaid their only cover. Dangerous rivers had to be forded and there was the hazard too of an unexpected change in the weather leading to blizzards.

Tailors too were often on the tramp. They went from one farm to another, altering clothes and making new garments from homespun cloth. The Revd Thomas Grierson, crossing from Glen Clova to Ballater with a companion, helped three tailors on the tramp from Alyth in Angus find the right way. Had they gone astray, their clothing was so poor, he judged, that they would not have survived the night. After consulting map and compass, Grierson left his companion and the tailors to carry on in the Ballater direction, while he digressed on a venture of his own in the high ground south of Lochnagar. This resulted in him being benighted, but fortunately he was better equipped than the tailors to spend a night on his own. When dawn came, he was astonished to see the upper half of Lochnagar white with snow, 'which had descended on me in slight showers of rain'. Continuing his journey, he reached a small farmhouse at the foot of Loch Muick. There he discovered his previous day's companions; his friend still snug in bed and the three tailors hard at work. 'I found them all, cross-legged, plying their needles, in order to defray their board and lodging; and delighted they were to be so comfortably housed after the labours of the previous day.' Not surprisingly, the three tailors had been as worried for his safety as he had been for theirs. Since the Reverend had had nothing to eat the previous night, the porridge hottering over a splendid peat-fire was another welcome sight. After breakfast Grierson and his friend went off to climb Lochnagar (3,789 feet). Their route took them past the simple three-roomed house called the 'The Hut', which Queen Victoria and Albert used mainly for picnics and as a halt-point for excursions. Grierson facetiously termed it 'the smallest of Her Majesty's palaces'.

Walking for pleasure, as opposed to tramping for work, may have come into vogue, but it was a fashion limited to very few. The poet John Keats, walking through Scotland with a friend in 1818, found that they were mistaken for virtually every kind of itinerant worker or salesman. Coming into a town with a knapsack – Inverness in this instance – everyone stared: 'We have been taken for Spectacle vendors, Razor sellers, Jewellers, travelling linen drapers, Spies, Excisemen & many other things.' Since his companion Charles Brown wore spectacles, that may have accounted for the first item in the list. To avoid being mistaken for a pedlar, the Revd Thomas Grierson carried a largish angler's basket. This, plus the staff-rod that he carried, gave him 'a light and gentleman-like air'. He had the basket covered with waxcloth, so he could carry his spare garments in safety. Good footwear he considered essential. He recommended 'a pair of Hornell's double-soled shoes or something similar' and to wear with them long worsted stockings. A small flask of whisky was also deemed to be a must.

The pedestrians of those days certainly travelled light. James Hogg, setting off with a companion on a jaunt from the Borders into the Highlands in 1804, took just a small portmanteau, 'Which we stuffed with each a clean shirt and change of stockings; a pocket travelling map, and a few neckcloths. Thus, nobly equipped, with each a staff in his hand, and a flashing tartan cloak over his shoulder, we proceeded on our enticing journey.' Keats and Brown also had staffs and also regarded a map as essential. If for nothing else, they would have needed their sticks to ward off troublesome dogs. Charles Brown described his outfit in a letter to a friend: 'Imagine me with a thick stick in my hand, the knapsack on my back, with spectacles on my nose, a white hat, a tartan coat and trowsers, and a Highland plaid thrown over my shoulders.' The plaid he praised as 'the best possible dress ... It is light and not easily penetrated by the wet, and when it is, it is not cold'. Long-distance walkers like Hogg, Grierson, Keats and Brown, and climbers too of a later generation, could afford to travel light because they could generally rely on getting to a place of shelter each evening where a fire could be lit, if necessary, to dry wet clothing.

Most pedestrians were of necessity male, though there were exceptions. According to Mrs Grant of Laggan, John Wilson (Christopher North) was minded to take his wife on a walking tour in the summer of 1815:

> This gentle and rather elegant Englishwoman is to walk with her mate, who carries her wardrobe and his own... through all the odd bye-paths in the central Highlands, where they propose to sleep in such cottages as English eyes never saw before. I shall be charmed to see them come back alive.

Undoubtedly there were risks in undertaking long-distance walks. Exposure to cold and wet and an inadequate diet prolonged over many days was one. Keats and Brown certainly found the food inadequate. Brown wrote:

> We have sometimes been nearly starved; for 3 or 4 days together we have not been able to procure a morsel of meat, and their oat-bread I thought my dainty stomach never would accept of, but I contrive to eat it now; all this is hard work in such long walks.

Apart from oatcakes, eggs were the other staple. By the time they reached Inverness, Keats was suffering from a violent cold and ulcerated throat, which he had contracted earlier while on Mull. Despite his illness he had insisted on climbing Ben Nevis. On reaching Inverness, a doctor considered him too thin and fevered to continue the journey. Keats therefore abandoned the tour, returning to London by sea. It has been suggested that the privations he endured on his journey contributed to his death from tuberculosis three years later, aged twenty-four. It may be noted, however, that both his mother and brother Tom had earlier died of tuberculosis; Tom at the even earlier age of nineteen. At that time it was not known that consumption, as it was called then, could be spread by human contact. By the time Keats and Brown reached Inverness they had covered, Brown estimated, 628 miles. Starting at Lancaster, they had walked through Northern England and the south-west of Scotland, made a short visit to Ireland from Portpatrick before carrying on through the Western Highlands. After Keats gave up, Brown carried on with his tour. Whether or not he reached John o'Groats, which had been their target, is unclear, however.

Keats and Brown were only two of the young gentlemen of leisure, Sassenachs mostly, who were venturing into the Highlands and other parts of Scotland on pedestrian tours. The Revd Thomas Grierson, himself a prodigious pedestrian, wrote his book *Autumnal Rambles among the Scottish Mountains*, subtitled *Or Pedestrian Tourist's Friend* as a guide for the younger generation of rambler. Grierson recommended early rising and covering 15 or 20 miles before 9 o'clock breakfast! Grierson, as is often the case with the older generation, considered the modern Scottish youths both unwilling and unfit for the kind of physical activity that his generation had been accustomed to. The ease of travel by steamboat and coach meant that the young gentlemen 'in these modern times' had adopted habits of indolence and effeminacy. He added, rather carelessly for a clergyman, that 'they can scarcely be prevailed to extend their rambles beyond the regions of silk stockings and feather beds'. Grierson did admit that, despite 'these times of rapid journeying' there were still some, chiefly young Englishmen 'not afraid to pad the hoof'. In the preface to the second edition (1851), Grierson commended these young men he had met in the wildest places making light of their discomforts, and it was largely for their benefit that he published his little handbook.

Judging by the account he gave of his various expeditions, the Reverend Thomas Grierson achieved some amazing feats of walking and mountain climbing. It is no wonder he found few companions on his Highland expeditions. Well-heeled tourists, though, had been climbing the more accessible mountains since the mid-eighteenth century. The first recorded tourist ascent of Ben Lomond was in 1758 and the first of Ben Nevis in 1771. The first recorded ascent of Ben Lomond was made by a party of Scottish gentry accompanied by Sir William Burrell. Though the others walked, Sir William had the use of a pony, which carried him as far as the steep part of the hill. It all proved to be rather much for Sir William, as he had a dizzy spell just 100 yards from the top. While the others caroused on the summit, Burrell, as he frankly admitted, crawled downhill on all fours. Another not too intrepid mountaineer, the Marquis de Custine, climbing Ben Lomond in 1822, had his guide carry him over the burns that were in spate – Noblesse obliged, so to speak!

For the early tourists, if physically active, climbing the best-known peaks seemed to be on their equivalent of a 'bucket list'. The great majority, however, required the assistance of local guides. Keats did not climb Ben Lomond as he considered the guide's fee to be exorbitant. Keats and his companion Brown did, however, hire a guide – a tartan-clad local man – to lead them up Ben Nevis. Apart from the professional guides, a number of local people were climbing Ben Nevis around that time. John Leyden, who climbed the Ben in 1800, met some gentlemen at the summit, Camerons of Glen Nevis, who accompanied him on his return. It seems that some women, unfortunately nameless like the guides, did go to the high tops. One author, who used the pseudonym 'A Lady', visiting the Highlands in 1775, had wanted to ascend Ben Lomond but found no one willing to accompany her.

Nor would she have been the first female to climb it, as her Loch Lomondside host, Sir James Colquhoun, told her of a young 'Scotch' lady who had walked up in the morning and returned to dinner without appearing tired. In later years it was common for ladies to use ponies to climb the big hills. Queen Victoria ascended Lochnagar, Ben Macdui and other mountains using a pony much of the way.

People climbed the mountains for a variety of reasons. In 1818 Keats found a large cairn at the summit of Ben Nevis, built by 'some soldiers of artillery'. It is likely that these soldiers were sappers of the Royal Engineers whose uniforms were fairly close to those of the Royal Artillery. The Royal Engineers had started in 1802 to make a trigonometrical survey of Britain as part of the Ordnance Survey's mapping work, and this work was extended to Scotland in 1813. The cairn on Ben Nevis would have served as the base for a theodolite. To carry out accurate measurements clear weather was essential. Accordingly, sappers had to live in tents or rough huts on or near the summits for prolonged periods. Indeed there were times when surveyors had to wait several weeks for a clear day, meanwhile suffering gales and being bombarded by rain and sleet. A sappers' station on Ben Nevis, for instance, was occupied from 1 August to 14 November 1846. One of the pioneer mountaineers, John Hill Burton, climbing Ben Nevis, came across an unexpected sight: 'A whole crowd of soldiers occupying the whole table-land of the summit! Yes, there they were: British soldiers with their red coats, dark-grey trousers and fatigue caps ... busy erecting a sort of dwelling – half tent, half hut.' While they were on Ben Nevis, other sappers were in the Cairngorms on Ben Macdui at the same time to establish which was the higher. Their surveys led to the publication of the Ordnance Survey maps, which are for mountaineers today potentially life-saving. The walls of some of the sappers' huts still survive – on Ben Macdui in the Cairngorms and on Mam Sodhail north of Glen Affric, for instance.

Some of the bolder tourists saw that there were other high tops that might be climbed. The Revd Chauncy Hare Townshend, touring in 1846, boasted in a letter: 'We have been to the very tip-top of Ben More [near Crianlarich], and have been standing a matter of four thousand feet above your head. Think of that!' In relating his adventures, he states that: 'We were forced to part company with our guide; were bewildered in a mist; and stumbled half the day amongst precipices.' Unfortunately he rather spoils the effect by going on to say they were on horseback until the path disappeared. Climbing steeply up, they kept on in thick mist, setting up stones to guide their way back. 'There was something really novel and exciting,' Townshend continued, 'in this ascent in a dark unknown ... The gray mist gathered on our hair, and stood in drops upon our garments. Pretty exploits these for a nervous gentleman!' When they got to a point where the ground began to slope downwards, this they judged, rather optimistically, to be the summit. Guided by their way-marks, they made their way down, until they were able to see Loch Dochart below them in the glen they had left: 'So we returned to our inn [Luib], tired and pleased.'

Guidebooks like Murray's 1875 handbook started to include advice for mountaineers. A light waterproof was deemed essential, 'or, what is better than all, a good Scotch plaid.' The guidebook quotes 'a Scotchman', expatiating on its many uses, who concluded by asserting that as a garment the plaid has superiority over every other, inasmuch 'that there's room in't for twa'. The guidance on what to carry included what was quite common then – a flask of whisky. Maps and compass were deemed essential – Black's *Large Tourist Map of Scotland* available in twelve separate sheets being recommended. The Ordnance Survey (OS) maps were admitted to be excellent but in 1875, we are told, were completed for only part of Scotland. By 1894 *Murray's* was now recommending *Bartholomew's* half inch to the mile maps. But the mountaineer, it was stressed, should get the OS one inch to the mile maps for the districts where he was to climb.

The availability of the new Ordnance Survey maps was revolutionary, inasmuch as hiring guides was an expensive business. Now the less well-heeled members of society could go off into the hills without a guide. The OS maps also allowed hill walkers to be more adventurous by leaving the beaten track. Thus a contributor to the Cairngorm Club Journal in 1897, while acknowledging the excellence of the Ordnance Survey maps, regretted that they had, to a large extent, 'superseded the fraternity of guides to the mountains'. He did concede that, 'A superannuated guide may still occasionally be seen with his ponies in Glen Derry, conveying ladies to the summit of Ben Muich Dhui.' But ladies, he continued, 'Now one-inch map in hand do the Lairigs without masculine escort, and scramble up the stony slope of Coire Clach nan Taillear in corrugated footwear.'

The early middle-class mountaineers had the leisure time and the money to spend on travel, hotels and the necessary equipment. It was the Alps – 'the Playground of Europe' – that became their Mecca, with British climbers attempting to 'conquer' the highest and most difficult peaks. In time some British climbers turned their attention to the more challenging of the Scottish hills. Railway and steamer services, much more extensive than today's, brought easier access and thus encouraged the founding of climbing clubs. In 1887 a group of Aberdeen climbers gathered at the Shelter Stone in the heart of the Cairngorms for a celebration, and there and then founded the Cairngorm Club. The Scottish Mountaineering Club (SMC), an elite organisation for experienced climbers, followed two years later. A landmark event in mountaineering circles was the publication in the 1891 edition of the 'SMC Journal of Munro's Tables', a list of the Scottish mountains over 3,000 feet (914.4 metres). This list of 'distinct mountains' was compiled by Sir Hugh Munro, one of the founding members of the SMC. Consequently, these 3,000-foot hills soon came to be labelled 'Munros' and many hill walkers and climbers ever since have had the ambition to climb them all (or as many as possible). With more accurate mapping and methods of measurement, the number of Munros has varied over the years, 282 being the present tally.

Hill walkers and other pedestrians, however, were finding that with more and more areas in the Highlands being converted to deer forests and grouse moors, access to the hills was becoming more and more difficult. The custom for gentlemen pedestrians was to write in advance to landowners requesting permission to walk on their land. Grierson, who wrote favourably about deer forests, was ingratiatingly grateful to the Duke of Leeds for granting him a pass to climb Ben Macdui and its neighbours. Townshend, arriving at Blair Atholl in August 1846, was anxious to see Glen Tilt. His *Scottish Tourist* guidebook had raved about its wild Alpine scenery and for it being 'famous in ancient times for its race of warriors'. Accordingly, he sent a note to the owner seeking permission to visit Glen Tilt, but the request was refused since deer stalking was in progress. Townsend and his friend were, however, able to visit Glen Fender. Even then, when they sought to see a waterfall mentioned in the guidebook, they found the access gate locked, so they had to find someone who had the key. The ancient race of warriors may have gone from Glen Tilt, but the warrior spirit was still there, when just a year later the Duke of Atholl and his minions sought to keep a party of students from gaining access to Glen Tilt. Professor John Balfour and his Edinburgh University students had approached the glen following the ancient drove road from Braemar. This was the same route that Pennant had followed in his 1769 tour, though he went in the opposite direction. In 1847, however, the Duke tried to turn back the professor and his botany students who, after a great deal of argy-bargy, bypassed the Atholl men by climbing over a dyke and storming down the glen. This 'war with the Duke' was continued in the courts, but the Duke lost this battle too. The Scottish Rights of Way Society, founded just two years earlier in 1845, had succeeded in its assertion that the route through Glen Tilt was a traditional right of way.

Asserting access to hills and glens was an unrelenting battle, however. In 1887 the Society had another major dispute on its hands, which went right to the House of Lords. This battle involved access to a trail, Jock's Road, which formed part of an old drove road from Glen Doll in Angus to Deeside. Previous landowners had posed no problem, but a new recalcitrant landowner, Duncan Macpherson, took a harder line. The Scottish Rights of Way Society won this case, but the huge legal costs left it bankrupt. The members did have the consolation of knowing that their opponent was likewise bankrupt. The Society too was successful with another traditional route that had been blocked for many years. This was the Lairig Ghru (the Savage Pass), which connects Aviemore to Braemar. An article in the Cairngorm Club Journal in July 1898 tells that, even when the right of passage was conceded, it was restricted to the narrowest possible line. With no deviation permitted, the constant pressure of feet in exactly the same places rendered the Lairig Ghru path extremely difficult and tiresome. The landowner's pettiness even extended to stationing so-called 'deer watchers' in huts to ensure that walkers did not stray from the path. One of these simple bothies at Corrour in the Lairig Ghru is now maintained by volunteers of the Mountain Bothies Association as a shelter for walkers and climbers.

With many landowners only too ready to ban hill walkers even outwith the stalking season, the Scottish Rights of Way Society (now ScotWays) continued and still has to fight to keep traditional paths open to all. Objections to the presence of walkers and mountaineers came not just from landowners but also from those wealthy individuals who were renting or leasing deer forests. W. L. Winans, an enormously wealthy American, was one notorious example of that breed. Winans, after leasing a number of estates in the northern Highlands, employed a small army of gamekeepers to keep interlopers out. Sir Hugh Munro, himself a landowner, sometimes tried to avoid disturbance by climbing at night. In 1889, on a visit to Glen Affric, although he had been granted a passport by the head stalker, he was accosted every few miles by one of Mr Winans' sentries who asked, quite civilly, where he had come from and where he was going. Sir Hugh Munro knew that, since he was on a public right of way, he had no need to answer, but that kind of experience would have deterred, and was meant to deter, less experienced pedestrians. Even more extraordinary, one of these sentries, carrying out instructions, followed Sir Hugh up Sgurr na Lapaich (3,401 feet), then on to Mam Sodhail (3,862 feet), and then back down to the glen. Sir Hugh carried on westward via the Falls of Glomach to Shiel Inn, where he had to waken the landlord. 'When I found,' he confessed, 'they were out of beer, I sat down and cried – or nearly so.' Winans brought ridicule on himself by taking out an action against a crofter for failing to prevent a pet lamb from straying on to his land. This nonsensical trespass case went to the Court of Session, which wisely rejected Winans' action of interdict.

On the plus side, steamship services and the railways had made access to the hills easier. For Ben Lawers, guidebooks told how the foot was reached from Killin by Loch Tay steamer, and that 'an active man should find it easily possible to manage the climb between the arrival of the morning boat and the departure of the last one'. With Fort William enjoying regular steamship sailing, many tourists came whose main purpose was to climb Ben Nevis – all the more so since its status as Britain's highest mountain had been confirmed. In 1883 the way to the top of Ben Nevis was considerably eased when a bridle path was constructed. This was not built for the benefit of tourists but to service a meteorological observatory. Its purpose was to collect weather observations at the summit, day and night, all the year round, no matter the conditions. Initially, the observation details were despatched to Fort William by pigeon, then by telegraph and latterly by telephone, and from there to London. The observatory staff over the years encountered some unusual visitors, not a few in difficulties and seeking help. Any tourists climbing the Ben came by the bridle path and then only in the tourist season. However, the observers got a shock one winter day when one of them chanced to look over the cliffs and was amazed to see two tiny figures, about 1,500 feet down, climbing up the snow- and ice-covered precipice. Roped together, they cut steps in the snow, and were slowly making their way up to the top. Winter mountaineering had arrived at the Ben. These two were the first of the many 'Alpinists', Scots and Sassenachs, who were to pioneer new ways of climbing these most formidable cliffs.

Since the path had been built by the Scottish Meteorological Society, the society, to help pay for its upkeep, levied a toll of one shilling per head on those using the path to climb the mountain. As happens nowadays, many tourists found that the upper section of the climb can be far more challenging than they expected. This was the case with an Edwardian visitor, the Revd A. N. Cooper, a doughty walker on the flat, but, climbing in May, was taken aback by the amount of snow at the upper level. Fortunately, on the way up the self-named 'Walking Parson' had encountered the superintendent of the road at his daily work, keeping the road in good order so that supplies could be brought up to the observatory. The clergyman was warned that on reaching the first snow-pole he should follow the footsteps but not to attempt to keep to the path. The depth of snow posed problems for him, but the Revd Cooper pressed on until he reached the top. The three men manning the observatory welcomed him in, even offering him a meal. This was not their usual practice, but perhaps they were impressed that he had walked all the way from Yorkshire. As the observatory was linked to Fort William by telegraph wire, the parson sent messages by it to friends and family.

When constructed, the path to the top was 6 foot broad, but, after the closure of the observatory in 1904, it deteriorated badly. It was still good enough in 1911 for a Ford Model T car to be taken to the top and back again as a publicity stunt. Various boulders and other obstacles, it must be said, had to be blasted away first. The presence of the path in conjunction with the opening in 1894 of the railway to Fort William brought even more visitors. William Brown writing in the *Cairngorm Club Journal* in 1896 regretted that Ben Nevis, with the observatory and the easier path to the summit, had become a 'show mountain': 'Worse still, he [man] has planted a hotel; and round the hotel has grown up a crop of broken bottles and sardine tins, the memorials of the 6,000 odd tourists that visit it every year.' The Temperance Hotel, as it was usually known, had been built by a local hotelier in 1885 and was run by two sisters.

The first climbers were men, but with women asserting themselves in political action – like the suffragettes – and in other ways, they too began to enter this male-dominated sphere. The formation of the Ladies' Scottish Climbing Club in 1908 was a landmark in this respect. As with the male clubs, it was a middle-class preserve. Even so, the women had many prejudices and difficulties to overcome. Writing in the late 1920s, Mrs Inglis Clark, the club's first president, recalled the club's early days:

There were no sports clothes for women in those days. It was almost impossible to get suitable strong boots, and for a long time I had to wear boys' boots or buy them in Tyrol! The whole tyranny of clothes has disappeared since then. Clothing for women is now practical and hygienic … Let us hope that gone for ever are the skirts that trailed in dust or mud, the hats that did not fit but had to be held on firmly – sometimes with both hands.

The packs carried by American pedestrians, Joseph and Elizabeth Robins Pennell, look to be far from ideal – likewise the lady's garments.

This book by the pedestrian parson, the Revd A. N. Cooper, describes his walking holidays in Britain and the Continent. The best preparation for a walking holiday, he wrote, was to harden the feet, and the only way to achieve that was by walking. If wet feet was a problem, his solution was 'two pennyworth of whisky' – not to be drunk but poured into the shoes!

When Victorian climber Sir Hugh Munro climbed Sgurr na Lapaich (3,401 feet) in Glen Affric, he was followed by one of the landowner's gillies right to the summit and then on to the other mountains in the view – Mam Sodhail (3,862 feet) and Carn Eige (3,880 feet). The first two peaks were key observation points for the Ordnance Survey's triangulation of Scotland in the 1840s.

An 1896 view of the Ben Nevis observatory and hotel built in 1883 and 1885 respectively. A volunteer helper described this 'so-called hotel' as 'a wooden erection open during the summer months only – for it is quite buried in snow in winter – with four small bedrooms, to enable tourists 'if they choose to stay all night to see the sun rise'.

The Ladies' Scottish Mountaineering Club was formed in 1908. This 1929 image shows the advance made in ladies' climbing clothing.

The Shelter Stone in the heart of the Cairngorms has long been a place of shelter and refuge for climbers. The Cairngorm Club was founded here in 1887.

By the 1930s female climbers could avail themselves of more practical clothing, as shown here in the hills looking down on Loch Long.

The remote Loch Avon in the Cairngorms is well-nigh surrounded by some of the highest mountains in Britain.

Chapter Twelve

Alternative Travellers by Land and Sea

Afoot and light-hearted I take to the open road,
Healthy, free, the world before me,
The long brown path before me leading wherever I choose.

(Walt Whitman)

There were many tourists who, like Walt Whitman, took to the open road, scorning the conventional ways of touring. From the 1880s onward increasing numbers of cyclists were to be seen on the Highland roads. They rode a type of bicycle called the 'Ordinary', better known as the Penny Farthing. Cycling as a sport for racing and for record-breaking became increasingly popular. Cyclists were numerous enough to form associations to protect their interests. The Cyclists' Touring Club (CTC) and the National Cyclists' Union (NCU), both with large memberships, had clout when negotiating terms for members. A metal sign with the initials CTC or NCU allowed cyclists arriving in a strange place to identify establishments that gave concessions on the production of a membership card. Touring cyclists brought custom to country inns that had suffered since the railways drove the stagecoaches off the main highways. Even large hotels like Macdonald's Atholl Hotel in Pitlochry welcomed the custom of cyclists and in Perth the Salutation Hotel, in an 1892 advert claimed to be the local 'Headquarters of the Cyclists' Touring Club by appointment'.

With its very high front wheel, the Ordinary demanded a fair degree of athleticism just to mount it. There was, however, an alternative that was favoured by those of a shorter stature or the less athletic – namely the tricycle. This was the type of steed selected by one of the most adventurous of the Victorian tricyclists – Commander Charles Edward Reade. In 1882, under the pen name 'Nauticus', he wrote the book *Nauticus in Scotland* about his travels. Starting in Newcastle and riding a Coventry-made 'Cheylesmore' tricycle, he covered an incredible area of Scotland, including Skye and the far north in sixty-nine days – a total of 2,446 miles. This total, he admitted, was calculated from distances given to him by local people, so he could not vouch for its complete accuracy. He had a companion for a short period, but most of the time he was on his own.

During his sixty-nine-day tour Reade stayed at many different hotels and inns. Generally, being careful of his bawbees, he gave the more palatial hotels the go-by, the small country inns being his usual choice. Although he received a frosty reception at the Inveruglas Inn at Loch Lomond, the landlady being suspicious of cyclists, and at Tyndrum a poor and expensive lunch, 'the remains of a scraggy rib', most were like the Arrochar Inn in providing good, comfortable, reasonably priced quarters. His conclusions reflected the changes that had occurred in the standard of accommodation available to tourists since the time of the pioneer travellers like Pennant and Johnson. Highland innkeepers and hoteliers had to be adaptable, especially when they had people like Sir Hugh Munro and Commander Reade turning up at ungodly hours and expecting to be accommodated. Reade, cycling into Dornoch in the dark, 'astonished the good people at the old-fashioned inn by arriving at 10.30 pm.' That, however, was early compared to his arrival at Achnasheen Hotel at 1 a.m. and having to knock up the landlord.

Reade found the Highland roads to be generally excellent. He did have some problems with his tricycle, however. At Killin, where incidentally he first heard the Gaelic language, one of the trike's solid tyres kept slipping off, so he improvised by tying it on with leather bootlaces. That evening he glued it back on, but the glue needed seventeen hours to dry. Having further problems, he ordered a new lighter model, 'Cheylesmore', to be despatched north. Meantime a blacksmith at Blair Atholl repaired his old trike to let him continue his tour. On arriving at Strome Ferry, his new Cheylesmore was waiting for him at the railway station, so he arranged for the old one to be sent back by rail to the maker's at Coventry. Unfortunately, Reade crashed soon after receiving the new tricycle, leaving one wheel badly twisted and out of shape. Back he went to Strome station and managed to retrieve his old machine. Though it was of a different pattern, he took a wheel off the old tricycle. At Strome Ferry he luckily found a blacksmith to attach the old wheel to the new machine, and, though the wheels were not an exact match, he was able to continue his tour. He then sent a telegram to the Coventry Machinists' Company for another wheel to be sent to Achnasheen station, four stops along the line, as quickly as possible. All credit to the Victorian tricycle manufacturer and to the railway service, as he was able to collect the replacement wheel at Achnasheen as planned, just three days later.

In the 1880s the introduction of the so-called 'safety bicycle' brought a huge increase in the number of cyclists. There was a further boost to the sport when, in 1888, the Scottish vet J. B. Dunlop patented the pneumatic tyre. With two equal-sized wheels, the rear one chain driven, the safety cycle was far more user-friendly than the Penny Farthing. The new type of bicycle was liberating for women – middle-class women at any rate – as it gave them greater mobility and freedom. A popular novelist of the day, H. G. Wells, summed up this social revolution. The sight of a woman on a bicycle, he said, was 'the picture of free, untrammelled womanhood'. The CTC even gave advice on ladies' dress. Avoid a tight-fitting bodice, it recommended, which 'however well it may look, must of necessity be hot and uncomfortable'. Female cyclists began, therefore, to adopt more 'rational' dress and that was part of another minor revolution.

In the late nineteenth century advice on cycling began to appear in the general tourist guides. The 'Cycling in Scotland' section of *Black's Shilling Guide to Scotland* (thirteenth edition, 1906) occupies no fewer than eleven pages out of 167. As a pocket-sized book, this guidebook would have been very popular with cyclists and pedestrians. It is advice, though, was penned with the comparatively well-heeled in mind. It is assumed that the cyclist would be making use of the railways and steamers and would also be accommodated in hotels. Significantly, in the tenth edition published just eight years earlier, there is very little on cycling.

Guidebooks and maps were essential companions for cyclists and pedestrians, especially those going off the beaten track. Reade had with him *Paterson's Tourist Hand-Guide to Scotland*. Its excellent pull-out maps would have been useful for general purposes, but he also had the Sutherland sheet of Black's four inch to one mile map. Just as mountaineers came to regard the one inch Ordnance Survey maps as indispensable aids, cyclists likewise gained from the production of maps designed for their use. The most famous of these were the colourful half inch to one mile maps of Edinburgh mapmaker John Bartholomew & Co. Bartholomew's maps were based on the Ordnance Survey but covered a wider area than the one inch series and, above all, were designed with tourists and cyclists in mind. Roadside hotels and inns were identified as were steamer routes. You could also find which railway stations had refreshment rooms. Roads were categorised, ranging from the first class to the indifferent. Making their maps cyclist-friendly gained Bartholomew the support and co-operation of the influential Cyclists' Touring Club. Early Bartholomew maps bore the winged wheel emblem of the CTC and the annotation 'Roads revised by the Cyclists' Touring Club'. Club members assisted the map-maker by sending in corrections and suggestions for other improvements. In return CTC members were able to purchase copies at a discount. The maps of another Edinburgh publisher, Gall & Inglis, also graded the roads, and their maps' simplicity and clarity provided strong competition to Bartholomew & Co. They also published *The 'Contour' Road Book of Scotland*, a very useful work for cyclists and early days motorists.

Whereas Reade on his Scottish tour stayed in inns, others preferred to camp. It was cheaper, more free-and-easy and allowed more flexibility in choice of destination. The new safety bicycle proved to be a better load-carrier than the Ordinary, as a specially designed luggage pack could be fitted within the frame, and other bits and pieces could be attached in a variety of ways. T. H. Holding, a pioneer camper, designed and made a lightweight tent. His book *Cycle and Camp* (1898), as well as describing his camping experiences in Ireland, provided plans and diagrams so that anyone could make their own. Other open-air enthusiasts were exploring the Highlands around the same time. E. E. Henderson and J. Walker wrote *Cycle, Camp and Camera in the Highlands* based on their travels. Like Holding they used lightweight tents of their own design, learning what to do and what not to do. They learned that leaving a tent door half-open at night meant that midges could enter. Having a home-made veil to protect the head and face from midges was, they discovered, an invaluable safeguard. Walker took a lot of photographs on his tours, using a plate camera and tripod. The tripod came in handy to support the tent, so that it could be used as a dark room. Initially, his primitive tent had been supported by string tied to two trees, but that system failed in a treeless landscape. His remedy was to use 'sticks' as tent poles.

T. H. Holding dedicated his book *Cycle and Camp* to the memory of John MacGregor, a Scot based in London, who had pioneered canoeing as a pastime. Beginning in 1866, MacGregor wrote a number of books describing his travels in different parts of Europe and the Middle East, using his own design of canoe, which he called the 'Rob Roy'. MacGregor popularised canoeing as an adventurous means of travel, with the result that canoe clubs were formed all over Britain. As a student in Edinburgh, the young Robert Louis Stevenson was an enthusiastic 'paddler' on the Firth of Forth. His first published book, *An Inland Voyage*, describes a canoe trip made in 1876 on continental inland waterways. About that time some of these pioneer canoeists took their 'Rob Roy' canoes by steamer to Stornoway. From there they explored the Outer Hebrides coast before making a hazardous return, paddling via Skye to Tobermory.

As well as pioneering cycle camping, T. H. Holding was also an enthusiast for canoeing combined with camping, and he preached the merits of the outdoor life in a short book entitled *Watery Wanderings 'mid Western Lochs*. The book is an account of a canoeing trip with four companions, in August 1885, up the west coast of Scotland from the Clyde to Oban via the Crinan Canal. Each evening they had to land and seek out a suitable place for a camp. Faced with the problem of drying garments soaked through by rain or spray, their procedure, once settled in an overnight camping spot, was to ask the occupants of a nearby cottage if they would be so good as to light a fire to dry their clothes. When they landed on the shore of a Loch Fyne estate, their requests were amicably received:

> The good women at the lodge very readily granted us permission to camp, undertook to cook chops, while we should fix the tent, to wash somebody's white unmentionables, to dry our towels, and generally to play the matron in the most agreeable fashion.

As with the pioneer pedestrians and cyclists, the cycle-campers were gentlemen travellers and that usually eased their way to a considerable extent. Gents expected, and usually received, the kind of deference that was not available to more humble tourists.

In the nineteenth century, and for a long time after, it was only the well-to-do who had the leisure time and the money to enable them to enjoy the simple life. Tourists of this class – and this goes back to the time of Johnson and Boswell – felt they had the right to enter Highlanders 'huts' without so much as a by-your-leave. Walking along the side of the Crinan Canal (their canoes went by barge), the canoeists espied a number of 'wretched huts' and determined to enter one. They got their comeuppance, though, when the crofter sold them eggs and charged them, they bemoaned, the same price as in an Oxford Street shop. It would not have occurred to these cocky tourists to ask why these crofters were poverty-stricken and why they had to live in 'wretched' hovels. Social class, however, did not keep the better-off tourists from suffering from the scourge of the Highlands – namely the dreaded midge. In wet weather they filled the tent: 'They bit our hands, neck and face so that scarcely a square inch of our complexion remained unshorn of its beauty.'

Enthusiasm for canoeing was not sustained. The 'Rob Roy' type of canoe was fairly expensive and heavy to carry. As the vogue for canoeing began to fall away, small boat sailing gained increasing favour. Holding had already observed a decline in the vogue for canoes and this was confirmed by his experiences on the West Coast: 'Not a canoe had been on the waters we selected for our cruise this year.' On the other hand, when he arrived at Oban in August 1885, he found the bay crowded with 'over thirty yachts at anchor of various sizes, from the modest two tonner to the 800-ton schooner'. Water sports were still in favour, but the well-to-do young men of the day were turning towards small yachts and sailing boats. The sport of canoeing was eventually revived, but that had to wait until the general introduction of lighter and more portable vessels.

The west coast of Scotland, with numerous islands to explore and spectacular scenery, was ideal for cruising and Oban was an ideal base for yachts. Oban, 'the Charing Cross of the Highlands', enjoyed good steamer access to the south and to the neighbouring islands. It had good hotels, shops and other services. With its sheltered bay, it provided good sheltered anchorages. The founding of the Royal Highland Yacht Club at Oban in 1881 indicated that it was a sport that had local support.

When Holding and his canoeing friends arrived at Oban they saw it at the height of the 'season'. Its streets, Holding wrote, were crowded with 'Saxons' promenading the streets, travelling from the shore to the yachts and filling the hotels and shops:

> In fact the accent in speech of Regent Street, and the affectation of style of dress of Belgravia were too, too apparent. The boating costumes of the Thames were all exhibited here ... to remind us of that other and higher civilisation which we had sought, for a time, to free us.

It is doubtful whether the Highland people he encountered would have appreciated this comparison with his 'higher civilisation'. Some Highlanders, accustomed to sailing small boats and fishing craft, did find short-term employment on the big yachts. In the 1901 census for Tarskavaig in the parish of Sleat in Skye, eleven men are listed as part-time crew on yachts. The big racing yachts had such a huge spread of canvas that they required a crew of at least twenty. Crews too were needed for the steam yachts, which were another form of rich man's toy and another manifestation of a 'higher civilisation'.

Murray's Handbook Scotland (1875) contained seven pages of Hints for Yachtsmen in the Hebrides and West Coast of Scotland. The sailing directions and hints included, not surprisingly, those two tourist hotspots, Iona and Loch Scavaig in Skye; the latter giving access to Loch Coruisk, made famous by Scott's poem *Lord of the Isles*. While the owners of big yachts could employ skippers and pilots with local knowledge, the small boat owners relied on Admiralty Charts, supplemented from 1909 by *Sailing Directions and Anchorages* published by the Clyde Cruising Club.

Not all yachts were for leisure purposes. In July 1845 a holidaymaker, Hugh Miller, boarded a small yacht, the *Betsey*, in Tobermory Bay. Looking round the cabin, he took note of the contents. These included a well-thumbed chart of the Western Isles and the latest edition of *The Coaster's Sailing Directions*, as well as some religious works. Hugh Miller, former stonemason turned geologist and writer, was one of the best-known figures in Scotland. Miller may have been on vacation, but for the skipper, the Revd Mr Swanson, this was both office and pulpit. In 1843 the Church of Scotland had split, with a large number of the clergy and congregations breaking away to form the Free Church of Scotland. The Revd Swanson of Eigg was one of the breakaway ministers. He, however, lost his manse and the owner of the island refused a site to build a new one. Determined to keep on preaching to his flock on Eigg and neighbouring islands, the Revd Swanson procured this 30-foot-long vessel, the *Betsey*, otherwise known as the Free Church Yacht. Using this tiny craft he visited the islands to preach and minister to those islanders who had followed him out of the established Church of Scotland. Miller used his time on the cruise to write a series of articles for the Free Church newspaper, *The Witness*, on the perilous nature of the Revd Swanson's work and also to describe his own geological rambles on the isles. These articles formed the basis for a posthumously published book, *The Cruise of the Betsey*.

The *Betsey* provided Hugh Miller with accommodation and mobility for his holiday, thus enabling him to visit Eigg and the other Hebridean Small Isles. However, it took another Scotsman to find what he conceived to be the solution to providing both mobility and a reasonable amount of living space while on holiday on dry land. This was W. Gordon Stables, CM MD RN, who was born in Aberchirder, Banffshire, but was then living in Berkshire. His solution was a horse-drawn caravan, but not one with the limited space of the gypsy caravan. Showmen and road-workers used caravans too, but his was the first built purely for leisure and as such Stables has been hailed as the originator of caravanning as a leisure pursuit. His caravan was specially built of mahogany and it was designed to his own demanding specification. As an ex-naval doctor with a lot of maritime experience, he called his van a Land Yacht. When he wrote a book about his travels in it through England and Scotland, the title he chose was *The Cruise of the Land Yacht 'Wanderer'*. This book, first published in 1886, was subtitled *Thirteen Hundred Miles in my Caravan*. So successful was it that other open-air enthusiasts followed suit, having their own caravans built.

A fresh-air enthusiast he may have been, but for Stables, heading for the open road did not mean dispensing with all comforts. His Land Yacht was a heavy vehicle, weighing just under 2 tons when loaded and needing a pair of horses to haul it. This 'gentleman gypsy' had two staff with him – his 'crew' as he termed them. There was a coachman who, when they stopped for the night, took himself off with the horses to an inn where he was accommodated and the horses stabled. If there was no inn nearby, he bunked down on the driver's seat, which had a canopy. The other 'crewman' was a young man who was Stables' valet, but also served as cook and odd job man. The valet slept in the van's pantry while Stables was accommodated in what he called the saloon. The valet's tasks included acting as a scout. He rode ahead on a tricycle to give warning of oncoming vehicles that might not be able to pass Stables' cumbrous vehicle. When passing through towns the valet rode close behind to keep wee boys from hanging on for a free ride and to prevent tramps from opening the drawers at the back. Also on board were a Newfoundland dog and a cockatoo.

Included in Stables' gear were a revolver and his naval cutlass! One night when some gypsies were on the prowl he had his sword ready and the revolver loaded. Hearing noises at the back of the van he sneaked out of the front with his sword, then crawled under the van. Seeing what looked like two pairs of legs, he slashed at them with the back of his sword. The result was that two very alarmed cows galloped off into the night. Like Nauticus, he tried to avoid the haunts of more conventional tourists, as at Pitlochry, which he thought, while picturesque and lovely, almost too civilised for his gypsy ideas of comfort: 'The people had too much of the summer-lodging caste about them; there were loudly dressed females and male mashers, so I felt inclined to fly through as I had done through Perth.' He did change his mind, however, and enjoyed his overnight stay and even recommended it to others for a prolonged stay.

Sadly, the good doctor could show a sadistic temperament. In his hints to would-be caravanners he wrote: 'I had the utmost satisfaction once this year in punishing some country louts. Butler, my valet, was innocently riding on about a hundred yards ahead and no sooner had he passed than three blackguards commenced stone-throwing.' But they had no idea that he was connected to the following vehicle. Stables slipped off the van, whip in hand, 'And for several seconds I enjoyed the most health-giving exercise. Straight across the face and round the ears I hit as hard as I knew how to. One escaped Scot-free, but two tumbled in the ditch and howled aloud for mercy.' This he generously granted after he got tired: 'The beauty of the attack was in its suddenness, and these roughs will remember it to their dying day.'

Stables' account of the Highland part of his journey ends with his arrival at Inverness. This was only after surmounting fearful climbs over the Grampians. With the horses struggling, Stables and his valet had to push at the steepest sections. He had to admit that, even with such powerful horses as his, crossing the Grampians 'was, to say the least, a risky experiment'. Twenty-one years after the publication of Stables' book, the Caravan Club of Great Britain and Ireland was formed with Dr W. Gordon Stables as Vice-President. The Land Yacht *Wanderer* still survives and can be seen at the City Museum, Bristol.

Commander C. E. Reade (Nauticus) fording a river.

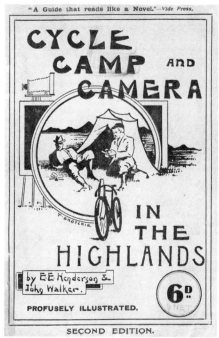

The booklet *Cycle, Camp and Camera in the Highlands* provided valuable information for the cycle tourist.

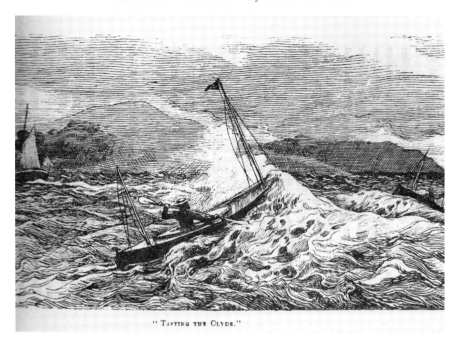

" Tasting the Clyde."

T. H. Holding in a 'Rob Roy' type canoe, battling the waves in the Firth of Clyde.

More conventional tourists on the Oban seafront. (Courtesy of Alan Brotchie)

Gall & Inglis emphasised safety in this Graded Road Map of Scotland. Road users would presumably wish to avoid the bad roads and dangerous hills.

The Pentland Hotel, Thurso, is one of many hotels that still have the Cyclists Touring Club's Flying Wheel on their exterior walls. This showed that cyclists would receive favourable terms in their establishments.

This sketch gives a grossly exaggerated image of the kind of terrain covered by the Land Yacht *Wanderer*.

Chapter Thirteen

The Quest for Health

'People come into this neighbourhood [Dunkeld] to drink goats whey, & ride on horseback for their health, here are very good accommodations at a house, prettily situated on the other side [of the] river, for such temporary inhabitants; & such summer lodgings are advertised in various parts of the highlands.' (Quoted from the 1788 Tour Journal of Elizabeth Diggle in Alastair J. Durie *Travels in Scotland 1781–1881*)

The people drawn from work and business to drink goats' milk at Dunkeld and other Highland places came, in the great majority of cases, from the cream of society. For instance, once the London season was over and Parliament was in recess, landed magnates like Lord Fife headed for the countryside. Writing from London in 1794 he confessed, 'A two weeks goat whey at Mar Lodge will do me much good.' Medical practitioners had been accustomed to recommend patients of 'weak constitution' to take themselves off to the country, the more mountainous the better, to avail themselves of whey derived from fresh goats' milk and drunk 'in its natural warmth'. Country dwellers at Dunkeld and other places on the edge of the Highlands profited by letting 'summer lodgings' to valetudinarians who sought benefit by drinking goats' milk whey. As this advice from Dr William Cullen makes clear, exercise and fresh air were also restorative: 'Nothing secures the good effect of Goat whey more than being in the Open Air & taking a great deal of gentle Exercise on horseback or in a Carriage.'

Though it still had its adherents, by the end of the eighteenth century the vogue for goats' whey was on the wane. Robert Heron, visiting Dunkeld in 1792, noted the change in medical and social fashion:

Goats' milk is now less valued, as a specific, than it formerly was. Watering places have at the same time become more fashionable: and at these, accommodations have been provided, which are not to be expected at the sequestered abodes of goat-herds.

Mineral waters were now the favoured cure-all. The principal types of mineral or spa waters were chalybeate (iron), sulphur, and saline (salt). The latter two, among other supposed benefits, were purgative. The fashion for saline mineral wells had far-reaching consequences. It provided the impetus that led to the rise of the seaside resort.

In the Highlands there were chalybeate springs at Pannanich in Deeside. Thomas Pennant on his 1769 visit to Scotland noted that, during the summer months, great numbers of people afflicted with a variety of ailments were going to Pannanich mineral springs to drink the waters. Though discovered only a few years earlier, several commodious houses to accommodate visitors had already been built. As with many such springs with a local reputation, it needed someone with finance and influence to exploit its potential. In this case it was the local laird, Francis Farquarson of Monaltrie. Francis Farquarson had led a chequered life. He had been a Jacobite rebel in 1745, fought at Culloden and was captured there. Sentenced to death, he was fortunate to be reprieved. After enduring a far from arduous exile in England, which included marrying a rich English lady, he was permitted to return to Deeside in 1776. Some years later he was able, thanks to his wife's funds, to repurchase his forfeited lands. It was on his return to his ancestral home that he involved himself in developing the Pannanich springs, providing baths and accommodation for visitors – the kind of accommodations that Robert Heron mentioned.

With increasing numbers of visitors, spas or watering places like Pannanich became in effect the first holiday resorts. If they retained their initial popularity, entrepreneurs provided hotels, pump rooms, bathing establishments and assembly rooms where 'polite society' forgathered. The social elite included young George Gordon Byron, the future Lord Byron, who around 1795–6 was brought to Pannanich Wells by his mother. Young George had been ill with scarlet fever, so his mother, Catherine, took him to Deeside to the farm of Ballaterach for the goats' milk cure. With the wells less than a mile away, it is likely that he and his mother sampled the Pannanich mineral water as well.

Pannanich Spa in itself did not expand to any extent, the main benefit going to the new town of Ballater erected on moorland about 2 miles away on the other side of the River Dee. The growth of the village was aided by the construction of a bridge over the Dee where previously there had been a ford and ferry. The destructive powers of the river meant the original bridge of 1783 had to be replaced no fewer than three times. In 1830, according to the *Edinburgh Philosophical Journal*, Ballater was always crowded during the summer months with invalids and other visitors. They were drawn not just by the fame of the Pannanich wells but also by 'the magnificence and beauty of the surrounding scenery'. As a planned village Ballater was, according to Robert Chambers, a striking contrast in its neatness and regularity to the usual Highland village. Ballater, Chambers noted, was well served by coaches from Aberdeen and now (1837), 'A communication has been opened through Glenshee to Edinburgh.'

Thanks to guidebooks many visitors would have been aware that the legendary romantic hero Lord Byron had spent part of his youth on Deeside, climbing the local hills – notably Morven and Lochnagar – and extolling their beauties. Majestic Lochnagar (3,789 feet), popularly known as 'the Queen of the Deeside Mountains', exemplified for him the beauties of the land of his youth. These he praised in his verses 'Dark Lochnagar':

Yet, Caledonia, beloved are thy mountains,
Round their white summits though elements war,
Though cataracts foam 'stead of smooth-flowing fountains,
I sigh for the valley of Dark Loch na Gar.

Though he had left his Aberdeen home in 1798 aged ten, Byron never forgot his Scottish roots – 'born half a Scot and bred a whole one'. Ballaterach Farm, where the young George lodged, became a place of tourist pilgrimage. The Revd Thomas Grierson was informed by the farmer of Ballaterach that the house once occupied by Byron was now his barn and that he still had the bed occupied by the poet. This bed, a box bed, was later accidentally destroyed. The Pannanich springs, too, remained popular for many years, as a mid-Victorian guidebook tells us:

Here, at all times, but more especially in summer, is a most immense concourse of people from all parts of the country, afflicted with all manner of diseases ... all flock here to drink the waters in whose efficacy they have great faith.

The author added that some people thought that the Pannanich waters would be a much better cure if they were taken with less whisky than commonly was the case.

Queen Victoria's arrival at Balmoral just 8 miles away was another step in the transformation of Ballater into a tourist Mecca. Soon the hill slopes above the original planned village were dotted with new granite villas and cottages. Landmark dates were the inauguration of the Ballater Games in 1864 and in 1866 when the Deeside Railway reached the town. An 1861 guide described Ballater as, 'A kind of pet place for the people of Aberdeen and so does credit to their good taste. The houses are well built, the streets regularly laid out, there are good shops and an excellent inn.' Between 1841 and 1891 the population of Ballater grew from 271 to 983. It also gained burgh status in 1891, by which time Pannanich Spa had dwindled in importance.

Another Highland spa that developed into a fashionable resort during the nineteenth century was Strathpeffer where the landowner exploited a sulphur spring (alternative name 'stinking well'), which the locals were already familiar with and utilised. Its reputation was boosted by the Revd Colin Mackenzie, parish minister and factor for the Cromartie estate, who told of two remarkable cures. Two local men, he wrote in 1777, who were both so lame and feeble that they had to be transported to the well on feather beds on carts, drank the water for some weeks, and had recovered to such an extent that they were able to walk on their own legs for miles. For wider acceptance, medical endorsement was essential. Various medical men duly praised the water's virtues. In 1819 a Pump Room was opened, with poor people allowed to drink free of charge. The crowds of poor people making their way to Strathpeffer was indicative of its popularity. Some came in hope of a cure, others to beg from the more well-to-do visitors. Writing in 1840, Catherine Sinclair observed: 'It is most melancholy and depressing to observe the crowds of poor, decrepid [*sic*], miserable objects who assemble at Strathpeffer.' By then a hostel had been built to house the ailing poor.

Guidebooks gave advice on how to take the waters and which of the four wells to use. Manson's *Guide to Strathpeffer Spa* (1884 edition) emphasised the necessity for patients, prior to drinking the waters, to take proper scientific advice; otherwise there could be 'serious consequences'. The doctor would decide what type of water – sulphur or chalybeate – was appropriate for each patient to drink. Likewise, he – always 'he' of course – would select the kind of bath – sulphur or peat – that would assist the patient to recover. Iron was recommended for a wide variety of conditions and ailments, ranging in alphabetical order from anaemia to uterine troubles. They included the perennial 'nervous disorders caused by overwork or worry'. While the four sulphur wells, which were of varying strength, were in or near the Square, the water for the iron or chalybeate well was piped from a spring at the foot of Ben Wyvis 3 miles away. All these treatments necessitated a fairly rigid regime. At the Spa Hotel slacking was seemingly not encouraged, as early each morning the hotel piper marched round and round waking all the guests. At 7 a.m., as one patient recalled, the omnibus was ready 'to carry all comers down to drink the awful water, and to undergo various baths'.

Patients with infections, the guidebook stressed, were instructed to stay away, as it would be 'an act of a diabolical nature ... to visit a crowded spa'. Too many patients dying was always a problem for a health resort, as its reputation could easily be ruined. According to the guidebook, Strathpeffer as a sulphur spa was the equal to any Continental resort. That there were no language problems was a bonus, since the English-speaking visitor had 'the advantage of hearing and using his own language'. However, for anyone looking for a taste of the foreign element then there was enough Gaelic spoken among the hills and glens around 'to interest, amuse, and afford him beneficial excitement'.

The arrival of the railway in 1885 stimulated further growth and development including more hotels being built, the clientele coming from the ever-expanding ranks of the Victorian bourgeoisie, many from south of the border. As with other railway companies, the Highland Railway Company (HR) had a strong interest in promoting tourist traffic on its lines. A fast train from Aviemore, 'The Strathpeffer Spa Express', was introduced in 1911. At Aviemore this express connected with trains from London. The Highland Railway could thus boast of its 'Through Lavatory Carriages and Sleeping Cars right from Euston Station in London to Strathpeffer'. Lavatories on HR trains, incidentally, were a fairly recent innovation. This service lasted only until 1915, with wartime exigencies bringing it to an end. But hopes of more visitors induced the HR to invest in its own hotel in 1911 named, not surprisingly, the Highland Hotel.

For the 'After-Cure', there was a wide range of diversions including orchestral music in the Spa Gardens and romantic walks and drives, and there was always the possibility of a real-life romantic encounter. The notorious 'wickedest man in the world' and exponent of Black Magic Aleister Crowley met his wife there, enticing her to elope with him to nearby Dingwall. Balls and concerts were held in the Baden-Baden inspired Spa Pavilion (1881). Eminent Edwardians gave lectures there, including Ernest Shackleton, the Antarctic explorer, and suffragette leader Emmeline Pankhurst. Both had problems – Shackleton seemingly with his magic lantern and Mrs Pankhurst with some obstreperous listeners. For the sporty visitor, there was fishing, shooting, golf, cricket, and the ascent of Ben Wyvis (3,429 feet) – 'a good test of the amateur climber's staying powers'. For those without staying power, ponies and guides were available. For anyone seeking a guide, Dr Manson recommended Geordie Munro of Park, 'who knows every turn, and who is not without something to say'.

'The Strath' remained a popular bourgeois resort into the 1900s. After a syndicate of London doctors took control of the spa, the facilities were renewed. The spa survived by adapting to change, with Strathpeffer Spa being the first to use peat baths as a form of treatment. Strathpeffer also offered hydrotherapy, the latest form of water-cure. For this treatment only ordinary water was needed and in the Highlands, like peat, this commodity was not in short supply. To compete with rivals the latest medical fads were adopted and in the 1920s there were eleven types of bath to choose from. Although the spa remained reasonably busy between the wars, the boom days were over.

In the nineteenth century, Strathpeffer, like other spas, had to meet competition from the hydropathics, which were being built all over Britain. Since hydropathics (hydros for short) did not need water with a mineral content, they could be built anywhere so long as there was a copious supply of good clean water. The hydropathic system used water applied internally and externally combined with exposure to fresh air and adherence to a simple diet. At the core of the system was the external application of water as, for instance, with high-pressure cold-water jets and then often followed by streams of hot water. Swaddling the patients' entire body in cold sheets ('the wet sheet treatment') was another favoured method, the purpose being to soothe the abdominal organs by maintaining moist warmth.

The initial popularity of the water-cure led to a rise in the number of hydros being built, including some in, or on the fringes of, the Highlands. They included Callander (1882), Dunblane (1870), Crieff (1868), Deeside (1874), and Pitlochry with two (the Pitlochry Hydro in 1879 and the Atholl in 1880). Commander C. E. Reade, pedalling round Scotland on his tricycle in 1882, was surprised by their size and number. 'In England,' he wrote, 'any imposing detached building is pretty certain to be either a lunatic asylum or a workhouse. In Scotland it is the hydropathic establishment.' Lunacy perhaps best describes some investment decisions at that time. As had happened with the railways in the 1840s, there were a number of rash speculations. The outcome was that the supply exceeded demand. There were far more bed spaces than customers to fill them. Though some like Crieff Hydro were profitable, others failed. Callander Hydro, according to a report in *The Scotsman*, was sold in April 1886 for £12,000 – about one-fourth of the original cost. Two years earlier Dunblane Hydro had gone into liquidation and Deeside Hydro at Murtle shared the same fate in 1917. What had happened at Oban was even worse. In their preliminary prospectus the developers had confidently predicted that the company would pay dividends of 15 to 20 per cent. In 1878 work commenced on what was to be a magnificent establishment; a great deal of money was spent but the company ran out of money. The result was a partially built structure which, because of its commanding position, stood for many years sticking out like a sore thumb.

While not exactly dead, the hydropathic movement gradually lost favour, with most hydros either disappearing or being altered out of virtually all recognition. It was not totally the end for hydros, however. Some, like Dunblane and the Atholl at Pitlochry, were turned into high-class family hotels. We catch a glimpse of the kind of changes that allowed the better-run hydros to survive from the message on the back of a postcard sent from the Atholl Palace Hotel. It is evident that the sender, Aunt Rhoda, writing in July 1932 to a niece in Yorkshire, had not gone to this hotel for any health cure. She stayed at the hotel for two nights while on a tour of Scotland in a 'Pullman Motor Coach'. The coach trip was, she said, 'A free and easy way of travelling, seeing different places of interest.' Most customers by then were like Aunt Rhoda; they came as visitors rather than as patients. Their facilities, entertainments on offer and large grounds – Callander had 30 acres of ground – made them ideal for family holidays. Hydros like Crieff were the forerunners of today's all-inclusive resorts. The services available at the hydros appealed to overburdened mothers and other carers. With everything done for them at the hydros, visitors could more readily throw off the cares of everyday life. Other attractions included balls and concerts. The various activities allowed parents, as one commentator remarked, to avoid 'the sometimes troublesome difficulty of providing amusements for their daughters'. As temperance establishments, fond parents saw them as places where their offspring might meet respectable potential mates, in those days obviously of the opposite sex. In theory alcohol was banned but enterprising clients could always find ways to smuggle in alcohol. In the Atholl, bottles of spirits could be surreptitiously stored in the billiard room lockers. Unfortunately, the revived Callander Hydro was destroyed by fire in 1893 and had to be rebuilt, and indeed survived until the start of the Second World War. Requisitioned for military use, it suffered much damage and was subsequently abandoned.

The fate of the Deeside Hydropathic illustrates some of the twists in medical fashion. Opened in 1899, it was in liquidation just eighteen years later. This ninety-two-bedroom hydro then became Tor Na Dee Sanatorium for the treatment of pulmonary tuberculosis. This was a time when fresh air, preferably high in the hills, was the conventional treatment for that dreaded disease. Once tuberculosis (TB) had been more or less eliminated by modern drugs and treatment, the sanatorium became a convalescent hospital. Another sanatorium, Nordrach on Dee, so-named from the German methods used, had been opened at Banchory in 1900 and this was Scotland's first specialist sanatorium for tuberculosis. The best-selling novelist Somerset Maugham was one of its fee-paying patients. In 1934 it then became a luxury hotel and was renamed Glen o'Dee. It fulfilled several different roles thereafter, before ending as a community hospital.

In 1901 a sanatorium was built on Swiss lines at the other side of the Cairngorms at Kingussie. Here, as at other contemporary sanatoria, the open-air treatment was favoured, with some patients sleeping in wide-open huts in the grounds, sometimes even in the winter. The sanatorium was well equipped with electric light and an X-ray room. The use of antibiotics in the 1950s meant that sanatoria of this type were no longer needed for the treatment of TB. The building is now an NHS-run nursing home for the elderly. Although TB sanatoria and the water-cure in its Victorian form have lost favour, the name hydro still retains some currency – such as with vibrant establishments of the Hilton Dunblane Hydro, the Pitlochry Hydro and the Crieff Hydro – all of course with modern spas.

As for Strathpeffer Spa, as happened with a number of other early spas, the tide of fashion moved on. As the railway network developed, other watering places and forms of holiday-going came into favour. During the First and Second World Wars, the large hotels and other public buildings were requisitioned. After the Second World War the railway station was closed to passengers. Spa treatments fell out of fashion in Britain, but not on the Continent. However, with the expansion of touring coach travel, Strathpeffer had the hotels large enough to house large groups. Its central position and heritage made it a suitable staging point for travellers heading further west and north, and, to quote a 1920s guidebook, 'Strathpeffer is the key to one of the most wonderful districts of grandeur in Britain.'

The Highlands also had its seaside health resorts. It was in the eighteenth century that health seekers started to go to the seaside for what they called 'the salt-water cure'. As with the spas, fashionable medical men were recommending immersion in salt water for a variety of ailments. Lord Fife was a believer in the beneficial effect of bathing in the sea. In 1784, he wrote from London to his factor at Banff: 'I shall leave the Stinking hot streets soon and get to the Sea bath at Macduff, which I long to be plunged in.' It was not just the saline quality of the sea that was important; sea air too was judged to have a restorative effect, particularly for pulmonary complaints. In June 1791, Mrs Grant of Laggan brought her daughter 'who had a threatening illness' from Badenoch to her father's residence at Fort George.

The growing popularity of sea-bathing saw towns like Nairn and Oban develop into seaside resorts. Although Elizabeth Grant of Rothiemurchus thought it an 'odious fisher place', Nairn became in time one of Scotland's premier golfing resorts. Places like Nairn and Dornoch with natural links courses had a head start when the vogue for golf spread to the English middle-classes. Dornoch Links had been lauded as superlative golfing ground as far back as 1618 – 'the fairest and lairgest linkes of any pairt of Scotland'. In 1886 Old Tom Morris, one of the country's leading golfers, laid out an eighteen-hole course. 'There canna be better found for gowf,' he declared. The real boom came when Dornoch was connected to the railway network by a branch line in 1902. It was only possible because it had financial backing from the Duke of Sutherland and other bodies. Seeing Dornoch's potential as a seaside and golfing resort, in 1906 the Highland Railway, which operated the line, opened a sixty-five-room hotel. Two other Sutherland villages, Golspie and Brora, also gained fine golf courses, with both being laid out by another notable professional, James Braid.

Over in the West Highlands, Gairloch is an example of a small beach resort that thrived despite having no direct railway connection – the nearest station being Achnasheen 45 miles away on the Dingwall to Kyle line. Baddeley's 1915 guidebook said that there were two principal ways of reaching this beautiful district. One was to travel by rail from Inverness to Achnasheen, then continue to Gairloch by motor car. The other involved an eleven and a half-hour journey from Oban by fast steamer – three times a week during the season. Since the largest hotel, the seventy-room Gairloch Hotel, was apt to be crowded, tourists were advised to book ahead for rooms. This hotel has an interesting history, as a block at the rear used for staff quarters was once the area Poorhouse. For today's visitors Gairloch has a short golf course, a museum and sites for tents and caravans. The National Trust for Scotland's Inverewe Gardens at nearby Poolewe should also not be missed.

In 2015, when this photograph was taken, the Pannanich Spa Hotel was no more – the building seemingly divided into flats. The mineral water, bottled now, is still valued for its therapeutic qualities and is available for purchase.

THE BEN-WYVIS HOTEL,
STRATHPEFFER SPA, ROSS-SHIRE, N.B.

VISITORS to this popular Watering Place will find this the Principal Hotel, replete with every comfort, combined with "Moderate Charges." It stands within its own grounds, which comprise Tennis and Bowling Greens, is surrounded by grand scenery, and commands a splendid view of Ben-Wyvis, the ascent of which can be made from the Hotel in a few hours.

The BEN-WYVIS HOTEL, which contains Public and Private Apartments *en suite*, Billiard, Recreation, and Smoking Rooms, is within two minutes' walk of the Mineral Wells and Baths, and of Post and Telegraph Offices, Pavilion, &c.

The Hotel is within a mile of the Strathpeffer Station on the Dingwall and Skye Railway, and is a convenient point from which to visit Skye, Loch Maree, &c.

The Terminus of the Proposed Branch Line from Dingwall to the Spa will be about two minutes' walk from the Hotel.

ORDERS for APARTMENTS & CARRIAGES PUNCTUALLY ATTENDED TO.
APPLY TO THE MANAGER.
N.B.—POSTING CONDUCTED IN ALL ITS BRANCHES.

✦ DEESIDE ✦
HYDROPATHIC ESTABLISHMENT
HEATHCOT, NEAR ABERDEEN.

THE Climate of Deeside is the healthiest in Scotland. Residents at this Establishment have the privilege of

Preserved Salmon & Trout Fishing in the River Dee

which runs through the Estate of Heathcot.

THE TURKISH AND OTHER BATHS

are constructed with all the latest improvement necessary for the practice of Hydropathy.

Terms per week, £2 10s. ; for two having same Bedroom, £2 each.

For Particulars, apply to
Dr. STEWART, Medical Superintendent, Heathcot, near Aberdeen.

Adverts for the Ben Wyvis Hotel, Strathpeffer, and for the Deeside Hydropathic.

Strathpeffer Square with the Ben Wyvis Garage charabanc ready for excursions to local beauty spots. On the board in front of the 'chara', tours to the Kilmorack Falls and Glen Affric are on offer. White-capped drivers are close by.

The Sanatorium, Kingussie

The Grampian Sanatorium in Kingussie was set among pine trees and this was one of its strong points, since pine-scented air was claimed to bring health benefits. Today it is an NHS care home for the elderly. Alice, who sent this card to a friend in Fife, was, 'Still improving <u>very</u> slowly, always in bed yet getting a little stronger. I am very weary for home and I am afraid I will not be home for the winter.'

On the Beach at Brora

Brora in Sutherland became a modestly popular resort thanks to its fine beach and golf course. In this 1914 image some of the children are visitors, while others are local.

Chapter Fourteen

Islands West – The Hebrides

'The steamboat is now established to the Western Isles, so I have heard lately, and therefore much of the difficulty becomes removed ...'

The steamship, as already noted, greatly increased the number of travellers to Scotland's islands. The above quotation comes from a letter by the romantic artist J. M. W. Turner, who had been invited to provide illustrations for a new edition of Sir Walter Scott's *Collected Poems*, but who had hitherto been reluctant to travel to the islands by sailing ship. In fact, a steamboat service to Iona and Staffa had been in existence from at least 1822 when, we are told, parties of tourists 'were sailing from Glasgow once a fortnight, by the steamboat *Highlander* to visit Fingal's Cave on Staffa – an island which until then had been but rarely visited'. By the late 1820s there was a twice-weekly service from Oban in the holiday season. Now that Staffa could be reached by steamboat, Turner accepted the commission. Unfortunately, his Hebridean voyage in 1830 was marred by bad weather, and, in the event, only one painting emerged from his short visit to the Hebrides – namely, his dramatic depiction of Staffa entitled *Fingal's Cave*. Nevertheless, for Turner, as with Southey and Wordsworth, the steamship had become a necessary but unloved feature of everyday life. He sailed in the *Maid of Morvern* and it featured in his painting – a tiny vessel belching a great deal of smoke while braving an angry sea. The year prior to Turner's visit (*as noted in Chapter 6*), the German musician Felix Mendelssohn had sailed to Iona and Staffa in this same vessel.

John MacCulloch's experiences some years earlier illustrate some of the difficulties earlier travellers to the isles had had to endure. Although MacCulloch, a pioneer geologist, was an experienced traveller he was continually frustrated when trying to procure a boat and boatmen to take him from Arisaig to Skye. After a long search the best he could find was a ramshackle vessel: 'All the arrangements were of the usual fashion; no floor, no rudder, no seat aft, oars patched and spliced and nailed, no rowlocks, a mast without stay, bolt, or halyards.' Later at sea, he realised that the boat was actually going backwards: 'I did not care; it was a fine day and a long day, and an entertaining coast:

they were good-natured fellows, and I was as well at sea as Sky [*sic*] or Arasaik [*sic*].' Visiting Skye in 1802, Sarah Murray found that there was no vessel available for her use because it was the herring fishing season and all the boats were needed for this vital fishery. Knowing how important herring were to the Gaels' subsistence, she accepted this without demur.

London Scot and retired bookseller John Knox (1720–1790) was one tourist who could empathise with the oppressed Gael. In his economic and social survey *A Tour Through the Highlands of Scotland and the Hebride [sic] Islands in 1776*, Knox criticised the landlords who did not allow their tenants 'to raise their heads, and are continually crushing them, by new impositions upon their industry'. If the tenants made improvements, there was no guarantee they would have the benefit of them. Improvements they carried out themselves probably meant a rent rise. Having made a number of journeys through the Highlands, Knox was troubled by the degree of poverty he saw there. Knox was not content just to describe the problems of destitution, but he also sought ways to resolve them. More encouragement for the West Highland fishing industry, with new planned fishing settlements, was part of the solution he proposed. Some of his proposals were later adopted by the British Fisheries Society, which was incorporated in 1786. A number of new settlements were created by the Society, among them Ullapool, Tobermory and the most successful of them – thanks to the herring boom of the early 1800s – Pultneytown, now part of Wick. As ever, the government in London had its own agenda. The Act of Parliament setting up the British Fisheries Society envisaged the proposed fishing stations as 'the Means of forming a Nursery of hardy seamen for His Majesty's Navy, and the defence of the Kingdom'.

Where tourists began to arrive in numbers as at Oban, a marked improvement in facilities began to be seen. In 1797 an English visitor, E. D. Clarke, found at Oban 'a very pleasant and commodious boat, neatly equipped with sails, and mounting four oars, for the express purpose of conveying passengers to the different islands and places in the neighbourhood'. By that time, of course, Iona and the Isle of Staffa were beginning to be established as tourist magnets. This new source of income meant that there was now money available in this area to invest in new and better-equipped vessels. Perennial poverty meant that the ordinary Gaels lacked the capital to invest in decent boats, whether for fishing or other purposes. The lack of capital for investment also meant that there were few piers or manmade harbours. In their absence boats had to be stored on land and dragged to the shore or other landing place, and this process, of necessity, meant the participation of many people in the community. John Knox in his 1786 tour related how a crowd of men, women and children – some of them up to their shoulders in water – were needed to launch a boat to take him from Coigach to Lochinver.

Skye had already attracted a few intrepid visitors, but, as in many other parts of Scotland, it was Sir Walter Scott who put it on the tourist map. In 1814 Scott was asked to accompany the Commissioners for the Northern Lighthouses on an inspection tour of the lighthouses under their control.

While on this tour, Scott kept a journal where he recorded his impressions of the places and people he and his friends encountered. On his return he completed his new verse-drama, the *Lord of the Isles*, which was published in the following year. While he had commenced writing it before going on the cruise, he now had first-hand experience of the wonders of Skye's mountains and coast – the Cuillin range's astounding pinnacles and jagged peaks, 'apparently inaccessible to human foot', and its 'precipitous sheets of naked rock, down which the torrents were leaping in a hundred lines of foam'. As for Loch Coruisk, that lonely loch in the heart of the Cuillin range, Scott saw it as breathtakingly bleak and savage:

> Rarely human eye has known
> A scene so stern as that dread lake,
> With its dark ledge of barren stone.

As with the Trossachs, the imagination of Sir Walter Scott determined how tourists should view Loch Coruisk and the Cuillin. Many writers and artists followed his example, exaggerating the bleakness and gloom. Scott at least had the excuse of poetic licence in his portrayal of Loch Coruisk, but there is less justification for John MacCulloch's overblown and erroneous description: 'Here the sun never shone since creation.' Dr John MacCulloch, a well-regarded pioneer geologist, had gone to Skye to study its geology, thus preceding his friend Sir Walter Scott. Locals directed him towards Loch Scavaig, the outer sea-loch, where he 'should find rocks enough'. Like Scott, MacCulloch was elated by the sight of Loch Coruisk: 'I felt as if transported by some magician into the enchanted wilds of an Arabian tale.'

By the early years of the twentieth century the Cuillin range had become a magnet for climbers, but half a century earlier, as the noted writer and mountaineer W. H. Murray remarked, artists were more numerous around Loch Coruisk than climbers. Starting in 1838 steamers en route to other islands began to call at Loch Scavaig – a very impressive sea-loch in its own right, surrounded as it was, in MacCulloch's words, by mountains 'dark, uncertain and mysterious'. From a ship anchored in the loch, tourists could then be rowed ashore and a short walk then brought Loch Coruisk into view. Alternatively, tourists could get a boat from Elgol.

While they were in Skye, Scott's party, after visiting Loch Coruisk, sailed into Loch Slapin in the Strathaird peninsula, where they went ashore to see 'the late discovered and much celebrated cavern, called Macallister's Cave'. They found, however, the way was blocked by a dyke erected by the landowner because tourists had been breaking the stalactites and stealing them. There was a door in the dyke, but the key was 3 miles away at the laird's house. Since time was short, the only remedy was to scale the wall, which they managed to do with the aid of a rope and, on Scott's part, thanks to 'some ancient acquaintance with orchard breaking'. Later visitors didn't need to emulate the climbing feats of Scott and his companions, as a passing gunboat had used the dyke for target practice.

Scott was so impressed with the cave's interior that he brought it into the ballad that he was then writing. In his fertile imagination, a pool in the depth of the cave became a grotto where a nymph bathed her limbs 'in sunless well, deep in Strathaird's enchanted cell … where dazzling spars gleam like a firmament of stars'.

By 1836, according to the *New Pocket Road Book of Scotland*, the Spar Cave, as it was then called, was 'the principal object of curiosity' in Skye, and the best way to reach it was to hire a boat. Fashions change, however. The cave was difficult of access and, furthermore, it was still being vandalised, with souvenir hunters continuing to remove the stalactites. By 1860, according to *Nelson's Hand-book to Scotland for Tourists*, 'the splendours' of the cave had been damaged by thoughtless tourists. Fifteen years later, *Murray's Handbook for Scotland* was also half-hearted about the cave. While conceding that the cave was curious and of interest to geologists, it otherwise was 'scarcely worth the visit'. Furthermore, the difficult approach meant that ladies found it 'particularly disagreeable'.

For Scott, the Cuillin peaks, the Black Cuillin as they were called to distinguish them from the more rounded Red Cuillin range, were seemingly inaccessible and very few would have disagreed. The most prominent hill on the north side of the Black Cuillin group is Sgurr nan Gillean. Although close to the Sligachan Inn, tourists deemed it impossible to climb. It was, however, climbed in 1836 by Professor Forbes and his guide, local gamekeeper Duncan Macintyre. Nevertheless, it was to be many years before the rest of the Cuillin peaks were conquered. For tourists seeking to view Loch Coruisk, there was a route from the north via Glen Sligachan but this was only suitable for hardy pedestrians or by hiring ponies from the Sligachan Hotel. That hotel, a former drovers' inn, was a popular stopping point for tourists and later became the main centre for the climbers who, by the end of the nineteenth century, were arriving in Skye to climb the Black Cuillin's many still-unclimbed peaks. Sgurr Alasdair, the highest at 3,257 feet, was first climbed as late as 1873. Poor transport links to and within Skye help explain why Britain's climbing elite had hitherto neglected the Cuillin. The extension of the Highland Railway to Kyle of Lochalsh in 1897 and then the rival West Highland line's arrival at Mallaig in 1901 brought mountaineers flocking to the Black Cuillin, which was now recognised as a climbers' mecca par excellence.

After Skye, Scott and the Commissioners of the Northern Lighthouse Board set sail for Harris in the Outer Hebrides to inspect the Eilean Glas lighthouse on the Isle of Scalpay. With Scott in thrall to all things medieval, St Clement's Church at Rodel was also on the agenda. To add to the drama, their guide here was a pistol-packing exciseman who, in fear of the local smugglers, carried a loaded pistol in each pocket. When Scott toured the islands, he was in an exceptionally privileged position. The Outer Hebrides, in particular, were well out of the reach of the ordinary tourist, with the transport links being so poor. In the travellers' guides of that period, the outer isles received but scant attention (in his otherwise comprehensive guidebook *The Picture of Scotland* (1837), Robert Chambers was miserly in the space devoted to the

Outer Hebrides). Although Stornoway, the only town in Lewis, was judged to be thriving and neat in appearance, the islands in general were described as low, bare and dreary, with little 'to engage the attention of one who travels to gratify his curiosity'. The sole island described in some detail was the one that was 'one of the smallest and least important', namely St Kilda. The transport links to the Outer Hebrides, Chambers stated, consisted of packet boats which sailed from Dunvegan in Skye to North and South Uist and a similar service from Poolewe in Ross-shire to Stornoway. We see the hint of change in a Glasgow advertisement in 1835 with 'delightful pleasure excursions' being offered covering a great deal of the West Highlands, including not only Iona and Skye, but also Jura, Islay, the Sound of Mull and 'even distant St Kilda'.

In the course of the nineteenth century, communications to the outer isles were gradually improved, with Stornoway having a weekly steamer from 1846. David Hutcheson and Co. and its successor company run by David MacBrayne and other companies, most notably McCallum Orme, operated a variety of services to the Western Isles. By 1860, according to *Nelsons' Hand-Book to Scotland for Tourists*, Stornoway and Lochmaddy in North Uist were regularly served by steamers from the Clyde and Oban, in addition to the aforementioned sailing packets. The *Hand-Book*, however, forewarned 'strangers' that none of these services 'nor any internal communication' provided any continuous routes. In other words, tourists could not expect to find the kind of interconnecting transport services that were now in place in popular areas like the Trossachs. 'Few strangers, except sportsmen, are attracted to the islands,' we are also told, 'and these rarely find better conveyance from place to place than local fishing-boats and ponies.' Nevertheless, Harris, we are further informed, had deer and grouse in abundance, and with three of its streams teeming with salmon and trout there was plenty to keep sportsmen happy.

By 1894, we learn from Murray's guidebook that communications to and within the islands were much improved. In 1870 a railroad had been built from Dingwall to Strome Ferry in Loch Carron, thus giving Stornoway a direct link with the railway network. When in 1897 the Highland Railway extended its line to Kyle of Lochalsh, Kyle replaced Strome Ferry as the railhead. The Outer Isles' internal links and accommodation for visitors had been improved by that time, but tourists were still few in number. Many Hebrideans, at any rate, found it difficult to understand why strangers would want to visit their part of the world, as amateur yachtsman Robert Buchanan (1841–1901) discovered when he dropped anchor at Lochboisdale in South Uist. The fact that he and his friends had dared to cross the Minch in a cockleshell craft for pleasure was met with incredulity. The islanders of South Uist were baffled by their presence, nor could they understand why anyone would seek to linger in Lochboisdale for longer than necessary. Lochboisdale was at times a hive of industry, but that was in the herring season. Even the landlord of the inn was unable to comprehend that anyone would arrive without some business purpose, and certainly the dreadful weather they endured for the next few days would have reinforced the natives' impression that they were quite mad. The locals Buchanan met in the inn were cynical about the merits of their community, 'its principal beauties, in their opinion, being ague, starvation, and weariness'. Robert Buchanan saw it differently, doubting whether the lover of beauty could find anywhere 'more exquisite than opens out, vista after vista, among these wondrous isles of the North'.

If Buchanan found weariness and apathy in South Uist, there was good reason for it. Between 1838 and 1851, South Uist, like neighbouring Benbecula and Barra, had been brutally cleared by autocratic Aberdeenshire laird Colonel John Gordon of Cluny. His barbarous methods of clearance aroused criticism as far away as Quebec, whose authorities had to deal with over 1,000 poverty-stricken Highlanders dumped on their shores. The Colonel even offered Barra to the government as a suitable place to dump convicts. In South Uist, while crofters were being evicted, wealthy tourists were welcomed. A steamer pier was built at Lochboisdale and then in 1882 a hotel, with shooting and fishing as the main attractions. Murray's 1894 *Handbook* rated the hotel good and the fishing excellent. A further attraction for well-to-do tourists came in 1891 when Sir Reginald and Lady Cathcart commissioned Old Tom Morris of St Andrews, the most famous golfer of the day, to design a golf course. Lady Emily Cathcart (1845–1932) had inherited considerable land and properties in the southern isles from her first husband Captain John Gordon, son of the egregious Colonel John Gordon. Lady Cathcart was another arrogant bully who tried to pressurise the remaining crofters of South Uist and Barra to emigrate. Her treatment of her tenants made her as disliked as her father-in-law had been. Ironically, it is said that she visited the islands only once in fifty-four years. Francis William Clark of Ulva (1800–1887) was another Lowland incomer who cleared two-thirds of the people of that island in an equally brutal and ruthless fashion. Nor is he forgotten there. Clark was 'the most hated man in the history of the island', as this author was informed on a recent visit to the island. It must be said that some of the native Highland lairds had been equally dictatorial. As far back as 1803, Lady Sarah Murray, on a tour of the Inner Hebrides, had accused the landowning proprietors of the Highlands of trying to maintain a way of life that they could not afford, and to pay for their luxuries 'they have screwed up their poor tenants to a far higher pitch than they can possibly bear'.

Most tourists to the isles, it would seem, gave little thought to the problems the Highlanders were facing. Whether 'sporting gentleman' or sightseeing tourist, few visitors seem to have been too concerned that many thousands of crofters had been dispossessed and their lands absorbed into a shooting estate. Robert Buchanan was one of the exceptions who took up the cudgels on behalf of the disposed Gaels. Writing in about 1871, he anticipated the Pennells (*see Chapter 10*) by comparing the condition of the Highland population to the former slaves of the United States:

... there exist here if not the name and law of slavery, at least slavery itself – that the home is laid waste here, the poor family driven to all the corners of the earth, the children starved, the ignorant man cheated out of the very crust he is raising to his lips. These people are called lazy and unenterprising; so they may be, for they know too well that, with their system of land tenure, no amount of exertion would much ameliorate their condition – that, let them improve their little scrap of land as they may, they are liable to be ejected at any moment to serve the interest or caprice of their landlord or their agents ...

The islanders did eventually rebel, and violent resistance to evictions in Skye and other islands brought a government-appointed inquiry, which was followed by the passing of the Crofters' Act in 1886. The Act brought security of tenure for crofters and a partial amelioration of their situation. Landowners' power was not greatly diminished, however. Halliday Sutherland, writing in 1939, described how, when on board MacBrayne's *Lochmor*, he was refused permission to land on one of the Small Isles. The ship's First Officer told him, 'No one is allowed to land on that island without permission in writing, signed by the proprietor himself.' Shades of feudalism! The island was Rum, long known as 'the forbidden island', and its then proprietor was Sir George Bullough, heir to a Lancastrian mill fortune. An old Highlander also on board gave his verdict on what Rum had become: 'Desolation, desolation!' 'When I was a young boy,' he continued, 'I met an old man who once was there ... and he told me there used to be good arable land along the shore, plenty of black-faced sheep, and fertile valleys between the ranges. Now it's only the deer and the estate servants.'

Nevertheless, steamer trips to the other Hebridean islands were popular with the affluent middle classes. Though carrying cargo was their main function, most steamers serving the isles also had room for passengers. For instance, the McCallum Orme Company's *Dunara Castle* had room for forty-four cabin-class passengers, thus offering opportunities for a sightseeing cruise round the islands. Tourists could leave Glasgow at noon on Thursdays on the *Dunara Castle*, calling at Colonsay, Iona, Bunessan on Mull, Tiree, and then at various points on Skye. From Skye the steamer sailed directly across the often tempestuous Little Minch to Tarbert in Harris. Sunday was the then strictly enforced biblical day of rest and that was spent at Tarbert. The return journey involved calls at Lochmaddy on North Uist, Lochboisdale on South Uist followed by return visits to Tiree and Colonsay. The *Dunara Castle* reached Glasgow once again on the Wednesday. The fare for the round trip including meals was, in 1915, a little over £3.

The *Dunara Castle* and her sister ship the *Hebrides* were now also calling at the hitherto little visited island of St Kilda. Until the *Dunara Castle* made its initial call in 1877, very few people had visited St Kilda. It was not only remote, but uncertain weather meant that landing could not be guaranteed. Nevertheless, for such a distant and difficult-to-get-to island group, St Kilda attracted the curiosity of the outside world. It has been calculated that over 700 books, articles and other pieces of writing have been devoted to St Kilda.

It was Martin Martin's first book, a *Voyage to St Kilda*, published in 1698, which first drew the attention of the wider world to that remarkable isle. Until the steamer trips started, the people of St Kilda had been largely self-sufficient, but regular visits meant more visitors and, therefore, an opportunity to earn ready money. During the winter the St Kildans were now busy knitting garments and making hand-woven tweed to be sold to summertime tourists, and this brought them for the first time into a cash economy. Access to the outside world meant that, as happened in other remote and fragile island communities, younger, able-bodied people were tempted to leave. As the population dwindled, the remaining islanders petitioned the government to be taken off the island and to be resettled on the mainland. On 27 August 1930 the islanders' sheep and cattle were taken aboard the *Dunara Castle*, and then two days later the last thirty-six inhabitants left the island on HMS *Harebell*.

With the evacuation of St Kilda, an ancient way of life came to an end. This was just one indication of how the modern world was impinging on the Gaels' way of living. Nevertheless, people from outside were increasingly fascinated by the Gaels' traditions and culture. Commencing in the late nineteenth century and continuing into the twentieth, there was a surge in the number of tourists to the Highlands, and they were not just sportsmen. More and more descendants of the Gaels who had left the islands, whether voluntarily or otherwise, came to see the land of their forebears – ancestry tourism it is called nowadays. The contemporaneous revival in Celtic art, literature and other cultural forms also helped to create a wider interest in the Highlands and its way of life. The more sentimental forms of this revival, as expressed in song and story, have often been denigrated. Hugh MacDiarmid, a critic like James Joyce of the transnational 'Celtic Twilight' movement, deplored the constant succession of sentimental books and articles about the 'Immortal Isles'. Sentimental many of these literary and musical effusions may have been, but they were undoubtedly popular, enticing tourists in increasing numbers to take the road to the isles.

Where no suitable pier existed, landing on small islands like Iona and Staffa meant that tourists had to be taken ashore in small boats, as here at Craignure in Mull.

Passengers leaving Loch Scavaig, Skye.

Photo.D.K. MacIntyre's Series. Fort William.

Above: Following the publication of Scott's *Lord of the Isles*, many tourists visited Loch Coruisk, either landing off a steamer or from a launch coming from nearby Elgol. Once ashore, the tourist, according to *Murray's Handbook for Scotland* (1875), would make his way towards the loch, 'the most savage scene of desolation in Britain'.

Right: The author's son, Moray, on Sgurr na Banachdich, Cuillin main ridge, in June 1990.

Group of St. Kilda Women

A group of St Kilda women in a late Victorian image.

The author's daughter, Rhona, in a kayak on Loch Slapin. (Photographed by Magda Gutowska)

The Spar Cave in Skye, photographed by the author's daughter, Rhona.

Chapter Fifteen

Islands North – Orkney and Shetland

We observe ... that the Leith and Clyde Shipping Company's steam yacht *Velocity* starts on Friday next on her first voyage to Kirkwall ... To those who travel either on business or pleasure this mode of conveyance must prove highly advantageous. We have no doubt that the Orkneys will in consequence have many visitors who would not otherwise have thought of taking such a voyage. (*The Aberdeen Journal*, 12 June 1833)

For the island communities of Orkney and Shetland, improvements in access to the Scottish mainland were vital for the development of the tourist business. From the above quotation, we can see that the introduction of the steamboat ensured that travellers to Orkney whether 'on business or pleasure' would, from 1833 onward, enjoy the benefit of a much faster mode of travel. Tourists now could sail to Kirkwall either from Leith or Aberdeen. Alternatively, travellers could catch a ferry across the often tumultuous Pentland Firth. The main crossing place was from Huna in Caithness across the firth to South Ronaldsay, the most southerly of the Orkney group. In an open boat – indeed any kind of vessel – it could be a terrifying journey. When English clergyman C. Lessingham Smith sought passage to Orkney in 1835, embarkation was from the beach, and there was no standing on ceremony. As he described it, the reverend gentleman was carried 'a-pick-a-back' through the waves and pitched into the boat like a sack. Steamboat sailings were introduced to the Pentland Firth in 1856, the crossing being made by the Stromness-built *Royal Mail* sailing from Scrabster near Thurso to Stromness in the West Mainland. With a stagecoach service to Thurso since 1819, Scrabster had the advantage of relatively good overland connections. When the railway reached Thurso in 1874, communications were transformed not only for Thurso but for Orkney as well.

A few tourists had been arriving in Orkney long before the steamboat era. Sir Walter Scott arrived in the archipelago in 1814 while on the Lighthouse yacht cruise. While in Stromness, Scott learned the story of Gow the pirate. This he got from 'an aged crone', Bessie Millie, 'whose principal subsistence was by a trade in favourable winds which she sold to mariners at Stromness'.

Although for a sixpence fee Bessie guaranteed that a favourable wind was sure to arrive, she took care not to be too precise about the date. The story of Gow gave Scott material for a historical novel, *The Pirate*, which was published in 1822.

Orkney's many prehistoric monuments such as standing stones and tumuli (burial mounds) always aroused attention. Although they had no archaeological expertise, some of the lairds even made a hobby of opening tumuli and removing the contents. When Lady Franklin, the widowed wife of the Arctic explorer Sir John Franklin, visited Orkney, a prehistoric burial mound was opened for her 'amusement'. Charles Weld, who arrived in Orkney in 1860, gave a full account of the various standing stones, stone circles and tumuli in the Stenness and Brodgar area – relics, as he described them 'of a people whose history is lost in the misty past'. Weld made no mention of the largest and most notable of the Orkney tumuli – namely Maes Howe. It was not till the following year that it was excavated, revealing its remarkable interior complete with Viking runes.

Weld had experienced rough weather in the Pentland Firth when sailing from Scrabster to Stromness. While up on the deck struggling to hold on, he heard 'deep moans and groans' from the seasick passengers in the cabin below. Once ashore in Stromness, Weld, however, was delighted to find a first-class hotel: 'In few English towns will you find so well appointed an hotel ... you will find in every bedroom combs and brushes, night-caps and slippers.' When Weld arrived at Kirkwall, it was the time of the annual Lammas Market – a great event in Orkney. The town was packed with Orcadians and Shetlanders 'from even the most distant isles' for this fair, which could last up to a fortnight. A notice attracted his attention:

> It is ordered by the Sheriff of the Orkneys, the Provost of Kirkwall, and the Chief Magistrate of Stromness, that all Lodging-house Keepers, Publicans, and others, within the Burghs of Kirkwall and Stromness, receiving strangers during the ensuing Fair, shall make out a list of the names of such strangers and the dates of their arrival, and send them to the Superintendent of Police.

This reads as if Orkney then was almost a mini police state!

With regard to communications, Shetland was even less well served than Orkney. In 1833, according to *Leigh's Guide*, travellers to Shetland could sail from Peterhead to Lerwick by the Post Office packet-boat, 'which generally performs the journey in a couple of days'. Alternatively, there were two trading vessels sailing from Leith, taking anything from three to five days. At that time potential tourists, the *Guide* continues, would have found but limited accommodation, as the principal town, Lerwick, had no inns. Travellers, however, could find good accommodation at the boarding houses, 'particularly in that of Mrs Scoller, under whose roof he will be comfortably provided for'. In 1836 a weekly steamer from Leith came into service, but for the summer months only. In 1844 an anonymous tourist published an account of his stay in Shetland. As in the Outer Hebrides, the usual mode of travelling round the islands, he found, was by pony and local fishing boat. 'What the camel is to the Arabian, the pony is to the Shetlander', he concluded. Although some of the Shetlanders overindulged in alcohol, this tourist judged their conduct to be generally good. If there was a fault, it was their passion for tea: 'No kind of beverage is so relished by the female peasantry of Shetland as tea. To get tea they will venture as great and as unprincipled lengths as any dram-drinker will go for his favourite liquor.'

By the time Murray's 1875 *Guide* was published steamers were arriving at Lerwick twice-weekly; but, according to this guidebook, there was not much for visitors to see, the cliff scenery and some buildings of historic interest like Mousa Broch, 'the most perfect specimen of its kind', excepted. There were features of interest in some of the other islands, but the poor transport links meant, we are told, that it would be a waste of time to try to reach them. Nevertheless, by 1891 Lerwick had two hotels and numerous lodging houses full to overflowing during the tourist season. Murray's 1896 *Guide* pinpointed the coastal scenery of the north-west Mainland as Shetland's main attraction and Hillswick the best centre for this (Mainland is the correct name for the principal islands of both Shetland and Orkney). Four years later, the North of Scotland, Orkney and Shetland Steam Navigation Company (usually just called the North Company or North Co.), which already had a vessel calling at Hillswick, opened a splendid new hotel there – the St Magnus Hotel. This hotel featured in the North Company's tour programme. The shipping company offered holiday packages, from a three-day cruise to a '12 Days' Holiday', which included three days on the boat and seven days at the St Magnus Hotel. The guests there could enjoy, as well as magnificent scenery, boating, sea and loch fishing, golf, and for the very hardy, sea bathing. One wonders how many of the hotel guests sought out another local 'attraction' – namely a gravestone in a lonely kirkyard with an epitaph to one Donald Robertson who died in 1848: 'His death was very much regretted, which was caused by the stupidity of Laurence Tulloch, of Clothester, who sold him nitre instead of Epsom salts, by which he was killed in the space of three hours after taking of it.'

By the 1890s, Orkney had good accommodation for tourists, with Kirkwall boasting five hotels and Stromness two, and there were also a number of inns. At that time Stromness was served by the mail steamer from Scrabster and from 1876 a weekly call by a steamer from a Liverpool company, Matthew Langlands & Sons. The Langlands steamer sailed from Liverpool to Leith, calling at a number of ports en route. During the summer months the Langlands vessels carried tourists, and Stromness, being quaint and picturesque, proved to be a popular destination. The North Company's boat sailing up the west side of Mainland en route to Shetland also called at Stromness. In addition, from 1907 the Antrim Line of Belfast offered cruises to Stromness, taking in the Hebrides en route. George Mackay Brown recalled the tourist ships of the interwar years when the wealthy on board tossed pennies for peedie (wee) boys like George to scramble for. Once arrived, the visiting tourists could enjoy good fishing in the lochs, plus rough shooting on land and sea.

A pamphlet entitled *Stromness (Orkney) as a Summer Residence* called upon the Stromness folk to wake up and seize the opportunities offered by tourism:

> The inhabitants of Stromness may not be as yet fully aware of the special attractions of their native town … but the demand will soon create a supply, and in a few seasons hence 'apartments', 'furnished lodgings', 'private rooms' and like notices will meet the eye of the passenger when he lands from the boat …

When the forty-bedroom Stromness Hotel was opened in 1901, it was almost as if the pamphleteer's appeal was being answered. It was kept up to date by having four bathrooms and by the bedrooms being connected to reception by telephone. Access to the fishing rights to the best lochs in the island was an important selling point for the Stromness Hotel and likewise for the Kirkwall Hotel. In 1914 John Mackay (who built the Stromness Hotel) purchased the slightly older Kirkwall Hotel. The Standing Stones Hotel at Stenness, a popular hotel with anglers, was another of his properties. Just for good measure, in 1905 Mackay took a lease of the Queen's Hotel in Lerwick in Shetland. Mackay was a good publicist issuing his own *Illustrated Guide to Orkney and Shetland*, which boosted the islands' value as holiday resorts.

Among the tourists drawn to Orkney were two young men who were to make names for themselves in different fields. One was Duncan Grant, who was to have a career as an artist and designer, and the other was John Maynard Keynes, who was probably the most influential economist of the twentieth century. Keynes enthused over the view from Brinkie's Brae, the wee hill that backed Stromness: 'The view above this town is of the Bay of Naples and the Island of Capri.' Some tourists came to the islands not so much for the view but to shoot, and that meant virtually anything, even seabirds and seals.

Although the islands' Viking past and historic buildings like Kirkwall's St Magnus Cathedral had long featured in the tourist literature, the islands' archaeological relics also began to receive more attention. Paterson's late Victorian *Guide to Orkney and Shetland* gave Maes Howe, by then on the tourist map, a full page, and likewise for the Stenness and Brodgar stone circles. Although it was first partially exposed in 1861, Skara Brae, the Neolithic village on the Bay of Skaill, did not attract much attention until Professor Gordon Childe made the first proper excavation in the late 1920s. It is only in recent decades that Skara Brae and Maes Howe have become crowd-pulling attractions, even to the extent of limitations now being placed on access. Shetland, on the other hand, had on the tiny island of Mousa the best example anywhere of a 'Pictish' broch (it is really Iron Age). The author of a mid-1930s Official Guide to Shetland raved about it: 'Were such a ruin found on the ancient sites of civilization, such as the valley of the Nile or Euphrates, it would still excite interest and even wonder.'

The spectacular Up Helly Aa January jamboree, which celebrates Shetlanders' Viking inheritance, attracts a great deal of attention nowadays. Early guidebooks like Paterson's ignored it, but a tourist in Lerwick in January would have been a very rare specimen indeed. Black's *Guide to Scotland* of 1907 described it as the, 'Curious festival of Uphellya ... supposed to have once marked the conclusion of the Yuletide rejoicings.' Two hundred or so mummers, it continued, dressed in every kind of costume paraded through the town by torchlight. Once the youth of the community had marked the end of Yule by dragging burning tar barrels through the streets, but this practice was banned in 1874 as being too dangerous to life and property. The organised burning of a mock galley was a safer substitute and helped to glorify and sanitise Shetlanders' Viking inheritance. Even if it had been designed as a tourist entertainment, which it definitely wasn't, a winter festival would not have boosted the fledgling Shetland tourist economy in those days. Hugh MacDiarmid, writing in 1939, regretted that so few holidaymakers came to Shetland. As a resident in Shetland himself, MacDiarmid argued that the essence of a holiday was complete change, and this the Shetland Islands offered to mainland dwellers at a reasonable cost. Nevertheless, MacDiarmid, contradictory as ever, had no wish to see Shetlanders embark on a 'mere tourist industry'.

If Hugh MacDiarmid recognised that comparatively few tourists ventured north to Shetland, another poet, Orcadian exile Edwin Muir, could admit that his beloved isles were not for everyone. While Muir recognised that Orkney lacked the spectacular beauty of the Western Highlands, he was at the same time able to write persuasively about 'the spectacle of the quickly changing skies and brightness of all the colours' and the other charms of the islands. Orkney's rich prehistoric heritage and other relics meant that anyone staying long 'is consequently bound to turn into an amateur archaeologist unless he has something more pressing to do'. Since the time of MacDiarmid and Muir, both groups of islands have seen a great increase in tourist numbers. For Orkney this is shown by the number of cars now being carried across the Pentland Firth. In 1948 the *St Ola* carried a mere 248 cars across the firth. Twenty-six years later there were over 9,000 – this despite the fact that all vehicles had to be craned off and on the ship. When in 1975 a roll-on roll-off ferry, the *St Ola III*, was introduced to the Scrabster to Stromness route, the number of passengers and cars increased exponentially. Today there are other choices – a car ferry from Gils Bay in Caithness to South Ronaldsay and a passenger ferry from John o'Groats also to South Ronaldsay. This last is linked by express bus to Inverness, thus allowing tourists to enjoy a quick day tour of Mainland Orkney. In addition the Aberdeen, Kirkwall and Shetland boats are still popular with tourists wanting a short northern cruise. Also, there has been a quick alternative to sea travel ever since aviation pioneer Captain E. E. Fresson commenced an air service from Inverness to Kirkwall in 1933 and then a similar service to Shetland three years later.

For long, as various observers commented, Orcadians and Shetlanders, while helpful to outsiders, were diffident about tourism. It is noticeable that the John Mackay who was involved in so many tourist-related enterprises in the early 1900s was 'a self-made Highlander'. In recent years, however, the islanders have shown themselves adept at developing niche markets, including bird and whale watching and diving in Scapa Flow to see the First World War German wrecks. In both Orkney and Shetland there are excellent museums and heritage centres. Marinas and other facilities for visiting yachtsmen have also been provided, with Lerwick attracting around 500 visiting yachts each year. Lastly, Orkney's tiny island Papa Westray can boast of a unique attraction – the shortest scheduled airline route in the world.

SCRABSTER & DUNNET HEAD, THURSO.

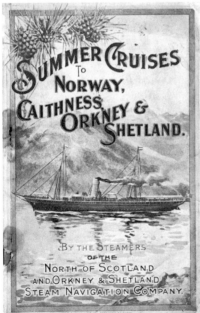

Above: The Orkney mail boat from Stromness, the well-loved first *St Ola* (1892–1951), entering Scrabster Harbour in 1925.

Left: The front cover for the North Company's 1906 Summer Cruises brochure. The cruise ships sailed from Leith and Aberdeen not only to Caithness, Orkney and Shetland but also for a time to the Norwegian fjords.

A photograph of Scalloway on Shetland's west coast, with a North Company steamer at the pier.

The author's car being craned aboard the North Company's MV *St Ninian* at Kirkwall in 1962. The advent of roll-on roll-off ferries to Orkney and Shetland brought a great increase in the number of vehicles carried.

This 1888 photograph would have been bought by tourists as a souvenir of a holiday in Shetland.

'Bird Catching at Orkney': unusual customs attracted the attention of eighteenth-century tourists.

Chapter Sixteen

Motorists and Mountaineers

At the start of the twentieth century, apart from visitors to some of the Clyde resorts, which still had a tinge of the Highlands about them, and the islands, most holidaymakers used the trains for at least part of their journey. The railway companies therefore continued to issue their own guidebooks. Indeed, new lines and extensions were still being opened. A line from Crieff to St Fillans in Perthshire was opened in 1901, reaching Lochearnhead three years later. Further west, the West Highland line to Fort William had been completed as recently as 1894 with an extension to Mallaig in 1901. The Highland Railway was also pushing west at that time, reaching Kyle of Lochalsh in 1897. These changes had far-reaching effects. Just as inns had grown in size to meet the needs of the growth of coach travel, so too were new, more comfortable hotels built for tourists arriving by train. However, not all of the new railway lines paid off. The line from Connell Ferry just north of Oban to Ballachulish on Loch Linnhe certainly did not. On opening day in August 1903, one over-optimistic speaker envisaged the merchants of Edinburgh and Glasgow building holiday homes along the new line. It was an expectation that unfortunately was not realised.

In the early 1900s we also see the first touring motorists come to the Highlands. Publishers of guidebooks and maps quickly adapted to this new market. Sections on automobilism appeared in guidebooks like *Black's Shilling Guide to Scotland* (1906) where a section on motoring and cycling was added at the end. This guide recommended that owners of large cars 'fitted with costly pneumatic tyres would do well to avoid certain of the rougher roads'. These included the road from Tyndrum to Ballachulish via Glencoe: 'Whatever the rugged grandeurs of the scenery, they scarcely compensate for the ruining of the tyres worth £20 apiece, so long as there are hundreds of better roads elsewhere and surroundings of equal impressiveness.' A mid-1920s advertisement for Pitlochry's Atholl Palace Hotel shows the changes wrought by the motor car. The hotel now had a large garage with space for forty cars, including thirteen lock-ups. There was also an inspection pit, presumably for the use of the chauffeurs rather than the owners. So many cars were chauffeur-driven that many large hotels had special 'quarters' for chauffeurs. It is not surprising, therefore, that people further down the social ladder felt that such posh hotels were not for them. Maisie Steven, growing up in Glen Urquhart in the 1930s, recollected that ordinary families like hers never went to hotels. They were well enough off to own a car and went on holidays, but when they did, they stayed in boarding houses. By the 1930s, the pattern of holidays had altered. With domestic servants hard to come by, the middle-classes were no longer renting houses for long periods. Consequently, many villas built to let were converted into boarding houses.

In the interwar years many visitors were now choosing to tour by car or motor coach, spending only one or two nights in any particular place. Consequently, an increasing number of guidebooks were now being written for tourists travelling by motor vehicle. Tourist routes were designed more with motorists in mind than rail travellers as hitherto. The specialist clubs like the Automobile Association (AA), Royal Automobile Club (RAC) and its Scottish equivalent, the Royal Scottish Automobile Club (RSAC), issued their own guidebooks. A popular AA publication was *Scotland for the Motorist*, which was first issued in 1910. The pioneering motorists, like Mr Toad in *The Wind in the Willows*, were entranced by the appeal of the open road – the sense of adventure and the freedom, as it seemed, to drive the length and breadth of the British Isles without let or hindrance. To J. Inglis Ker, the author of the fourth edition of *Scotland for the Motorist* (1925), the motor car was still a source of wonder, despite it having been around for a quarter of a century. 'Those of us,' he rhapsodised, 'who are old enough to have lived in a pre-automobile age – the horse age – cannot rid ourselves of the feeling that there is magic at work … we think of it as a magic carpet by which we are … wafted, gently and swiftly to "fairy lands forlorn".' Inglis Ker appealed to the adventure of motoring in the Highlands: 'There are mountain passes for the motorist where only the eagle and the shepherd on the hill shall mark his progress along the white road.' Such steep mountain passes presented a challenge to 'sporting' drivers and motorcyclists who competed in 'time-trials'.

With his 'grim' peaks, 'gloomy forests', 'mystic and silent island-dotted lochs', Inglis Ker's over-the-top prose tends to exemplify the kind of Celtic Twilight-style writing that Hugh MacDiarmid abominated. Otherwise the AA had produced a practical guide describing a variety of routes through Scotland with useful information, including small-scale maps and town plans, and a list of ferries with charges and other details. As ever, ferry crossings caused problems. In the AA guide we are informed that the Kylesku Ferry in Sutherland was not available on Sundays and did not run during the winter months at all. It seems, however, that the well-heeled members of the RSAC took matters into their own hands. *The Royal Scottish Automobile Club Year-Book* for 1926–27 tells us that a new motor ferry boat had been constructed by that club for the Kylesku Ferry, and it would be on service from the beginning of May until the middle of October. Unusually for the

West Highlands it was to operate on Sundays. This was in contrast to the ferries to Skye, where there were no Sabbath-day sailings until 1965. Loch Etive, north of Oban, was another sea loch that posed a significant obstacle. When the railway line from Connell Ferry to Ballachulish was built, a major bridge was needed to cross Loch Etive. This being expensive, the railway company constructed it so that cars could also use it, but only after the payment of tolls. W. Henry Menmuir, on a tramping tour in August 1911 with his wife, described how they crossed over to North Connell on the railway company's motor car, which ran on the rails.

Motorists and other road users travelling further afield also benefited from the new Ordnance Survey maps that were being issued in the 1920s. It was only then that the Ordnance Survey, hitherto greatly outsold by Bartholomew's attractive half-inch series, began to exploit the commercial potential of its maps. Producing attractively designed map covers by artists like Ellis Martin was one of its solutions. The picturesque covers of the interwar years invariably feature the Ordnance Survey's target customers – leisure motorists, cyclists, and hikers. For drivers covering longer distances, the Ordnance Survey's quarter-inch maps were a later addition to their range. Firms involved in the automobile industry – the petroleum companies most notably – were also to the fore in providing maps and guidebooks. The interwar years also saw a flood of travel books with Scotland as the subject. Probably the most successful works of that genre were *In Search of Scotland* (1929) by H. V. Morton and its successor *In Search of Scotland Again* (1933).

The very detailed advice to drivers contained in the RSAC Year-Book (1926–27) included a list of 'Courtesies of the Road'. Motorists were advised, for instance, to drive slowly when passing houses and cottages as well as other road users, so as not to cover them with dust or mud. The drivers Walter A. Mursell encountered on his cycling tour of the Highlands seemed not to have read 'Courtesies of the Road' as cars caused him a lot of problems: 'What with the stink of their petrol, the bray of their hooters, the bother of their dust, and the illimitable lordliness of their occupants, they added appreciably to the terrors of life.' The dust was a consequence of vehicles being driven at speed on macadamised Highland roads. Before the widespread use of tar (thus tarmac), the clouds of dust created by vehicles was a major problem. W. Henry Menmuir saw the Edwardian 'motor highwayman' as a scourge and the time was coming when motor-propelled vehicles would need to be confined to roads of their own, like the railway. Otherwise, he anticipated, the pedestrian, the cyclist and the horseman 'will soon find it impossible to use the roads which were made for them'.

The increase in the number of motor vehicles of all kinds brought a demand for major road reconstruction. The Great North Road between Dalnacardoch and Dalwhinnie was, according to a Burrow's guide, more or less a rough mountain track. The Tomintoul to Cockbridge Road via the Lecht was another to be dreaded – that 'fearful road', Victoria had called it. In the early 1930s Iain F. Anderson drove over the Lecht when it was undergoing reconstruction. The first few miles were tarmac but then 'the rough surface of the old Lecht Road appeared – a stream-riven channel, unbottomed, boggy and rocky ... the roughest going any car could have'. For H. V. Morton, the worst road in Scotland was the main west coast road to the Highlands from Tyndrum via Rannoch Muir and Glencoe to Ballachulish.

Local and national governments were eventually forced to embark on a programme of road improvement. Some of the new roads of the twentieth century impinged, however, on tourist hotspots like Glencoe and the Trossachs, and that created a lot of opposition. The proposal in the early 1930s to build a new highway over Rannoch Moor to Glencoe was highly criticised. Reams of papers were sacrificed in defence of the old road, with claims that the solitude and wildness of Rannoch Moor and Glencoe would be ruined. Matt Marshall, on the tramp through the Highlands, saw the work underway in Glencoe:

> Every two hundred or three hundred yards or so, I passed places where sections of the new road were under construction. In fact, the whole glen from end to end ... was ploughed up, raw and ugly, by these sections. Unsightly road-making plant, too, at intervals defiled the wayside, while workmen's bothies kept cropping up all along the road.

One stretch from Bridge of Orchy to the Kingshouse Inn was completely new. The writer and mountaineer Ernest Baker slated this 'speedway', which enabled the motor-fiend to 'rush through Glencoe in top gear without having his attention distracted – even by the scenery'. Others welcomed what was variously called 'The New Road' or 'The Great Western Highway', seeing it as a great work of engineering.

The end of the First World War in 1918 had meant that a flood of surplus military vehicles had come on the market, many of which were easily converted into motor buses or charabancs. No less important, many men and some women too had been trained to drive and repair vehicles. In consequence, many parts of the Highlands were now connected by motor bus. One by one, motor buses and charabancs replaced the remaining horse-drawn services; the last of the kind, the four-in-hand Trossachs coach service, was withdrawn in 1937. In towns like Fort William and Pitlochry cheap charabanc excursions were now available, and these could often take tourists to parts of the Highlands inaccessible by train. Improved roads and more comfortable buses helped boost the 'motor cruising' market, which meant that ordinary people could now tour the Highlands in comfort. The SMT Coach Company, for example, could now boast that the motor coaches used for their Perthshire Highlands Tour were fitted with pneumatic tyres and were noted for their swift and smooth running. Nevertheless, some hoteliers, who had been used to catering for an opulent class of tourist, were reluctant to accept coach parties. One coach operator recalled: 'I vividly remember that, in the early days, our applications for advance accommodation were coldly received, and in many cases met by a blank refusal. Some managers in those early days seemed unable to conceive that really nice people would travel in such parties.' Hotel-keepers in time found that this was a sector of the market they couldn't ignore. In the 1930s touring coaches were even reaching as far as John o'Groats. The Royal Hotel in Thurso had to be extended to provide more bedrooms and dining space to meet the increased demand.

In the interwar years open-air pursuits were all the rage. There was growth in all kinds of outdoor activities. Cycling and walking – hiking, as it was now called – were more popular than ever before. Canoeing, which had gone out of favour since the *Rob Roy* days, enjoyed a revival. In 1934 two young men, Alastair Dunnett and Seamus Adam, employing a new type of lightweight canoe, embarked on a well-publicised voyage to the Western Highlands. Successful in having their day-to-day exploits reported in the daily press, the 'Canoe Boys', as they came to be known, gave the sport a considerable boost.

Since many people still favoured the long-stay type of holiday, resorts like Grantown-on-Spey and Braemar provided improved facilities for golf, tennis and bowls. In such hill resorts, nearby woodlands and the old drove roads gave scope for walks of varying length. Even so, there were limitations. Straying from the path in the grouse and stalking season was not encouraged. The traditional summer visitors who came to resorts like Braemar for gentle walking or golf or tennis were acceptable. The hill gangrels (although a gangrel in Scots is a vagrant, it is a name many hill walkers have been pleased to adopt) who tramped the hills in all seasons of the year were another matter. In the early days, mountaineers had often written to the laird or head keeper asking permission to walk their hills. Then, they were invariably 'gents' – people like Sir Hugh Munro with free time and money. They too were often able to procure bed and food at remote keepers' or shepherds' dwellings. Some landowners, including Queen Victoria at Balmoral, banned their tenants from giving hill walkers a bed for the night. Some tenants in out-of-the-way corners of a big estate covertly ignored the ban. In lonely places they were often delighted to see a new face and have someone bring news from the outside world. Keepers could be friendly or the reverse, as Tom Weir testified, often depending on whether the owner was present on the estate or away. Where a keeper was hostile, it was usually on the owner's orders.

Landowners also had indirect ways of restricting the numbers of visitors who might trespass, accidentally or otherwise, on their shooting fiefdoms. That was by reducing the number of inns and other places where these hill gangrels and other wanderers could find food and shelter. The Shiel Inn, which had provided a welcome refuge for Sir Hugh Munro in 1889 (*see Chapter 11*), was closed, due, it was said, to landowners' pressure. For hill walkers Shiel Inn was, as one climber put it, the key to a whole series of cross-country routes and ridge walks. It was popular with hill walkers and other stravaigers and that ensured that landowners looked on it with considerable disfavour. Its loss to hill walkers was important in the days when there were no Youth Hostels or other equivalent accommodation. Ernest Baker, writing in 1932, complained of the scarcity of non-expensive hotels and other accommodation in the Highlands, especially beyond the Great Glen. Inns, he claimed, had been deprived of their licences or turned to other uses: 'A definite policy of keeping the visitor away has been imposed upon large areas of the highlands'. Owners, he stated, had turned most of the Highlands 'into a solitude' where a few rich men brought their friends to shoot and fish.

There were some places, Inverey (an estate village near Braemar) for one, where cottagers had traditionally been able to make a little extra money by accommodating summer visitors. In the 1930s Janet Adam Smith was one of the many hill walkers who found a ready welcome at Maggie Gruer's cottage at Inverey. For many years Maggie Gruer (1861–1939), like her mother before her, had provided a haven for hill walkers and other wanderers. When the Invercauld Estate tried to stop their tenants at Inverey from taking in summer visitors, a ban which would have meant a severe loss of income to the tenants, Maggie, as an independent householder, led the resistance campaign. Helped by press publicity and apparently with royal backing, the tenants got their way, and these restrictions were rescinded.

To meet the demand for a simple and cheap form of accommodation, the Scottish Youth Hostels Association was founded in 1931, with its first hostel opened that same year in the Borders. Access to the countryside was its aim, especially for young people 'of limited means living and working in industrial and other areas', and from the beginning the SYHA received the support of many of the great and the good. Hostel behaviour – including an alcohol ban – was strictly regulated. Members were required to help with the running of the hostels, with each hosteller being allocated a daily task. To avoid offending the landowning class, members had to respect sporting rights. Rule breakers could be expelled forthwith. Chains of hostels were soon established, with many of the hostels adapted from old contractors' huts. A number of substantial houses, even including a castle – Carbisdale in Easter Ross (1945) – were gifted by beneficent individuals. Much of the work of converting and adapting suitable buildings was carried out by volunteers. Caravan and camping holidays was another boom area. Cyclists and walkers found also that their range could be considerably extended when new, affordable, lightweight tents came on the market. Seeing that catering for open-air enthusiasts could be a useful source of income, some farmers set aside land for campsites.

In the 1930s, for working-class people eager to explore the great outdoors, there was another restriction – time. They did not have the kind of spare time enjoyed by the aptly named leisure class, nor indeed did they have much in the way of spare cash even if they had a generous amount of free time. For working people then a two-day weekend would have been a prize to be savoured. For Tom Weir (1914–2006) the lucky ones were those who, enjoying a Saturday half-day, finished work at midday or 1 p.m. Tom, who in later life enjoyed success as a climber, author and broadcaster, then worked as an assistant grocer for the Co-op, and like many in the retail trade had to work till 7.30 p.m. on Saturdays. While he did get a half-day off, it was in midweek and consequently of little use to someone whose hobby took him into the hills. The end of the decade brought one very significant development, however – the passing in 1938 of the Holidays with Pay Act. Although it was after the end of the war before it came into full effect, it was for many working people a life-enhancing measure.

The years immediately following the end of the Second World War were a time of austerity and difficulty. A number of the Highland hotels had been requisitioned by the military and needed substantial refurbishment. Shortages of materials for repairs and rebuilding posed problems in that respect, though. Food shortages also meant that wartime rationing was carried over into peacetime. There were, however, some items in plentiful supply – namely, surplus war garments and equipment. Climbers and hill walkers could equip themselves for the mountains very cheaply. This writer, for instance, bought his first climbing gear in this way – buying at a cheap rate a Commando rucksack, ice-axe, old army boots, gas cape for a waterproof and army tropical shorts for the summer. With many soldiers having been trained for mountain warfare in the Cairngorms, there was plenty of skiing equipment also available. In addition, quite a number of army veterans, having been trained to ski, were anxious to maintain their newfound skills. This cadre of domestic ski enthusiasts were to play an important role in the later development of the Scottish skiing resorts.

Writers have to stop somewhere, and this writer has chosen 1946 for several reasons. Firstly, just as the Battle of Culloden 200 years earlier brought one conflict to an end, so 1946 was the first full year of peace following a much greater war. Secondly, that was the year when the Scottish Tourist Board came into existence, with Tom Johnston (who had been an outstanding wartime Secretary of State for Scotland) as first chairman. This was the start of a more professional approach to tourism in Scotland. Thirdly, and this is very much a personal choice, 1946 saw the launch of the Paddle Steamer *Waverley*. It still survives and continues today, not as a static museum piece but as the last sea-going paddle steamer in the world. Hopefully she will continue sailing for many a long year, following in the tradition of the great pioneers of West Highland steamboat services – Henry Bell, David Hutcheson and David MacBrayne.

Left: A London, Midland & Scottish Railway advert – 'Scotland for the Holidays'.

Below: Cars could be taken across Connell Railway Bridge on payment of a toll. The cars were placed on flat railway trucks and were then hauled across the bridge by a tractor modified to run on rails. In 1914 the bridge was adapted so that cars could be driven across.

THE GRAMPIAN TEA ROOMS AND FILLING STATION, DALWHINNIE, ON THE GREAT NORTH ROAD
BETWEEN PERTH AND INVERNESS.

Above: On the Great North Road to Inverness, tearooms and petrol filling stations replaced stagecoach inns, as here at Dalwhinnie.

Right: Whether hiking, cycling or driving a motor-propelled vehicle, the tourist of the interwar years had a good selection of maps to choose from, many now coming with attractive covers.

Stromeferry looking North.

Above: Strome Ferry at the mouth of Loch Carron in Wester Ross. For motorists utilising this ferry it must have been a bit of an adventure.

Left: Scottish Youth Hostels Association Handbook Cover.

Acknowledgements

Grateful thanks are due to Anne Paterson for her meticulous proofreading and to her and Fraser Simpson for technical help.

Photographs are by the author unless otherwise stated. I am grateful to many people for advice and assistance. These include – for images – Alan Brotchie, Jennifer Pickering, Magda Gutowska, Martin Mills, Fraser Simpson and Rhona Simpson/Mackenzie. Other images, unless otherwise stated, are from the author's personal archive.

Over a long lifetime I have had help from the staff and volunteer helpers at numerous museums, libraries, archive centres and heritage centres. For this I am grateful; they do a marvellous job.

The references to the Astley sisters in Chapter Ten are from *Morvern Transformed* by Philip Gaskell.

Viscount Strathallan is due my gratitude for granting permission to copy the Parker family facsimile images from *A Tour in Scotland in 1863*. This book was published by the Roxburghe Club in 1984 with the permission of the late 17th Earl of Perth.

Thanks also to my family and friends for their company while traversing the Highland bens and glens over very many years.

Select Bibliography

Books

Anon., *A Visit to Shetland* (*c.* 1846)

Anon., *Burrow's Guide to the Scottish Highland* (N.D. but early 1920s)

Anon., *Leigh's New Pocket Road-Book of Scotland* (New Edition 1836)

Anon., *The Book of the Braemar Gathering and Scottish Annual 1924–1994* (N.D.)

Baker, Ernest, *On Foot in the Highlands* (1932)

Bangor-Jones, Malcolm, *Historic Assynt* (2008)

Bede, Cuthbert [Bradley, Edward], *A Tour in Tartan-Land* (1863)

Black, Ronald (ed.), *To the Hebrides* (2011)

Botfield, Beriah, *Journal of a Tour Through the Highlands of Scotland* (1830)

Bowman, J. E., *The Highlands and Islands: A Nineteenth Century Tour* (1986)

Brander, Michael, *A Hunt Around the Highlands* (1973)

Bray, Elizabeth, *The Discovery of the Hebrides* (1986)

Brendan, Piers, *Thomas Cook: 150 years of Popular Tourism* (1991)

Buchanan, Robert, *The Hebrid [sic] Isles: Wanderings in the land of Lorne* (1883)

Burrell, Sir William, (ed. John G. Dunbar), *Sir William Burrell's Northern Tour, 1758* (1997)

Burton, John Hill, *The Cairngorm Mountains* (1864)

Butler, R.W., 'Evolution of Tourism in the Scottish Highlands' in *Annals of Tourism Research* (12, 1985)

Carlyle, Alexander, *Journal of a Tour to the North of Scotland* (ND)

Chambers, Robert, *The Picture of Scotland* (Fourth Edition, 1837)

Cockburn, Lord Cockburn, *Circuit Journeys* (1975)

Cooper, Derek, *Road to the Isles* (1979)

Cooper, Derek, *The Road to Mingulay* (1992 edition)

Crane, Nicholas, *Great British Journeys* (2007)

Delaney, Frank, *A Walk to the Western Isles* (1993)

Donaldson, M. E. M., *Further Wanderings Mainly in Argyll* (1926)

Chambers, Robert, *The Picture of Scotland* (Fourth edition 1837)

Crawford, Henry J., *French Travellers in Scotland* (1939)

Durie, Alastair, *Scotland for the Holidays* (2003)

Durie, Alastair, *Water is Best* (2006)

Durie, Alastair, *Travels in Scotland 1788–1881* (2012)

Eden, Ronald, *Going to the Moors* (1979)

Fairweather, Barbara, *The View of the Traveller* (ND)

Fairweather, Barbara, *Highland Heritage* (1984)

Fleet, Christopher, Wilkes, Margaret, and Withers, Charles W. J., *Scotland Mapping the Nation* (2012)

Fontane, Theodor, *Across the Tweed: Notes on Travel in Scotland 1858* (1965)

Forbes, Robert, (ed. J. B. Craven), *Journals of Bishop Forbes* (1923 edition)

Gardiner, Leslie, *Stage-Coach to John o'Groats* (1961)

Gaskell, Philip, *Morvern Transformed* (1980 edition)

Gilpin, William, *Observations on the Highlands of Scotland, 1789*

Glen, Ann, *The Cairngorm Gateway* (2002)

Glen, Ann, *Old Kingussie and Badenoch* (2008)

Gordon, Anne, *To Move with the Times* (1988)

Graham, Revd Patrick, *Sketches descriptive of the Picturesque Scenery of Perthshire* (1806)

Grant, Elizabeth, *Memoirs of a Highland Lady* (ed. Lady Strachey, 1928 reprint)

Grenier, Katherine H., *Tourism and Identity in Scotland 1770–1914* (2005)

Grierson, Thomas, *Autumnal Rambles among the Scottish Mountains* (Second edition 1851)

Haldane, A. R. B., *The Drove Roads of Scotland* (1952)

Haldane, A. R. B., *New Ways through the Glens* (1962)

Hanway, Mary Anne, 'A Lady Journey to the Highlands of Scotland 1775 with some Remarks on a Voyage to the Hebrides'

Hedderwick, Mairi, *Highland Journey: A Sketching Tour of Scotland* (2009)

Hewitt, Rachel, *Map of a Nation* (2010)

Holding, Thomas Hiram, *Watery Wanderings 'mid Western Lochs. A practical canoe cruise* (1886)

Howitt, William, *Visits to Remarkable Places* (1890)

Hunter, James, *The Making of the Crofting Community*

Jackson, Dick, *The Deeside Line* (1994)

Jenkins, David and Visocchi, Mark, *Mendelssohn in Scotland* (1978)

Kelly, Stuart, *Scott-land: The Man Who Invented a Nation* (2010)

Kirk, Thomas and Thoresby (P. Hume Brown ed.), Ralph, *Tours in Scotland 1677 & 1681* (1892)

Knox, John, *A Tour Through the Highlands and Hebride (sic) Islands in 1786* (1787)

Kyd, James Gray, *The Drove Roads and Bridle Paths around Braemar* (1958)

Lenman, Bruce P., *Integration and Enlightenment Scotland 1746–1832,* (1981)

Lindsay, Maurice, *The Eye is Delighted* (1971)

Lindsay, Maurice, *The Discovery of Scotland* (1979 edition)

MacCulloch, John, *The Highlands and Western Islands of Scotland* (1824)

MacDiarmid, Hugh, *The Islands of Scotland* (1939)

Macgregor, Alasdair Alpin, *A Last Voyage to St Kilda* (1931)

Mackenzie, Donald W., *As it was An Ulva Boyhood* (2000)

Mackintosh, John, *History of the Valley of the Dee* (1895)

Mc Lintock, John, *West Coast Cruising* (1938)

Mc Connachie, Alex Inkson, *Deeside* (1985 edition)

Marshall, Matt, *The Travels of Tramp-Royal* (1932)

Marshall, Meryl M., *Glen Feshie: The History and Archaeology of a Highland Glen* (2013 edition)

Marshall, Rosalind K., *Columba's Iona A New History*, 2013

Martin, John, *SYHA's Youth Hostels 1931–2011* (2011)

Martin, Martin, *A Description of the Western Islands of Scotland* (1934 edition)

Menmuir, W. Henry, *A Walking Tour in the Scottish Highlands* (1912)

Michie, Margaret Fairweather, *Glenesk: The History & Culture of an Angus Community* (2000)

Mitchell, Ian R., *On the Trail of Queen Victoria in the Highlands* (2000)

Muir, Edwin, *Scottish Journey* (1935)

Murray, W. H., *The West Highlands of Scotland* (1977 edition)

Murray's Handbook for Scotland (1874 and 1894 editions)

Nairne, Campbell, *The Trossachs and the Rob Roy Country* (1961)

Parker, Mike, *Map Addict* (2009)

Pennant, Thomas, *A Tour in Scotland in 1769* (1979 edition)

Pennant, Thomas, *A Tour in Scotland and Voyage to the Hebrides in 1772* (1790)

Pennell, Joseph and Elizabeth, *Our Journey to the Hebrides* (1889)

Pococke, Richard (Daniel William Kemp ed.), *Tours in Scotland, 1747, 1750, 1760* (1887)

Reid, John T., *Art Rambles in the Highlands and Islands of Scotland* (1878)

Richards, Eric, *The Highland Clearances* (2000)

Rixson, Denis, *The Hebridean Traveller* (2004)

Rogers, Charles, *Leaves from my Autobiography* (1876)

Ross, David, *The Highland Railway* (2005)

Simpson, Eric, *Going on Holiday*, National Museums of Scotland (1997)

Simpson, Eric, *Discovering Moray, Banff & Nairn* (Second edition 1998)

Sinclair, Catherine, *Scotland and the Scotch, or the Western Circuit* (1840)

Smith, Alexander, *A Summer in Skye*, 1865

Smith, Janet Adam, *Mountain Holidays* (1946)

Southey, Robert A., *Tour in Scotland* (1972 edition)

Steel, Tom, *The Life and Death of St Kilda* (2011 edition)

Steven, Maisie, *The Heart is Highland: Memories of a Scottish Childhood in a Scottish Glen* (2010)

Stott, Louis, *The Waterfalls of Scotland* (1987)

Sutherland, Halliday, *Hebridean Journey* (1939)

Taylor, Alistair and Henrietta (eds), *Lord Fife and His Factor* (1925)

Taylor, William, *The Military Roads of Scotland* (1976)

Townshend, The Revd Chauncey Hare, *A Descriptive Tour in Scotland* (1846)

Victoria, Queen, *Leaves from the Journal of Our Life in the Highlands* (1973 Folio Edition)

Victoria, Queen, *More Leaves from the Journal of a Life in the Highlands, 1862-82* (1884)

Walker, Carol Kyros, *Walking North with Keats* (1992)

Wordsworth, Dorothy, *Recollections of a Tour Made in Scotland in 1803* (ed. J. C. Shairp, 1981 reprint)

Weir, Tom, *Weir's World: An Autobiography of Sorts* (1994)

Weld, Charles Richard, *Two Months in the Highlands, Orcadia and Skye* (1860)

Wilson, Bryce, *Stromness, a History* (2013)

Articles

O'Dell, A. C., *Travellers All* in 'The Scottish Geographical Magazine' Vol. 71, No. 2 (September 1955)

Hiley, Alison, *'Scotland's Name is Poetry to Our Ears': German Travellers in Scotland, c. 1800–1860* in 'Scottish Archives' Vol. 2 (1996)

Smout, Christopher, *Tours in the Scottish Highlands From the Eighteenth to the Twentieth Centuries* in 'Northern Scotland' Vol. 5 (1983)

Index